# PLANTING THE ANTHROPOCENE

# PLANTING THE ANTHROPOCENE

*Rhetorics of Natureculture*

**JENNIFER CLARY-LEMON**

UTAH STATE UNIVERSITY PRESS
*Logan*

© 2019 by University Press of Colorado

Published by Utah State University Press
An imprint of University Press of Colorado
245 Century Circle, Suite 202
Louisville, Colorado 80027

All rights reserved

 The University Press of Colorado is a proud member of the Association of University Presses.

The University Press of Colorado is a cooperative publishing enterprise supported, in part, by Adams State University, Colorado State University, Fort Lewis College, Metropolitan State University of Denver, University of Colorado, University of Northern Colorado, Utah State University, and Western State Colorado University.

ISBN: 978-1-60732-854-4 (pbk.)
ISBN: 978-1-60732-855-1 (ebook)
DOI: https://doi.org/10.7330/9781607328551

Library of Congress Cataloging-in-Publication Data

Names: Clary-Lemon, Jennifer, author.
Title: Planting the anthropocene : rhetorics of natureculture / Jennifer Clary-Lemon.
Description: Logan : Utah State University Press, [2019] | Includes bibliographical references and index.
Identifiers: LCCN 2018056065 | ISBN 9781607328544 (pbk.) | ISBN 9781607328551 (ebook)
Subjects: LCSH: Persuasion (Rhetoric) | Exhortation (Rhetoric) | Ecocriticism. | Nature—Effect of human beings on. | Tree planting. | Environmentalism.
Classification: LCC P301.5.P47 C55 2019 | DDC 809/.933553—dc23
LC record available at https://lccn.loc.gov/2018056065

Cover photograph courtesy of Replant.ca

*For Rapunzel*

# CONTENTS

*Acknowledgments* ix

Introduction: Inventing the Anthropocene    3

1. Nature, Wilderness, and the Environment: How Humanism and Efficiency Construct the Nature-Culture Divide    24

2. A New Materialist Environmental Rhetoric: Rhetorical Bodies in Relation    58

3. Affect and Intense Rhetorics: The Stickiness of Persuasive Entanglements    100

4. Persuasive Movement: The Rhetoricity of Things    132

Conclusion: From Anthropocene to Choracene: The Power of a New Materialist Environmental Rhetoric for Staying with the Trouble    167

*Appendix*    177
*References*    179
*About the Author*    193
*Index*    195

## ACKNOWLEDGMENTS

I owe this book—the peace and space and time to write it—to many humans, nonhumans, and places, the first of which is the Treaty One land on which I sit to write these words and those who have allowed me to settle here. I am indebted to the tree planters who took the time to talk with me, without whom this book would not exist: Lindsay Ainsworth, Ryan Boldt, Tamir Bourlas, Georgia Chappell, Dan Cheater, Sam Dyck, Nik Friesen Hughes, Sam Friesen, Thomas Kroeker, Thayer MacInnis, Ross McCannell, Luke Rempel, Erin Sawatzky, Jane Seniw, James Simpson, and Jon Sprohge. For your words, thank you. And for being the brave souls who have battled the blackfly season after season, I stand in awe of you. I am particularly grateful to both Lindsay Ainsworth and Jonathan "Scooter" Clark, who generously agreed to the use of their photographs in this book, and for the tree planters whose words have been published elsewhere but who join a chorus of tree-planting voices again here.

It takes many people to write a book. To Sarah Vaage and Gazel Manual, I am perpetually grateful for your exacting attention to detail in transcribing interviews. For being a steadfast reader of this manuscript and not getting impatient with having to read about trucks and bugs and plants, I am thankful to Erin Rand. I'd be remiss for not acknowledging the kindness of Casey Boyle, whose amazing personal library and willingness to engage my questions, as well as to read and respond to parts of this book, have been instrumental to its development. I am thankful to the two anonymous reviewers of this book and the time they took out of their lives to help shape it, as well as to the publishing team at Utah State University Press. The University of Winnipeg was a source of research and funding support in the writing of this book, allowing me a research leave and the resources to present parts of this work to my colleagues at the Western States Rhetoric and Literacy Conference, the Conference on College Composition and Communication, and the Rhetoric Society of America Conference. I'm thankful to those colleagues who heard and commented on this work before it reached print, notably Laurie Gries, a source of encouragement about ideas that sometimes seemed far-fetched. I am also thankful to the students in RHET-3155, who were patient with me when my excitement for these ideas leaked out of me and into the class, and for Tim Runtz, whose keen graduate student mind helped me read with fresh eyes the work of scholars whose ideas help make up this book. Fischer James indulged all my questions on metalwork and helped me see more clearly the ways lives and rings are fashioned together. I am so grateful for the patience and interest of these students and colleagues and friends.

Sometimes when we write arguments, it is for the sake of writing them and not always because we believe them. In writing this book, I've come to believe my own argument about the ways our entanglements persuade us into a different way of being in the world. To that end, I am thankful for the serendipities, nonhumans, and things that have helped me see my argument more clearly: for the stories whispered to me by the ōhiʻa lehua on the Big Island that were reminders of my own childhood; for the Garudas who helped guide me; for the cold-medicine–induced haze that writing in February required; for the heartbreak I experienced when trying to write about affect. For my houseplants, who are able to grow lemons indoors when it is -30ºF outside and for the aloe plant in my office who delayed the conclusion, I thank you. And for my sweet sixteen-year-old grandmother companion Chihuahua, Fuzz, whose gentle soul put up with mine long before I could see her for who she is, I am thankful. Finally, I am thankful to the bees, who I know will be the herald of some of my better work from now on.

And then there are the people so special to me that including them in an acknowledgment seems not nearly enough. I was knee-deep in wading through this book about trees when I realized that my late stepfather, the geographer Paul Sneed, whose work with tree rings and life spent carting around rocks, would have been tickled to know that my work wound up rubbing up against his own. To my mother, Ramona Mattix, who was (and is) so patient with me, who allowed me to crash her trip to Hawaii and was always willing to lend a parenting hand when I needed one more weekend afternoon to wrangle with messy ideas—thank you. For never letting me believe my ideas were as far-fetched as they sounded, for being my assuredly confident cheerleader, and for always being my soft place to land, I thank Derek Mueller.

Finally, for listening to me talk about crows and pea plants, for giving up free weeks and weekends so I could write and travel, for being an expert on spalling and lane sizes, for taking care of all the living things that make up our garden and our days, and for joining me in this life, I thank Chris Clary-Lemon. He and my daughter, Rapunzel, remind me of the best ways irrationality shapes us.

# PLANTING THE ANTHROPOCENE

# Introduction
## INVENTING THE ANTHROPOCENE

*I swat at black flies, horse flies—the sun scorching my already burnt neck and back. Even though I've already had five liters of water, I'm parched. I glance at my watch and groan. It's only noon. One more tree, one more tree, one more tree. One, two, tree! One, two, tree! The rhythm of tree planting resounding in my head. The silence of the clear-cut ringing in my ears; the only sounds are my breath, the thunk! of my shovel in the earth, the rustle of a tree in my bag as I pull it out . . . Three o'clock rolls around, and I've been replaying the same scene from* Mrs. Doubtfire *in my head for the past hour. Over, and over, and over, and over again. I'm going crazy, I think as I unwrap another 270 trees to put in my bags, and cram half a peanut butter and jam sandwich in my mouth. I've planted 3,000 trees at this point today, and there are still two? three? hours until quitting time. You plant until you're told to stop. As a tree planter, I am paid per tree that I plant—that is if it fits the specs that we are given: properly planted, no bent roots, not too shallow or deep in the ground, 1,400 stems per hectare, no leaning trees. There are a thousand ways to plant a tree wrong and only one way to plant it right, and you're only paid if it's planted right. Staring out into my land, I take a deep breath, and head out again. (Clement 2015)*

Planting a tree symbolizes for most an uncomplicated positive endeavor, whether in the name of Arbor Day or as a backyard carbon offset in an age of unprecedented global warming. This book is about a different kind of tree planting, a kind that takes place on an industrial, unimaginable scale. A kind of tree planting that invents place intimately connected to rhythm, motion, intensity, and economy, as Stephanie Clement writes in the excerpt above from "To Plant a Million Trees." A kind of tree planting that happens by the thousands, on clear-cuts so large they can be seen from space.[1] A kind of tree planting that requires human bodies, tree-bodies, and shovel bodies working in tandem to produce a seamless movement repeated hundreds of thousands of times in one planting season. This book asks you to understand industrial tree planting as something that tells the stories of both bodies and landscapes, as Anna Tsing (2015b) has it, stories that require considerations of human and nonhuman beings in the making of place. It asks you to understand industrial tree planting as a window through which we might view the constant invention and reinvention of the Anthropocene because without such windows, we have little way to grasp such an impossibly large human impact or even to attune ourselves to its scale.

This is a book about tree planting, but it is also a book about rhetoric, nature, culture, and environmental change and the ways they can be taken together to understand how it is that we are to live in ruin in the Anthropocene; and that it is not a static enterprise but rather a continual invention of particulars, situated in place and time. Such places of ruin are those that have been both simplified and abandoned in the quest to produce ever more material for consumption (6), as in the clear-cut as a space for replanted monocultured seedlings, a crop whose outcome and value in a human lifetime (it takes eighty years for the next harvest) are relatively unknown. It is a book about the ways human and nonhuman bodies make meaning of, dwell, and persuade each other to invent competing stories of the Anthropocene; to see humans as entangled with a range of nonhuman others; and to imagine what it means to be with each other in devastated landscapes.[2]

Our understanding of these landscapes is minor at best, since most of us live far away from the economic centers of the forestry industry—whose locations are, by design, remote—even if we do have everyday contact with its products, whether in the books we read or the toilet paper we use. By design, forest products seem completely disconnected from the trees they come from. Our national and provincial forests preserve relationships with trees that often separate cultural iconicity—the redwood forests of California, for example—from the facts of economic imperatives—8 percent of the world economy is made up of the forest products industry (Ross 2015); nonetheless, we know we must strike a balance between consumption and sustainability. We cannot continue to consume without somehow planning for how we might consume again, which is what has brought about the contemporary tree-planting industry as a sub-unit of industrial forestry. Forests, as "natural" spaces, must now be managed by humans; and trees, as a renewable resource, may be cut down, planted again, and harvested again. As Shaul Cohen (1999, 428–29) notes, trees have both instrumental and emotional value, whether symbolically (as with the Tree of Life), metaphorically (representing a connection to the natural world), or futuristically (a measure of hope for generations to come in an era of global climate change).

Some of the work to understand the "environmental panacea" brought about by planting trees in North America has been done by geographers and environmentalists who query its role in the nonprofit sector, examine the timber industry's public awareness campaigns, and investigate its successful message put forth by the US government;[3] others have sought to examine forestry's often exploitive labor practices by undocumented Latino immigrants on US federal lands.[4] Those who study tree planting as a social and cultural phenomenon have framed it in terms of gender, sexuality, and class; communities of practice; and nationhood and identity.[5] It has thus far been seen through an examination of human social life. Unlike these prior studies, however, this book situates tree planting differently: as an activity that is not only part of how humans manage forests but also of how forests manage humans.

It is said that we are in the age of the Anthropocene, where humans are the primary geological force that shapes life on the planet. Of course, creating a geological epoch named after ourselves suggests the impossibility of imagining our way through it—after all, the end of the *anthropos* suggests the end of human life on earth. Yet if we imagine the Anthropocene as always-already, as never-ending, as statically here and not something that is invented, maintained, and in constant motion, it becomes nearly impossible to imagine futures that offer alternatives to self-annihilation. In suggesting that we turn our attention to the sites, words, things, processes, and sensoria that invent the Anthropocene, then, this book is part of the larger political project, as Donna Haraway (2015, 160) calls for, of making "the Anthropocene as short/thin as possible." Examining what it means to plant trees—to alter landscapes into plantations by constructing a particularized nature of a monocultured tree in a forest ecology—carries significant weight. Yet the stories we tell about this particular kind of living in ruin, stories that include what we might call "more-than-human sociality" (Tsing 2013, 27) through which we might consider the discursive, rhetorical, and material realms of silviculture, remain un-remarked in favor of the social, environmental, economic, and geographic realms. Thousands of popular press and scholarly articles documenting climate change, increased circulation of media calling for sustainable environmental management, and popular environmentalist messages that urge us to "leave no footprint" suggest that we prefer to think about silviculture in simple terms of carbon offsets and sequestration. Yet this book seeks to carve out a role for *both* the discursive and the non-discursive, the rhetorical and the material, among what exist as the new "illogical landscapes" proffered by those who plant trees for a living (Gill 2011, 31). It is an attempt to provide, as

Nathaniel Rivers (2015, 422) calls for, a more *intense rhetoric* located in both human and nonhuman forces. Such a project must situate rhetoric, then, as the footprint itself: "*all* the ways we mark and are ourselves marked, bitten, or stung." Living in ruin is a state of being. As Rivers (2015, 438) suggests, "Avoiding footprints is both impossible and ethically suspect."

As such, this book is a footprint.[6] It is a mark on an Anthropocene that calls our attention to that which rests in liminal spaces—between human and nonhuman, intelligible and rational—as a move to examine place through the rhetorical act of placeholding. Such moves are acts of consequence because they ask us to understand the Anthropocene as made up of acts of constant *invention*, states of being and being-with, rather than a foregone conclusion. The Anthropocene marks an epoch and also an argument.[7] In other words, it is only possible to thin the Anthropocene when we are able to view it as one of many possible -cene-spaces—a shorthand that emerges through acts located in and over time, in constant action and motion, with varying levels of intensity, and with a constant need to catch up (since the now is already behind us). The casement for such a view, in Tsing's (2015b, 161) words, is the requirement that we "pay attention to the assessments through which we know disturbance . . . an open-ended range of unsettling phenomena" that "redesign the environment." Examining tree planting and its naturecultural entanglements is one such possible assessment. What better take on anthropocenic living? We raze forests to the ground. We plant millions of trees. Yet as Tsing reminds us, those acts are assemblages and in them are a million protagonists: pines, shovels, nation-states, muscles, resignation.

So what does it mean to plant a tree? In Canada, forested areas—that is, federally owned "public" Crown land available for logging and, later, planting—occupy 56 percent of the country, twice the amount in the United States and ten times more than Mexico. Between 12,000 and 15,000 Canadian reforestation workers plant trees on logged forests in any given year (Brown et al. 2004, 19), a markedly small number in an industry that represents the nation's largest source of export earnings. Yet in the national imagination, tree planting looms large as a rite of passage in Canada. Unlike the American silvicultural industry, which relies heavily on immigrant labor from Mexico (*pineros*), or the Mexican silvicultural industry, whose tree-planting *ejidos* and *comunidades indígenas* often live in extreme poverty (Brown et al. 2004, 19), Canadian tree planting—while seasonal contract work—is dominated by postsecondary students, a result of the stigma and refusal by local populations in the

1960s to do the work (Sweeney 2009, 77). As a result of a young, upwardly mobile, white, middle-class demographic engaging in the physically laborious work of planting trees, it is not hard to find stories of nostalgia, of connection to the homeland, of a "grueling but highly coveted job" (Luke 2014), and versions of an authentic experience of what it means to be Canadian.[8] Unlike a parallel American demographic that has not heard of silvicultural work, since around 1990, unprecedented years of logging and increased reforestation employment have resulted in nearly every Canadian becoming connected to it in some way—a brother, a niece, a parent. It is a uniquely Canadian phenomenon in this way.

Thus to situate a study of tree-planter's discourse is also to draw upon Canada's historic struggle with defining itself as an independent, authentic nation: as Catriona Sandilands (2000, 169) suggests, the national project of "'Canada' is questioned by U.S. and global cultural, financial, human and natural resource flows." As a result, the nation depends specifically on narratives of geographic sovereignty to bind itself; one of the strongest is that of *wilderness*, a "situated narrative of desires for human and nonhuman relationships, one that may be underscored by a series of natural events and processes but is only given meaning and relevance in particular social and political contexts" (Sandilands 2000, 177). What it means to "be Canadian" is tied up in common relation to this shared landscape, a marker of national specificity and personal identity. Thus in turning to stories of planting this landscape, there is an inevitable turn to both culture—identity, belonging, territory—and nature, interactions with nonhuman actors and an idealized a-historical, a-cultural wildness. Yet it is precisely this impossible bifurcation of the nature-culture split, a Cartesian refraction of the subject and the object in a time of ecological crisis, that must be held up to scrutiny.

What this book seeks to do is reduce the friction between the subject-object split by examining the rhetorical and the human in tandem with their interaction with other inanimate and nonhuman bodies, drawing on silvicultural work to make its case. Like other projects that seek to engage with inquiry into material sites,[9] this project seeks to zero in on rhetoric as an a-theoretical attunement to *being*, an attention to rhetorical energy, in order to better understand the world. In keeping company with scholars interested in ontologies that seek to include humans within (rather than separate from) their environments, a dwelling, ambient rhetorical perspective—which characterizes the framing of this book—does not aim to contribute to a Cartesian logic that absents nature from culture and concepts from things; nor is it intended to conflate description of material objects with the objects themselves. Yet unlike projects that engage a material ecocriticism, my interests here are less critical and more rhetorical: I seek to examine what has been parsed generally by materialist ecocritics as "narrative agencies" (Iovino 2012) by putting forth a productive, rhetorical lens through which we might view and understand anthropogenic labor.

Rather than see rhetoric as a simplistic opportunity to somehow separate what is persuasive from the circumstances that surround any given material-discursive act, I promote an ambient rhetorical view (Rickert 2013), which, like other scholarship that lends credence to affect[10] or to materiality,[11] moves those who study language and material closer to navigating both from a *dwelling* perspective. Dwelling, for rhetorical scholars like Thomas Rickert (2013, xiii), suggests "how people come together . . . in the continual making of a place; at the same time, that place is interwoven into the way they have come to be as they are." This notion of dwelling is no doubt influenced by the anthropological; Timothy Ingold (2000, 5) notes that the overarching endeavor of his book is to have readers adopt a dwelling perspective, in which they might accept that awareness and activity are rooted in the engagement between persons and environment for understanding perception and cognition, architecture and the built environment, local and global conceptions of environmental change, landscape and temporality, mapping and wayfinding, and the differentiation of the senses.

Ingold (2000, 5) insists that to adopt a dwelling perspective, we must acknowledge that "humans . . . are brought into existence as organism-persons within a world that is inhabited by beings of manifold kinds, both human and non-human." This call has been taken up in varied ways by rhetorical scholars interested in, for example, indigenous studies, object-oriented ontology and new materialism, as well as scholars in feminist science studies, the environmental humanities, and relational archaeology.

## THE LIMITS OF THE ANTHROPOS-: SITUATING NATURECULTURE

The Canadian (and indeed, Western) notion of wilderness has specific connotations; that is, people know what they mean when they talk about it, and it has become a universalizing discourse. William Cronon (1995, 70, 80) suggests that the discourse of wilderness itself, filled with memories, images, and sensations of interacting with things "irreducibly nonhuman"—that is, *wild*—reproduces that which it seeks to protect and "embodies a dualistic vision in which the human is entirely outside the natural." That is, a forest cannot be both wild and inhabited at the same time because wild spaces are natural spaces, and natural spaces are those where humans do not dwell.

Like other grounding modern Western dichotomies, culture/nature has kept good company with dualistic splits such as the mind and body or the subject and the object. The postmodern shift to deconstruct these dichotomies has provided deep framing for moving beyond these oppositional categories. However, as feminist scholars Stacy Alaimo and Susan Hekman (2008, 2–3) point out, postmodernism and its linguistic turn have served to make "the discursive pole . . . the exclusive source of the constitution of nature, society, and reality"—leaving material reality an entirely separate realm and thus "forclos[ing] attention to lived, material bodies and evolving corporeal practices." Turning again to a silvicultural "wild," if we accept the impossibility of separating landscapes from the bodies that change and are changed by them, we are forced to see the linguistic and material as part and parcel of living both in nature and against it—the tree, the talk, and the shovel as an assemblage of humans, nonhumans, and things. *Planting the Anthropocene* joins scholars in feminist science studies, indigenous epistemologies,[12] and the environmental humanities[13] who view nature and culture as mutually constitutive and who engage possibilities beyond dichotomous thinking—whether in providing the continuum of *natureculture*, acknowledging the role of the intuitive, spiritual, and moral (Berkes 1993, 4); engaging the discursive-material as an alternate framework;[14] or taking on nature as agentic. As Alaimo and Hekman (2008, 5) suggest, engaging possibilities beyond these dichotomies also asks for new ways of understanding the world that turn from human-only instances of agency and consequence toward an accounting for "'intra-actions' (in Karen Barad's terms) between phenomena that are material, discursive, human, more-than-human, corporeal, and technological." To push ourselves away from the nature/culture dichotomy or to imagine nonhuman agency or to accept the fundamental role affect plays in connecting humans to nonhumans is to move toward a new kind of environmental rhetoric that does not imagine the *anthropos* as its only center.

The problem with contemporary environmental rhetoric, which leaves humans with only two options with which to consider the environment—to either be its savior or consume it as a commodity—is that "both [options] reduce environments to what we can say and do about them" while over-privileging human control (Rivers 2015, 427). The difficulty in ascribing a hubristic agency to human environmental action commits us to these same problematic bifurcations. In a tongue-in-cheek critique of humanistic environmentalism, Nathaniel

Rivers (2015, 427) notes: "With the right amount of data and the correct political will, humans can reverse the trend of global climate change and save the earth. Through our awesome technological might we have rewritten the face of the Earth. Through our awesome scientific might we can now, finally, read the earth and see the true effect of our awful agency. But fear not, for it is that agency that will allow us to re-write (or right) the earth again." In his skepticism, we can read Rivers's frustration alongside that of Alaimo and Hekman's framing of a linguistic turn that has reestablished human beings from outside nature and situated the environment as "a code that can be read, mastered, and controlled" (Rivers 2015, 428). His call to engage Jane Bennett's (2010) vital materialism while considering issues of environment and environmental rhetoric similarly resonates with material ecocritics' call to consider nature as agentive, to examine the wildness and "thing-power" of objects. Swayed deeply by these arguments, my aim here is thus not simply to interrogate discourse and make grand claims about language and the construction of human reality in thinking through anthropocenic industry; instead, it is, as Bennett (2010, 116) urges, a "giving up" on "the futile attempt to disentangle the human from the nonhuman" in an effort to "engage more civilly, strategically, and subtly with the nonhumans in the assemblages" in which we participate. It is an attempt to recognize the invention of the Anthropocene while engaging with those who work through spaces of environmentalist-developmentalist polarities with their bodies.

I chose the title *Planting the Anthropocene* to recognize the tension inherent in the *anthropo-*, not a simple acceptance of its human-dominated hubristic naming that recognizes and frames the existing idea that global environmental change has been and continues to be precipitated by human activities. Instead, its use is a signifier of boundaries and shifts. It stands, on the one hand, for arguments in Earth sciences that suggest its use represents a paradigmatic shift from thinking about Earth ecology, defined as "the science of the relationship between organisms and their local environments," to Earth System science, defined as "the science of the whole Earth as a complex system beyond the sum of its parts" (Hamilton 2015, 1). In thinking through the Anthropocene as metaphorical, the first ecological use, as Lauren Rickards (2015, 4) suggests, "equates the concept to 'global environmental change'; the second [systemic use] sees it as having exploded the modernist human-nature binary that underpins global environmental change science." The Anthropocene is noticed here as a "boundary event",[15] as a discourse,[16] as a slice of time that is one among many competing options: the Plantationocene, the Capitalocene, the Chthulucene.[17] Through choosing the scope, process, and framework of this examination of natureculture by explicating narratives of silviculture, then, I recognize that to do so under the umbrella of "Anthropocene thinking" is to invoke throughout the "explosion" of the nature/culture bifurcation happening in both humanist and scientific fields.

### "SAVING THE PLANET" AND "PLANTING A CROP": PARTICIPANTS

I first began this project because the subject matter was completely unknown to me but seemingly common for everyone I met. As a dual citizen, born in Canada but raised primarily in the United States, I had never come across tree planting as something salient in my own life. However, after returning to Canada and as a university professor, I found myself in situations that invoked planting and were made strange by my ignorance: at faculty brunches, someone would talk about how her nephew was planting trees over the summer and ten other folks would join the conversation, or I'd get into conversations with students who described their summer plans for seasonal work. In other words, it seemed as though I had stepped into something no one else seemed to think was anything special. I had no grounding to the Canadian landscape as a particular kind of industrial resource; the closest I had come to understanding this particular topoi was in terms of the contract work and management of the Alberta oil sands. Curiosity and these problematic parallels drew me to silviculture.

Because tree planting is so common and networks of planters are so close, participants were easily recruited for the project. Although I gleaned through interviewing them that some of the planters who participated knew each other, none knew beforehand to whom I had spoken. Thus I began the project by interviewing a former student, who sent me names of and contact information for people who were interested in the project; I visited a forest wildlife management class and handed out my contact information; I sent an email to a local environmental listserv explaining the project. I did not place barriers on age, time spent planting, or gender. From these gestures, sixteen interviews took place with a variety of participants, yet most were white, young, and middle class. Five were women and eleven were men, though since the 1990s the female workforce in tree planting has risen in number to be nearly equal that of men (Sweeney 2009, 69) and interviewees were not meant to represent the particularities of silvicultural demographics. What all participants had in common, despite experience planting often in Canada's western provinces that dominate the industry (British

Columbia and Alberta), was their connection to the prairie province of Manitoba, where the interviews were conducted. This is significant in thinking through geographies of planting, as Manitoba (as part of the west/central region of Canada) has fewer reforestation companies and plants fewer trees than most provinces to the west and even the eastern province of Ontario.

Generally speaking, there are fewer forested areas, less planting, and less data about the experiences of planters as one moves east.[18] The little research that exists on Canadian planting focuses on a specific region, usually British Columbia[19] or Ontario.[20] Thus participants' experience reflects a relative diversity of planting not relegated to a particular region, with slight additional information about planting in the East, something with which only a few planters had experience.

When I began interviewing planters, I was operating from the position that I was recording histories of their experience that others might use in the future; since this was an oral history project, all participants agreed to be identified by name.[21] Currently, data available about tree planters specifically (as opposed to forestry workers such as loggers, forest contractors, foremen, logging road construction workers, and mechanical repairpersons) are limited.[22] The voices I add to the existing literature on tree planters in *Planting the Anthropocene* take up the complicated position forestry workers hold about their relationship to the environment, documented notably by Thomas Dunk's (1994) work with loggers (or "cutters"). Dunk (1994, 17) suggests that both ambiguity and contradiction characterize forestry workers' relationship with the environment and their response to environmentalism; as he notes, these complexities in perspectives of those who work in the forest "highlight the need to break with economic-determinist ways of thinking about environmental debates." Although loggers depend on the forest for wages and report having "no use for" environmentalists (Dunk 1994, 24), they also report concern over widespread herbicide use, clear-cutting, tree waste, soil erosion, mechanical harvesting, and single-species planting (Dunk 1994, 21). Throughout the interviews, Dunk (1994, 23) notes that "many workers attempted to define the boundary between the natural and the unnatural (what anthropologists might think of as the distinction between nature and culture) and situate their own activities in relationship to this boundary." As he suggests, "We live both in and against nature but few of us have to live this contradiction in our everyday lives" (Dunk 1994, 22).

While Dunk's (1994, 23, 17) scholarship ultimately falls into the same privileging of the culture/nature divide (suggesting that "in the end it is culture that determines how one defines the boundary between nature and culture"), listening to the confusion and ambiguity produced by those who work in forests represented in his study suggests that there are more complicated positions inherent in rhetoric surrounding a "job-versus-environment narrative." It is not enough to assume, then, that humans who cut down trees for resource extraction do not see themselves as having environmental values; similarly, what became evident in talking with tree planters (who represent the last, rather than the first, stage of industrial forestry) is that it is not enough to assume that humans who plant trees in the name of resource management necessarily think of themselves as saviors of the forest.[23] As Thayer, one of the planters I interviewed, said, "Particularly earlier on in the season, I spent a lot of time thinking about myself planting a forest, and by the end of the year actually my perspective was altogether different. I was planting a crop, and it took me a while to reassess that" (T. MacInnis, unpublished data). This realization is echoed by nearly all the planters who participated in this project and represents, I argue, a call for a dwelling perspective that does not make the way forward for environmentalism as a simple separation between human impact and conservation, between culture and nature. Instead, it suggests that we can live both in and against nature, that we can grant "nature" (that is, nonhuman assemblages and materials) agentic force to change minds and resist human control or codification. It suggests, as I note in chapter 3, that human and nonhuman entanglements allow a more nuanced affectual engagement with environmental destruction and loss that does not fall simply between these two positions, an engagement that represents an opportunity for reckoning and reinvention. We might embrace the idea that, as Rivers (2015, 428) argues, "the environment is finally not a problem to be identified and then solved, but a fundamental agonism (a *krisis*) that we must always work through." Such a recognition is the basis for what I am calling here a new materialist environmental rhetoric, which brings together the work of material ecocriticism and critical affect studies as a frame with which to work through environmental *krises*.

## METHOD-METHODOLOGY: NETWORKED PRACTICES

Undertaking this project has meant accepting Donna Haraway's (2008, 159) argument that nature is both *topos*, a commonplace with which to order discourse, and *tropos*—a turn, or movement toward and away. This book does not attempt to pin down or construct an image of the Canadian "wild" or anthropocenic "ruin." Yet it does frame the attempt to order human and nonhuman actors in silvicultural narratives as a way of giving place to them and recognizes, in so doing, that "how to *give place* to something is an issue of invention" (Rickert 2013, 63).

To that end, my thinking through Canadian narratives of silviculture has been informed methodologically by theories of ambient rhetoric, which, like other theoretical perspectives from feminist science studies, political theory, posthumanism, ecological postmodernism, and new materialism, seek "ontological hybridity" (Gries 2015, 5). As a researcher of rhetoric, I am invested not only in what words mean but also in how they attune users to being in the world. *Planting the Anthropocene* is an effort of chorography that recognizes that "minds are at once *embodied*, and hence grounded in emotion and sensation, and *dispersed* into the environment itself, and hence no longer autonomous actants but composites of intellect, body, information, and scaffoldings of material artifacts" (Rickert 2013, 43). While some of the finer elements of chorography go undefined in Gregory Ulmer's (1994) original rhetorical use of the term, they've been taken up by scholars who have used this framing to situate the act of inventing place using associational and analogic thinking.[24] Thus this project, like others that invoke the chōra as a place where things begin and also as an organizing inventional principle, a "cultural space that emerges between metaphysical and physical space" (Hawk 2003, 75), also understands chōra as a continually invented place, attuned to the material and the affective.[25]

In positioning myself as a choric rhetorician, then, I recognize that *Planting the Anthropocene* has been shaped throughout with an intention to "attend to memory, networks, technologies, intuitions, and environments (places), because these things all touch on place as something generated, not statically present and hence prereceived" (Rickert 2013, 67). Much of the organizing principle of the book, then, relies on the choral word: an attunement to roots, dreams, flies, machines, thinking less "linear indexical" than "network associational" (Ulmer 1994, 36). What this has meant for the methodological framing of this book has been a different kind of listening to participants, an allowing for objects and nonhumans patterned through discourse to speak and arrange chapter content, allowing intuitions to count as data, to imagine material and affect as having both an organizing and a persuasive function, and to imagine the associations among these assemblages[26] to construct a character of a cut block, of an anthropocenic landscape, of a new Canadian geography.

Methodological support for choral thinking has emerged from a range of interdisciplinary work, much of which comes from both critical affect studies and feminist new materialism and from scholars who have worked to generously engage the work of Baruch Spinoza, Martin Heidegger, and Gilles Deleuze and Félix Guattari or to carry it forward (i.e., Bruno Latour and Graham Harman). While I primarily rely on the work of rhetorical scholars who have engaged this scholarship, writing this book has taken detours into philosophical thinking about the place of humans, animals, plants, and things that would be impossible without these thinkers and writers and those who have taken them up in a range of disciplines, whether in politics (Jane Bennett), anthropology (Anna Tsing, Annemarie Mol), plant neurobiology (Anthony Trewavas, Michael Marder), feminist science studies, affect studies, and new materialism (Karen Barad, Donna Haraway, Diana Coole, Samantha Frost, Sara Ahmed, Teresa Brennan, and Rosi Braidotti) or material ecocriticism (Serenella Iovino, Serpil Opperman). While I have read widely in a range of areas to help lay this groundwork, the scholars I've gathered here together similarly refuse to allow the codification of the nature-culture binary to unproblematically stand.

This interrelation of mind and matter, the interruption of logic as detour to reason, the acknowledgment of bodies as sets of relations, and a firm rootedness in Diane Davis's (2014) claim for an "underivable rhetoricity of being" constitute the methodological infrastructure that undergirds choices about research methods. Here my approach to interview data sees those data not only as a qualitative research method or a collection of oral and aural-historical accounts but also as collective acts of description by participants. In so doing, I wish to reclaim description as a central method for understanding complex systems. In the spirit of the scholarship of Sharon Marcus, Heather Love, and Stephen Best (2016, 11), whose work counters the contemporary intellectual view of description as filled with risk and even contempt, I view the descriptions provided by interviewees as complex attentions to messy details. Obviously, interviews with humans are not interviews with trees or crows or trucks, even as, perhaps, the humans from which these interviews spring are themselves multi-species assemblages of bacteria, microbes, and parasites and thus are always "speaking with." What these interviews are instead are outbreaks of assemblage thinking that allow us, as Bennett (2010, 108) suggests, an opportunity to "listen and respond more carefully" to the nonhuman elements within them. Humans only ever understand meaning making through the limits of the anthropos, even as other living and non-living bodies make meaning in other ways, whether through assemblage, bodily form, reaction, or transformation.

Yet humanness is also, as Tsing (2013, 34) reminds us, "a place to begin." Interviews with tree planters and the questions and intersections they invite with nonhuman others allow this book to delve into what Tsing (2013) calls *critical description*.[27] As an act of critical description, this book both asks urgent questions and demands a curiosity about bodies, affects, and things that implicate the material within the linguistic, see humanness as a way in, and networks such a method with the methodological interventions of those working in the disciplinary fields I've mentioned. In viewing interviews as a method that invites and sometimes bridges critical description, I am also urging readers to see such descriptions for their invocation of nonhuman worlds, to know that we "learn them and ourselves *in action*, through common activities"—a move, Tsing (2013, 34) suggests, "from technological and ethical object making to pursuing the social worlds of these objects in motion." She reminds us that projects like these "might begin with arrangements humans set into motion, but then [they] trust guides such as form and assemblage to tell us about social relations in which we are only indirect participants" (Tsing 2013, 34). Thus Stephanie Clement's opening invocation of the one, two, tree! motion of planters on the landscape, her encounters with black flies and horseflies, sun and thirst, tree seedlings and shovels, are all ways in—for the rest of us—to understand persuasive assemblages woven from human and nonhuman relations on the silvicultural landscape.

The descriptions provided by tree-planting interviews are a *way in* to the testimonies of the living and nonliving bodies they take up, the chōra they construct, and the forms and assemblages they ask us to consider. They are a beginning way—insomuch as any text-based project is not also a walk in the woods—for readers to engage in complex silvicultural worlds of humans, animals, plants, and things they are distanced from in the same way reading such descriptions captures our own distanced experience of connecting the page in our hands to the same pulp-paper-silviculture process tree planters are describing. We are, all of us, complicit in inventing this anthropocenic moment. Such a view emboldens description as a method that allows us to engage with the vitalness of material because stories contain affectual richness that is "responsive to the liveliness of material relationships" (Marcus, Love, and Best 2016, 8).[28] Such richness, in its most promising form, works to further unseat the subject/object divide and, it is hoped, draws us toward our own recognition of environmental loss and complex movement forward. It also suggests that these descriptions are simply a thickly dripping part of the chōra—words that planters speak are part of the assemblage of bodies and worlds that move, reflections of relationships and liveliness among humans and things. Thus, it is my intention for readers to acknowledge the (often lengthy) descriptions provided by tree planters "as a collective, networked social practice"—which here includes nonhuman sociality—or as Marcus, Love, and Best (2016, 9) suggest, as "neither the view from nowhere, nor simply the view from somewhere, but many views from many places, over time." In engaging interview data as views from many places over time—inviting human description as ways *in* to nonhuman forms and assemblages—such multiplicity also acknowledges the attendant uncertainties and messes that accompany figuring sensory worlds through words.

## DWELLING PLACES

The silvicultural workers and their experience as represented by interview data are often ambiguous, sometimes contradictory. It has been a messy practice to try to make sense of their words and worlds, wanting to construct a Canadian *topos*—some fixed insight about the land, about the people—but only being able to locate *chōra*, indeterminate and associational. In gathering together the details of the interviews—the human and nonhuman mentions, the invocation of the body and its movement, the realm of the affective—my purposes have been twofold. First, I have been looking to move through environmental rhetoric as an ongoing *krisis* by offering a rhetorical lens that provides insight into the ways theory and method interoperate, suggesting that rhetorical scholars and researchers might situate chorography (and ambient rhetorical approaches) as something not only relegated to the realm of unbounded, aleatory generativity but also as a grounding methodology for an extended research case. While some degree of this work has been accomplished, notably by scholars like Byron Hawk (2007) (in examining the film *The Fifth Element*), Jeff Rice (2007) (in examining the rhetoric of cool), and Thomas Rickert (2013) (in using examples of Toronto Island and the EV1 electric car), this book diverges somewhat from prior chorographical scholarship. Unlike the tradition of chorography used primarily in the realm of the digital—to "update the topoi" (Rice 2007, 33)—instead I use it here as a framework for the rhetorical-material. Second, this book seeks to use chorography as the principle that binds and gives meaning to a phenomenon—tree planting—through an extended examination of its discursive presentations. *Planting the Anthropocene* deviates from the usual chorographic approaches, then, in inventing the cultural space of silviculture rather than examining its appearance, for example, onscreen and online (as, for example, in the documentary *78 Days*). To that end, *Planting the Anthropocene* is an attempt to write silviculture "through its connections and meanings" (Rice 2007, 40) rather than as a definitive textual source or through new media, to travel the lines wrought out of tree dreaming and tendonitis to attempt to capture a particular perspective on dwelling in the Anthropocene. Scholars have named the gathering of these perspectives in different ways. Debra Hawhee (2017) argues for a "rhetoric of tooth and claw," Haraway (2016a) asks that we "make kin," and Haraway and Tsing (2015) argue for a storying of *resurgence*, the changing of an ecosystem by plants and animals that emerge after a quick, large-scale ecological disturbance (such as fire, flood, or farming). If, as Tsing (2015b) has argued, the Anthropocene is marked by the complete denigration of refuge, then examining the moment in which "cheap nature is over" for the precise outcome of thinning and shortening the Anthropocene is long overdue (Haraway 2015, 160).

As an extension of these observations, *Planting the Anthropocene* suggests that tree-planting discourses, as markers of dwelling and one human way to story resurgence, are representative of persuasive relations in human-disturbed forests that offer the possibility to rethink human relations to nature. One way to rethink our relations, I argue, is by engaging a *new materialist environmental rhetoric*. Such a rhetoric accepts the relational materiality offered by material ecocriticism and theories of affect as put forth by scholars of critical affect studies (CAS); however, in its emphasis on the *rhetoricity* of bodies—that is, the persuasive effects a multitude of bodies generates—such an approach can be distinguished from others that may differentially emphasize biosemiotics, ecopoetics, ecological postmodernism, or transcorporeality. Such a lens is one through which we might view the messiness of tree-planting descriptions: planters embrace in their narratives both the problematics of rhetorical humanism (which posits individual choices against an objective world) and efficiency (equating time with money and thing-capital) while at the same time countering them with alternative persuasive practices of body, things, machines, and affect that break down the separation of individual from material environment.

To understand the tensions between anthropogenic work and tree planting geographies, in chapter 1 I provide a historical overview of common discourses of nature, wilderness, and environment that have ruled human ways of thinking about the relationship between nature and culture to show how deeply rooted they are in the split of subject from object, self from other, and nature from culture. This divide is what constructs the availability of the common rhetorics of humanism and efficiency tree planters so often draw on to frame their narratives—rhetorics that, as Rickert (2013) notes, work as moves that further separate humans from the material world. Drawing on the work of David Harvey (1996) and William Cronon (1995) in complicating the idea of nature, environments, and landscapes and their relationship to human modification, disturbance, and thing-capital, chapter 1 focuses on the ways tree planters' discourse describes struggles with the dualism between culture and nature and between environmentalism and developmentalism. This is represented by the common invocation among interview participants of a particularized individualism, an idiomatic assessment of land value, and a consideration of trees as capital. It also explores the rhetorics of efficiency that run throughout the interviews, in which planters overwhelmingly equate time with money. Chapter 1 positions the expected and found problematic narratives of work, technological progress, humanism, and efficiency (which separate people and environments) against later naturecultural alternatives of *dwelling* (which enmesh people in lifeworlds), represented by taking up a new materialist environmental-rhetorical approach in chapters 2–4.

In chapter 2, I turn to the work of Diane Davis (2014), John Mucklebauer (2011, 2017), Debra Hawhee (2017), Brett Buchanan (2008), and Jeffrey Nealon (2016) to situate patterned planting references in the interview corpus that dwell on human-nonhuman interaction. In so doing, I put forward three major premises that guide the rest of the book: (1) that we need not depend only on logos to define a rhetorical way of being in the world, (2) that there is an "underivable rhetoricity" (Davis 2014, 536) that unites human and nonhuman bodies, and (3) that we understand bodies as sets of relations. Together, these ideas frame a new materialist environmental rhetoric by examining the role human and nonhuman interaction plays in tree-planting narratives, and they give rise to the book's main argument: reflective of human-nonhuman entanglement, such descriptions also complicate narratives of humanism and efficiency and challenge the nature-culture bifurcation. In turning to planters' unanimous descriptions of pain and pleasure, animal encounters that shape decision-making, and the rhetorical force of plant bodies, I argue that the realities of dwelling with nonhuman bodies both challenge the logos of efficiency and self-determination and reflect possibilities for environmental rhetorics that are attuned to messy and complex notions of timescale and bodythinking.

Building on these arguments, in chapter 3 I turn specifically to affect as a way to anchor an ambient perspective. Here I draw on rhetorical-ecological thinking put forth by Jenny Edbauer Rice (2005, 2008), as well as that of scholars invested in rhetoric's sensorium (Hawhee 2017) and critical affect studies (Ahmed 2004, 2010; Brennan 2004), to focus primarily on the non-rational as a source of dwelling. With the aim of embracing the "messiness" of affect rather than continuing to propagate theories of emotion that divvy it up between mind and sensation, chapter 3 locates itself within Sara Ahmed's (2004, 1) assertion that "emotions shape the 'surfaces' of . . . bodies" while acknowledging the range of bodies present in planting work, as situated in chapter 2. Planters categorize their experience of planting along affective axes: as an experience of bodily intensity, in the meditation and mindfulness or "infinite resignation" generated by repetitive movement, as a site of encounter with nonhuman bodies: trees, animals, shovels, weather, and water. In viewing affect as produced out of multi-species encounters and "contact with objects" (Ahmed 2004, 7), chapter 3 suggests that these complex entanglements allow us to recognize tree planting as an event that is not mired in the media creation of a pristine nature-fantasy but instead allows a naturecultural middle ground, a reflection on dwelling, and an intense environmental rhetoric (Rivers 2015, 422).

I extend this notion of intense rhetorics in chapter 4 by turning specifically to thing-bodies as they co-invent the planting landscape. Drawing primarily from the work of Jane Bennett (2010, 2012), who argues for the vibrant materiality of things, and from the work of rhetorical scholars in the area of rhetorical ontology (Barnett and Boyle 2017; Pflugfelder 2017), in chapter 4 I turn to the ways human entanglements with things—trucks, roads, and helicopters—draw attention to the ways persuasive movement co-constitutes the planting landscape and interrupts common assumptions about the nature-culture divide. Focusing on the ways everyday thinking about automobility, infrastructure, time, and speed is enabled and constrained by thing-bodies on the landscape, I examine the ways thing-bodies work to enable and constrain particular discourses about human efficacy and control. Examining the mythos of personal freedom, economic prosperity, and political integration suggested by the promises of infrastructure and automobility, in chapter 4 I move outward from the planter body and its circulating affects of efficiency and humanism to examine some of the ways these affects circulate in the world. In looking at some of the animating materiality of rhetoric, such as the way a road might enable an Indigenous fight against the fossil-fuel industry or the way a helicopter might promote efficiency discourses, I argue that these kinesthetic rhetorics (Pflugfelder 2017,

17) orient us in ways that no longer have the luxury of differentiating nature from culture.

In the fifth chapter I conclude that living in ruin in the Anthropocene exhorts us to account for the ways disturbance-based ecologies reveal themselves as subtle, nuanced, and in flux. In doing so, I offer the new materialist environmental rhetorical framework I have been articulating as one possible way we may learn to "stay with the trouble" (Haraway 2016a) of the Anthropocene so we can resist its discursive power, which presupposes impossible foundations for future living and being. In reflecting on this account of tree-planting work, I draw on the ideas of Haraway and Tsing, who entreat scholars to find ways of reconfiguring relations between the human and nonhuman to move beyond the Anthropocene. In putting forth a framework for a new materialist environmental rhetoric that acknowledges new networks of things, places, and being, I locate possibilities for chorography to disrupt the continuity of an Anthropocene that allows us only to envision outcomes that leave us filled with either hope or despair. I close by identifying other sites of anthropogenic work that would benefit from analysis that bridges the gap between ecocentrism—valuing nature for its own sake—and anthropocentrism: valuing nature because of material or physical benefits it can provide for humans.

Although I cannot claim for this book an approach to natureculture that has engaged with what is increasingly known as Indigenous research methods in its design (Chilisa 2012; Wilson 2008), I would be remiss if I did not acknowledge the ways the perspective and rhetoric I espouse here have long been at play among those whose voices we listen to the least. To that end, I recognize that many of the ideas from feminist science studies, the environmental humanities, affect studies, and new materialism owe a great debt to a worldview that encompasses all our relations[29] and comes from Indigenous people around the world. I hope that what I offer here will be seen as an effort at reconciling these relational ontologies to better attune us to sites of resurgence—accounts where we might better observe nonhuman arrangements and desires within them and better assert the impossible bifurcation of nature and culture. In granting readers a view of the Anthropocene through the dwelling space of tree planting, it is my hope to enable a reimagining and reconfiguration of the ways one might work and write through encounters and entanglements with nonhuman others. Although work in plant ecophysiology, botany, and forest ecology increasingly show us the ways forests themselves are resurgent creative and connected lifeworlds, I echo Haraway and Tsing's (2015) argument that these stories—stories of ruin, of disturbance, of "feral biologies"—need to be told, not just by scientists but also by humanists. In examining the ways the phenomenon of silviculture is given meaning across a range of bodies, things, affects, machines, and places, I align these knowledge-making practices with John Law's (2004, 3) assertions about method: that we must "find ways of knowing the indistinct and the slippery without trying to grasp and hold them tight." Shortening and thinning the Anthropocene, putting forth natureculture as the obvious and unavoidable epistemological choice in moving us forward, means living as rhetorical beings in flux and engaging in listening processes that are themselves as messy, recursive, and reflective.

## NOTES

1. See Natural Resources Canada (2002) for a discussion of remote-sensing (satellite) methods of mapping clear-cuts.
2. I take the term *devastated landscapes* from Catriona Mortimer-Sandilands (2010, 334), who suggests that spaces of ruin such as cut blocks or nuclear power plants are affective spaces of melancholic loss that foreground an acknowledgment of complex human-environmental relationships.
3. See Cohen 2004.
4. See Sarathy 2012.
5. For representative discussions of these approaches, see Ekers 2012; Sweeney and Holmes 2008; Ekers and Farnan 2010.
6. Rivers (2018, 186) suggests that the footprint trope might be better understood as a means of wayfinding rather than only transport. It is in that spirit that I suggest the metaphor.
7. The Anthropocene is noted by the layperson as often metaphorical, an age in which humans are causing large-scale environmental and planetary change. For scientists studying geological time through examination of Earth layers, the Anthropocene has yet to be registered. For a discussion of the distinctions between Anthropocenic and Holocenic time through an examination of stratigraphic records, see Waters et al. 2016. For a nuanced examination of an interdisciplinary argument of the Anthropocene beyond a geological time perspective, see Haraway et al. 2016.
8. See Plummer 2012; "Vintage" 2014; "Let's Talk" 2016 for further examples.
9. See, for example, Mazzolini's (2015) work with Mount Everest or Tsing's (2015b) work with matsutake mushrooms.
10. See, for example, Edbauer 2005; Micciche 2007; Gross 2006.
11. See Selzer and Crowley 1999; Gries 2015; Barnett and Boyle 2017.
12. For a discussion of the differences between Western ecological knowledge and what is known as "Traditional Ecological Knowledge," which draws from an amalgamation of Indigenous knowledge of ecology, see Berkes 1993.
13. For a discussion of current thinking on the environmental humanities, see Neimanis, Åsberg, and Hedrén 2015.
14. See Strathern 1980; Haraway 2008.
15. See Haraway and Tsing 2015.
16. See Crist 2013.
17. See Haraway 2015.

18. Eastern Canada is made up of Quebec and the Maritime provinces of Newfoundland-Labrador, New Brunswick, Prince Edward Island, and Nova Scotia; see "About the Regions" 2013.
19. Ekers 2012; Ekers and Sweeney 2010; Roberts 2002.
20. Sweeney and Holmes 2008; Sweeney 2009.
21. Ethics approval was obtained through the University of Winnipeg Human Research Ethics Board, #HE02559. See a list of interview questions in the appendix.
22. Everything we currently know about tree-planting work is represented by 46 planters in Sweeney and Holmes's (2008) study of tree planting in Ontario, 35 interviews with British Columbia planters in Ekers's (2012) work, 13 planters in Bodner's (1998) unpublished thesis, 6 pineros in the Jefferson Center for Educational Research's (2003) "Voices from the Woods" project, and 28 American forest workers in Sarathy's (2012) book-length work on pineros (although the exact number of planters is unspecified). Thus, what we currently know about tree planting, despite its cultural capital in Canada, can be summed up in ethnographic and interview-based studies of 100 people, slightly more if one considers data collected in the United States about pineros.
23. See Sandilands 2002 for a broader discussion of the privileging of consumptive constructions of nature over productive ones.
24. Morrison (2001, n.p.) clearly articulates that chorography is "(1) 'learning how to write an intuition [ . . . ] or is reasoning as intuition' (37). The chorographer is an 'active receiver' and writes with 'paradigms (sets), not arguments.' It's also (2) the 'generative potential of specific geography' and encountering 'unexpected and different factors and associations' affecting the character of a place—or a 'field,' 'premises' (in its various senses, including real estate and the logical grounds of reason or the propositions from which a conclusion is induced) (40). Chora (3) has to be approached 'indirectly, by extended analogies,' so [it] is inherently ambiguous; it's neither in the order of the sensible nor of the intelligible 'but in the order of making, of generating' (67). To locate the 'choral word,' (4) one must be attuned to coincidence" (n.p.).
25. See Hawk 2007; Holmevik 2012; Liestol, Morrison, and Rasmussen 2004; Gries 2015; Rice 2007.
26. I recognize here the groundbreaking work of Deleuze and Guattari (2003 [1987]) in coining "assemblage" as a conceptual framework for thinking through matter and material. For a larger discussion of its use and meaning, see Marcus and Saka 2006.
27. Tsing (2013, 28) defines critical description as follows: "critical, because it asks urgent questions; and description, because it extends and disciplines curiosity about life."
28. Marcus, Love, and Best (2016, 9–13) note that building better descriptions makes space for allowing knowledge to overlap with its knowledge object (rather than maintain critical stances of tautology), for embracing the uncertainty that characterizes trying to understand the sensory world through words, for engaging stray details that create possibilities from the strange, for "attending to the describers as much as to the described," for allowing the instability and changeability of description that encourages "responsive wandering," and for questioning objectivity as both "impossible and undesirable."
29. "All our relations," from the Lakota phrase Mitákuye Oyás'iŋ, is often used widely in Indigenous prayer, reflecting on the oneness of people with their surroundings. Both Powell (2011) and Chilisa (2012) mark such a premise as a starting point for research.

# 1
## NATURE, WILDERNESS, AND THE ENVIRONMENT
*How Humanism and Efficiency Construct the Nature-Culture Divide*

*The first feeling, I guess, out there was when Eric left me on my piece of land and said "plant" and walked away. I just remember looking around. I had a big swampy piece, and [I was] not seeing a single god damn bräcke.*[1] *And I'm thinking to myself, "where the fuck am I supposed to put the tree." And as soon as I thought that I was standing around and I thought: "oh my god you're supposed to be planting like fifty of these in a minute." And I started panicking, "I can't just stand here. Oh god, oh god!" and like looking around for anyone to help me. Finally Eric came along and he made the hole for me for the first little-whatever. But you know I mean the first two weeks weren't that bad (Kailen, June 12). (Bodner 1998, 85–86)*

The worlding of our contact with "nature" is filled with terminology that helps us separate ourselves from it with greater clarity. We often don't recognize the ways discourses of nature are pitted against culture or the ways such discourses depend on humanism or have been managed with efficiency in mind or even, perhaps, the ways those discourses constrain the stories we can tell. In this chapter I unpack some of the ways nature terminology—*nature, wilderness, environment*—contributes to a specific geography of tree planting. This geography not only depends on a particular understanding of spatial discourse and material relations but also helps explain the ways tree-planter bodies (as separate from a simple human body by virtue of their constant contact with both shovel and tree) are already attuned to particular arguments about these landscapes, as Kailen's excerpt above suggests. It is in the spirit of seeking to understand those specific geographies—and the way they invent particular anthropocenic moments—that I draw on contemporary definitions of these terms thoughtfully constructed by geographers, environmental humanists, anthropologists, and environmental historians who have sought to problematize nature-culture divides in their explanatory work.

What contemporary theorists of space and place have in common is recognizing a long Western tradition of accepting as true that humans are separate from their environments, commonly positioning "nature-as-other" (Sandilands 2000, 179). This separation is ubiquitous in everyday life: common invocations of distinctions between native and introduced/invasive plant species, the frequently urban-planted sugar maple tree and the old-growth sugar maple, the farm and the forest. It also contributes to common philosophical divides between environmentalists and ecologists, as David Harvey (1996, 118) points out, allowing environmentalists to "adopt an external and often managerial stance towards the *environment*" and ecologists to "view human activities as embedded in *nature* . . . constru[ing] the notions of human health in emotive, esthetic as well as instrumental terms." Increasingly, scholars are turning from this common divide, pointing to the historical ways these distinctions have emerged and the damage they have done by continuing the subject-object split between humans and the environments in which they live.[2]

The common separation of humans from environments sets up a naturalized discourse about the physical world that takes as foundational this disconnection of culture from nature. I use the term *discourse* here in its Foucauldian sense, that is, to describe "practices that systematically form the objects of which they speak" (Foucault 1969, 49), thus both enabling and constraining what is possible to say in any given moment and constructing specific realities about any given object—in this case, the natural world and human relations within it. The ways humans have circulated knowledge about their relationship with the natural world in the last 500 years have everything to do with the ways humans can or can't talk about these relationships today. Foucault (1969, 49) suggests that "one cannot speak of anything at any time; it is not easy to say something new." As such, the ways Western notions of nature, of wilderness, and of environment are constructed over time set up a fairly rigid script for thinking about the world in which we dwell, as I take up next. This nature-culture divide sets up a discourse and a rhetoric about nature that is nearly impossible to escape, particularly for forest workers. Thus a brief discussion of common nature terminology is useful for framing an understanding of how tree planters arrive at the particular discursive geography of planting that they do, which takes for granted humanism and efficiency as normalized. I take up these brief histories of *nature*, *wilderness*, and *environment* to recognize that these terms not only set up common patterns of description that invoke rhetorical humanism and efficiency but also construct patterns for us that are nearly impossible to avoid, given the anthropocenic commitment to situating humans separately from lifeworlds over a great deal of human history. As I turn in later chapters to arguing for the larger theoretical framework of a new materialist environmental rhetoric, it's important to note the discursive boundaries and constraints such a history embodies, since no human exists completely outside of them. In examining planters' discourse, I show how these patterns get articulated in the everyday experiences of replanting labor. Yet in revealing the inconsistencies of the logics of humanism and efficiency that also appear, I argue that there exists some possibility to imagine *dwelling* alternatives to these limiting rhetorics, which can invoke ambient ways of being in the world that are corporeal, affective, and material.

### THE WRONG NATURE

The nature-culture divide is attributed to the movement of rationalist thinking in the late seventeenth century, spurred by the scientific revolution and the work of Enlightenment thinkers. As Neil Evernden (1985) points out, Galilean thought, upon which much of the scientific revolution was founded, suggested that science depended on assessing the world as "if living creatures were removed" (Galilei 1957, 274). Galileo was the first to suggest a distinction "between what was measurable and therefore 'objectively' ascertainable—being the same for everyone—and what was not measurable and therefore varied from person (subject) to person (subject)—that is, was subjective" (Pepper 1996, 138). Galileo imagined a measurable world without humans, giving credence to the "inherent qualities of objects" (139), thus separating primary object-qualities (objects' qualities such as size, shape, number, motion) from secondary object-qualities (subjective qualities known only through human interference, such as color, taste, smell, sound, and perception of temperature).

This distinction between object qualities as those that exist "out there" and those that are "in here" was the foundation of Cartesian and Baconian thinking, which similarly bifurcated the mind from matter, just as Galileo had separated subject from object. This bifurcation is the fundamental ground on which the nature-culture split rests. As David Pepper (1996, 141) argues: "Nature became composed of *objects metaphysically separated from humans*. These objects had primary qualities and no others. They were reducible to atoms, whose unthinking, machine-like behavior was universally the same and explicable in terms of mathematical laws. Humans, by contrast, were defined as rational thinking beings—subjects who observed objects, including nature, and could impart secondary qualities to them." Here, the separation of self (human) from Other (nature) is the most basic distinction, played out as the acceptance of rational human/culture (subject) separated from mechanistic nature (object). Such a view, as Evernden (1985, 18) contends, has resulted in "people accepting as normal a view of nature from which they are excluded."

Although the impossibility of this "normal" view has been noted in contemporary studies of anthropology, geography, sociology, and ecology,[3] the common anthropocenic view of nature existing outside the realm of the human persists, as is evidenced by the major perspectives on nature put forth by rhetorical scholars M. Jimmie Killingsworth and Jacqueline Palmer (2012). In their useful model, they frame public rhetorics of environmentalism (mainstream science, news media, environmental impact statements, ecotopian discourse, and ecological economics) and construct a continuum of three human attitudes toward nature, from Nature as Object (the view of scientific objectivity) to Nature as Resource (the anthropocenic view) to Nature as Spirit ("mythic involvement with nature," or a deep ecological view) on a linear scale (Killingsworth and Palmer 2012, 11–12). Although they recognize that contemporary scientists are moving toward a more holistic model of this continuum, thus bending the linear continuum into a horseshoe in which Nature as Object and Nature as Spirit are brought closer together (Killingsworth and Palmer 2012, 14), despite that contention, the three major positions still generally place humans/culture outside of nature.

This constraining discourse of nature-culture separation persists whether humans approach nature as a measurable object, as a commodity, or as an emblem of the Divine. Yet for Killingsworth and Palmer (2012, 12), the Nature as Spirit pole is a position they insist brings nature and culture closer together, claiming for it "an identity in which the spirit of creation wraps the human and the nonhuman in an indissolvable unity with definite ethical consequences."

While Killingsworth and Palmer allude to this unity as fitting a monastic rather than a dualistic view of nature and culture, I suggest that their invocation of ethics and ethical consequences provides a humanistic binding to moral discourse and, as William Lynn (1998, 281) argues, gives us norms for "evaluating and directing our conduct . . . using principles about what is good, right, just, or of value." Rather than pre-Renaissance or, alternatively, "New Age" constructions of nature that hark back to monistic views of micro- and macro-cosmos using things such as the occult, magic, or astrology—or indeed, pre-modernist mindsets that conflated images, metaphors, and reality (Mills 1982)—Nature as Spirit views seem to invoke, rather, a mysticism that suggests a Judeo-Christian sacred and "moral universe" in which good environmental decisions depend on human attributes of desire for doing the right thing (Pepper 1996, 125–26).[4] Thus even as Killingsworth and Palmer suggest that Nature as Spirit has the capacity to bring nature and culture closer together, such a position is still bound by discourses of reason and anthropocentrism which suggest that only humans have the capacity to determine value and that such value is determined through moral reasoning about what is just or unjust.

A primary grounding of this schism between humans and nature can be attributed to the rise of the scientific method, primarily Bacon's development of inductive reasoning. Inductive methods move from scientific observations of nature out to generalizable laws, placing the human scientist in the position of control over nature and the purpose of science as having dominion over nature through observation and order. The resulting assumption is that *"scientific knowledge equals power over nature"* (Pepper 1996, 143).[5] This underlying notion has played out contemporarily in humans believing that nature needs to be not only controlled but also managed—central values in both the modern environmental movement and modern industry.[6] The connection of a scientific understanding of the world—in which nature exists only to benefit humans and its attendant notions of nature as a resource and progress as interminable and inevitable—remains pertinent to discussions of tree planting, as I take up later in this chapter.[7]

It is important to locate exactly where modernist conceptions of nature have led us, even as postmodern assertions that break down these bifurcations are clearly available. Scholars in the environmental humanities might consider, for instance, Donna Haraway's (2008, 159) assertion of nature as *topos*, a rhetorical commonplace, or Bruno Latour's (2004, 36–37) grouping of the natural and social worlds into assemblies and collectivities of human and nonhuman members that lend themselves far more easily to the inseparability of nature from culture. Yet even as contemporary scholarship may conceptually embrace the idea of natureculture, as Sarah Pilgrim and Jules Pretty (2010) point out, Western industry has not, remaining firmly rooted in notions of management, control, and progress. In addition, public environmental rhetorics have not accepted this position, as Killingsworth and Palmer (2012) establish. This is particularly true for English Canada, whose identity, as Catriona

Sandilands (2000, 179) asserts, is enmeshed in histories of settlement, narratives of adventure, domestication, dominion over, and industrialized wilderness.

## WILDERNESS TROUBLE

As William Cronon (1995) argues, wilderness and its associations, far from representing a place untouched by humans, constitute an entirely cultural construct as well as being a product of history, civilization, and—as others like James Morrison (1994) have noted—painful practices of colonization. Cronon (1995, 70–75; quotation on p. 71) points us to ways wilderness meanings have changed over time, moving from the connotive association with desolation, wasteland, barrenness, and terror in the eighteenth century—"the antithesis of all that was orderly and good"—to a romantic-religious association with power, sacredness, piousness, divinity, awe, and dismay by the first half of the nineteenth century. As he explains, by the twentieth century, much as a result of the works of John Muir, the piousness associated with a powerful and awe-inspiring wilderness was replaced with the domesticated sublime—associations with beauty, pleasure, and joy—as well as simplicity, primitivism, and a nostalgia for a waning American frontier, ideas circulated by the work of Frederick Jackson Turner (77). The last 300 years have witnessed a discursive "wilderness turn"—from desolation and terror to an appeal toward beautiful, "freer," and "truer" places that exist only outside the contamination of civilization, as "virgin" uninhabited land (79).

This turn created a number of cognitive associations in the public consciousness. First, as wilderness began to be associated with nostalgia and a diminishing frontier rather than dismay or fear, there was an increased push to preserve what was considered "wild" land—an emergence of a conservationist ethic in tandem with thoughts of wilderness. There was also an increased passion to seek out, find, and enjoy wilderness, not as a "site for productive labor . . . [or a] permanent home" but rather as "a place of recreation" to be enjoyed primarily by elites (Cronon 1995, 78). In a quest to mark off, preserve, and view wilderness as uninhabited, the move toward managing large parcels of land as national and provincial parks (as separate from productive uses of land) also continued the tradition of displacing and eradicating Indigenous peoples. This willful continuance of the European colonization of the Americas occured by "finding" land deemed "wild" and "uninhabited" and marking it either for development (as in first European contact with

Indigenous peoples) or, later, "saving" the land for preservation or conservationist purposes (and often breaking treaty rights and Indigenous land claims to do so).

This ongoing displacement of people already inhabiting "wilderness" is noted in Cronon's discussion of Glacier National Park (which is still enmeshed in land claim arguments with the Blackfeet people),[8] as well as in Morrison's (1994) discussion of Yellowstone National Park (which displaced the Crow and Shoshone peoples). Such a narrative is echoed by the creation of Algonquin Park in Ontario, which has a long history of rights claims with the Lac la Croix Ojibway people; Quetico Provincial Park in Ontario, which was created on reserve land of the Lac la Croix people; and Riding Mountain National Park in Manitoba, home to the Ojibway and Nakota/Assiniboine and site of a successful land claim by the Keeseekoowenin Ojibway people in 1991. Parks Canada (2016), the equivalent of the National Park Service in the United States, recognizes that the creation of Banff National Park in 1885 displaced the Stoney/Nakoda people and acknowledges that no indigenous people were consulted in the creation of the nation's first seven national parks.[9] The erasure of such histories of "wild" places as already inhabited, as Cronon (1995, 79) suggests, represents a "flight from history,"[10] serving up visions and practices of wilderness committed to the idea of landscape emptied of civilizations and devoid of work, of the wild as separate from humans, as culture divided from nature.

This separation continues today, made manifest in common attachments to wilderness represented contemporarily in, for example, ecotourist literature. Aimed at the elite world traveler and crafted to situate wilderness as providing access to "wild" places, such messages about modern wilderness represent it as something unspoiled, pristine, remote, secluded, and "true" (Black and Crabtree 2007, 491). Yet as Cronon's work reminds us, contemporary views that privilege an "authentic" wilderness experience are still very much a situated, human-made construct that ignores hundreds of years of material and discursive changes[11]—creating a very real divide between what counts as "nature" and what doesn't—and continues the bifurcation between culture and nature. This is perhaps nowhere as true as in Canada, a place in which wilderness is seen as a marker of "national specificity" that routes desire through stories of origin and universal national experience through narratives of non-domestication and deference,[12] despite the fact that 17 percent of the country's GDP is produced from its natural resource sectors (mines, forests, and oil)[13] and another 6 percent from agriculture (Agriculture and Agri-Business Canada 2014).[14]

## "THE ENVIRONMENTAL DILEMMA"

A term like *environment*, taken broadly, gestures to a situated being-in-place, an awareness of surroundings for descriptive, analytic, and meaning-making practices. However, environment broadly conceived has also been subsumed under environmental meanings: as David Harvey (1996, 118) suggests, this is a convention that relegates discussions of environments either to "the relationship of human activity and well-being or to (*a*) the condition or 'health' of the biome or ecosystem which supports human life, (*b*) specific qualities of air, water, soil, and landscapes, and (*c*) the quantities and qualities of the 'natural resource base' for human activity." Such a distinction that classifies human activity on the one hand and the ecosystem on the other is a common basis of the nature-culture divide, one that has been solidly critiqued, given that ecologies without human intervention are impossible to study and become arbitrary and ideological rather than objectively "true" (119). Yet embedded in definitions of the environment, *environmentalism*, *environmental issues*, and *environmentalists* are limiting narratives of human-based economic progress, technology, and development (the "natural resource base"), on the one hand, and ecological preservation on the other. Such a view pits Western liberal individualism (in the form of the "self-made" human) against "environmental values" that privilege protection and conservation of natural spaces while ignoring the very real ways natural spaces propagate and house particular technologies, labor, and infrastructures.

As Samuel Hays (1987) points out in his historical study of public environmental awareness, the development of environmental values—even preservationist ones—has always had economic roots. With a rising standard of living after World War II, Western concerns about the environment became transmuted into a concern for an elite environmental quality and was far more concerned about consumption and the construction of an additional "amenity" to be added to consumer life than about any sense of being-in-place (Hays 1987, 34–35). Expectations of a higher standard of living go hand in hand with an ideology that purports that an improved quality of life is accompanied by clean air, less noise, drinkable water, pristine recreational areas, and pollutant-free waterways in which to fish or kayak. Despite consumerist leanings that construct the environment-as-amenity (and thus worth preserving as a resource), such a position still establishes an "environmentalist-developmentalist" divide (Hays 1987, 9).

In this dichotomous setup, environmentalists "who seek long-term protection of endangered environments regardless of short-term economic costs" are pitted against developmentalists "who seek short-term economic gain regardless of long-term environmental costs" (Hays 1987, 9). This "good-guy"–"bad-guy" mentality not only presents an oversimplification of the fact that the system in which we live "produces both economic prosperity and environmental pollution" but also positions those without economic interest in the natural world ("environmentalists") against those who have such interests ("developmentalists") (Hays 1987, 9).[15] It leaves no space, then, for the worker with a clear economic interest to engage in what might, in other circumstances, be termed a "preservationist" act. The impediment of such binary thinking exists as more than only a theoretical problem; it simply doesn't describe or make sense of *well* the experiences those with a great deal of exposure to fragmented natural spaces actually have. Environmental studies scholars term the perceived incommensurability between these poles of unchecked growth and preservation a "dilemma."[16] And this sense of having two equally unfavorable choices from which to choose characterizes much of public environmental discourse. Yet on the local level, in focusing on the *inhabitant*—whether human or nonhuman—our attention may be drawn instead to the conflict and complement between, the middle way of being. Such a middle way has been embraced by both ecological postmodernists and material ecocritics; however, in drawing attention to a new materialist *environmental* rhetoric, I underscore a lens that inherently seeks to frame the suasive forces between preservation and growth. Until we recognize that the polarity between growth and preservation underwrites both rhetorics of efficiency (developing more efficient ways of using physical resources) and consumer consciousness (ensuring a quality of human experience that privileges pristine, untouched, and beautiful surroundings) in the very discourse of environmentalism,[17] we foreclose the possibility of developing nuanced forms of understanding and producing human attitudes toward the environment.

## HUMANISM, EFFICIENCY, AND INCONSISTENCY: GEOGRAPHIES OF PLANTING

From historical ideals of nature that exclude humans while creating it as a measurable object to the domination of modernist scientific worldviews that construct a mechanistic and rationalistic view of the material world, contemporary discourses of nature have, as Max Oelschlaeger (1991, 96) contends, left us with a nature converted "into a standing reserve possessing market value only." This constructed view of wilderness a-historically separates preservationist ideals of "untouched" *wild* land from already inhabited land, filled with biota and abiota, already teeming with productive uses. This gears human attention toward managing its treatment and development. Modernist notions that place humans in a position of control over their environment and position environments as no more than resources to be protected or exploited by humans have clearly taken hold as the most common discourse about the nature-culture relationship in contemporary life.[18] Separations of self/other, human/nonhuman, and developmentalist/preservationist are continually positioned against a backdrop of unending progress and technological advancement. The ways people have historically taken up these topics are central to understanding how pervasive both rhetorical humanism and rhetorics of efficiency are in characterizing what one might say about the environment, about nature, or about wilderness, and they similarly direct our attention contemporarily within the context of industrial forestry. If nature-out-there is only something to be managed and controlled by humans-in-here, this not only prohibits seeing humans as always affectively entangled with things and nonhuman others (for example, bacteria, food, chemicals, or animals) but also prohibits possible disruption of these discourses in favor of simplistic humanistic models of agency and persuasion.

Anna Tsing (2015a) draws our attention to patchy areas of the Anthropocene through the figure of the plantation, which she defines as "ecological simplifications in which living things are transformed into resources, future assets, by removing them from their lifeworlds." It's easy to see the world of the cut block, where tree planters live, work, and sow, through the figure of the anthropocenic plantation, complete with Tsing's assertions of the cultural work of alienation required to make resources out of living things—that is, trees to eventual lumber, pulp, or paper. Yet in bringing forth the plantation as a marker of the patchy Anthropocene, Tsing (2015a) notes that everywhere plantations are formed, they emerge through "vernacular histories, which tie them to the contingencies of encounters and the peculiarities of place," noting that plantations' proliferation "depend[s] on the multispecies assemblies they simplify." For Tsing and for the accounts I give throughout this book, places like cut blocks and those who do cultural work within them help us understand the Anthropocene as both an environmental dilemma and something that is only ever invented and enacted in place and through relations—as Tsing (2015a) has it, only ever "parochial, perspectival, and performative." Taking together the discourses we live and work within and the tensions they create on plantation landscapes also push us to more closely examine perspectival descriptions that emerge from them rather than to merely take for granted simplified rhetorics of efficiency or humanism. It is worth extending an examination of such performances to understand the Anthropocene not only as global but also as existing in the tension between simplified ecology, on the one hand, and the particularity of experience and multi-species assemblages on the other. If the Anthropocene can be invented, we can also reinvent it.

While tree planters creatively make space for the ambient and material in their narratives, they are also caught up in specific relations of selves to nature that are bound by modernism and yoked to notions of individual choices and industrial progress—the cultural work of alienation, as Tsing (2015a) might suggest. Tree planters are representations and disseminators of the *anthropos*, and as human actors they are enabled by and constrained in their discourse choices by what has come before them. Still, while it is "not easy to say something new," as Foucault has it, it is also not impossible to do so. In everyday vernaculars that depend specifically on place, planters give voice to everyday possibilities for imagining humans as enmeshed in lifeworlds that are articulated not only in terms of inevitable progress or individual choice but also in terms of persuasive nonhuman selves, affects and intuitions, and interactions with things. Such an argument relies on seeing planter descriptions through the lens of a new materialist environmental rhetoric, in which tensions between these seemingly incommensurate positions become generative sites of encounter. In the next sections I discuss how planters' discourses are caught up in rhetorics of both humanism and efficiency, which lay the groundwork for understanding geographies of planting in particular located ways in subsequent chapters. In them, you'll encounter descriptions of tree planting by planters whose voices make up the bulk of this book: Lindsay, Ryan, Tamir, Georgia, Dan, Sam (Dyck), Nik, Sam (Friesen), Thomas, Thayer, Ross, Luke, Erin, Jane, James, and Jon.

### RHETORICAL HUMANISM

While it is not the aim of this book to qualify all contemporary and historical debates about rhetorical humanism,[19] humanism's main tenets—an emphasis on human beings; on reason; on individual freedom, choice, and autonomy; on a desire to increase human happiness and on that happiness as the only "good"[20]—are already privileged in discourses about nature that position it as an object, favor scientific rationalism and decision-making based on knowledge and reason, and seek to preserve nature for the purpose of either future resource use (production) or gratifying human experience (profit). In this bifurcated view that characterizes the discourse, human choices about nature become, as Thomas Rickert (2013, 251) puts it, "ultimately subjective event[s] played out against an objective world." Here I frame the pervasiveness of humanism in tree planters' narratives as rhetorical, or, as Timothy Laurie (2015, 144) maintains, "humanism as a *narrative* about humans." The fact that planters appeal to humanism as they negotiate topics within their experience is a marker of anthropocenic worldviews; however, they simultaneously challenge such a binary framework by their inconsistencies. Such disruptions and messiness suggest vernacular alternatives to privileged binaries—places of fragmentation that request different kinds of attention because they are fractured with unreason, nonhuman resurgence and agency, rhetorical bodies, and sticky affects. I argue that paying attention to these patches of unreason works to resist the simplification that comes with the nature-culture split inherent in humanism and efficiency.

Attention to how these binaries function in common planting themes is initially necessary to demonstrate the suggestion that planters use common notions of humanism *rhetorically*—that is, for certain means and to particular ends. As they discuss their work, they set up a particular geography of planting that situates the human as a central element of the *anthropos*. This is perhaps nowhere more apparent than in planters' descriptions of the job itself and their visions of themselves as individuals, as well as in how they describe their "pieces"—what they term "good" and "bad" land.

### *"So You're a Dirtbag?"* The Prevalence of Individualism

Although tree planting is based on some communal experiences—planters live together in "bush" or "isolation" camps in groups of thirty or forty, where they share meals and evening hours for a three-month season—it is generally a job characterized by a great deal of social isolation and exposure to long periods of time people-free. As in this chapter's opening narrative by Kailen, a tree planter who took part in John Bodner's 1998 ethnography "*Slash Romance*," these experiences are encapsulated in moments—that is, "when Eric left me on my piece of land and said, 'plant' and walked away." A tree planter spends his or her ten- to fourteen-hour workday planting trees after being dropped off by bus or truck (within a two–three-hour drive of the planting camp) or helicopter (for longer distances). Although planters occasionally work in pairs separately on one large parcel of land (a "piece") and a planting contract's work will occasionally be assessed by a foreman, a planter generally works alone. Because of this, planters situate their work on highly individualized terms, which resonates with rhetorical humanism's emphasis on autonomy and personal responsibility. As Georgia, a planter with two years' experience, describes:

> I think, well, the thing about planting trees is that planting 1 tree isn't physically hard at all. It's like, anybody can do it. But what is hard is planting, you know, 300 trees and then doing that over and over and over again. And so, it's almost like more mentally challenging than physically challenging in some ways. Because it's like, you know, just planting that 1 more tree isn't hard, but you just have to convince yourself to do it over and over and over again. And there's like, you have kind of like a boss, like you have a foreman that comes by once in a while, but they're not there to make you do anything. If you don't want to plant no one is going to make you plant; you can just lay there all day if you really wanted. And so it's really just about convincing yourself to do it, and after like sixty days into the season it gets much harder, and so it's just like this constant mental game of like, "How I am going to convince myself to plant 1 more tree and then 1 more box of trees and then 6 more boxes of trees?" And, "How am I going to convince myself to get up tomorrow and do that?" (G. Chappell, unpublished data)

In Georgia's description, she captures both the nature of the work—grueling physical labor—and the laissez-faire approach taken in the job itself: no one will make you work (since individuals get paid per tree), yet the work needs to get done to fulfill the obligation of the contract agreed upon by the tree-planting company and a logging company to plant a particular block of land in a certain number of days with a certain number of trees. Tree planters often connect the motivation needed for the job to an individual work ethic. As Luke, a two-year planter, says: "The thing about tree planting is if you put a lot of work into it, you are rewarded because you're getting paid per tree, so you're getting rewarded based on how much work you put into it rather than another job where you could put, say in construction, where you could work harder than everyone else, but you'll still get paid the hourly rate. Where [with] tree planting it's really based on how much you put into it, you're getting out of it" (L. Rempel, unpublished data).

A similar sentiment was echoed by Tamir, a four-year planter, in attributing value to being a "self-starter": "Self-starting, you know, because you're on your own out there, no one helps you, even your first year it's sink or swim" (T. Bourlas, unpublished data). Thus the geography of planting, despite being embedded in a reforestation collective of other planters, foremen, supervisors and logistics coordinators and "checkers" (quality control staff), camp staff (e.g., cooks), contract negotiators, logging company clients, and the government, is boiled down in tree-planting accounts to an individual endeavor dependent on motivation. To tree planters, it amounts to individual choice, as Sam, a four-year planter, suggests: "Your time is your own. Obviously, you're encouraged to plant as many as you can, but if you feel like taking a three-hour break, you take a three-hour break, and, I mean that's really, you're losing out, you're losing out on probably, you know, close to a hundred bucks by doing that, but it's all your own choice really" (S. Friesen, unpublished data).

Similarly, those who choose to plant trees are understood within the community to be a certain type of individual. As Sam, a five-year planter, reports, "there are various types, sort of the young people trying to either earn some money or escape from something" (S. Dyck, unpublished data). This theme is often taken up by other planters in the data when they describe why they chose a job planting trees. Tamir, speaking of his first year planting, said "it really freed me from my parents, really freed me from having to go to school, having to get a real job" (T. Bourlas, unpublished data). Planters I spoke to often described themselves as loving adventure and challenges. Erin, a three-year planter, had "a tendency to try and challenge myself, pick things that are hard and just go for it" (E. Sawatzky, unpublished data), or, as Sam suggested, there was value in "pushing myself beyond the limits I think I have" (S. Friesen, unpublished data). Often, a reflection on the experience of planting became a narrative of growth and improvement stemming from hard work, represented by Jon's (a one-season planter and two-season logistics coordinator) sentiment: "I got challenged a lot, and I learned that I could deal with problems and overcome them, the 'adapt, improvise, overcome' kind of philosophy" (J. Sprohge, unpublished data). Here we see an emergent humanistic value on individual freedom: to make decisions, to live unbounded by the expectations of others, to address challenges and overcome them by adaptation, creativity, and improvisation. Taken together, these accounts are clear descriptions of the importance of the individual spoken through narratives of choice, motivation, personal responsibility, and freedom.

Humanism, for tree planters, is also realized through character and veracity. Planters consistently value integrity, decrying *stashing*, or hiding or throwing away trees—as Sam noted, "it would be really easy to just throw a bundle of trees over a cliff and just make your money that way" (S. Friesen, unpublished data)—but a responsible individual does the right thing. Yet this sense of personal responsibility is not simply attributable to personal integrity, attitudes of sink or swim, or the development of a simple entrepreneurial self. The pervasiveness of humanism through descriptions of individualism is complicated by companies' policies of planting, pay, and organizational structure that depend on a particular planting speed, as Lindsay (a single-season planter) suggests:

> I think the first, was it the first two week[s] or first two shifts or I don't know, for a set amount of time at the beginning they would just top you up [to minimum wage] and it was fine, but after a while, after the grace period was up, they'd still top you up, but it would start coming out of your foreman's paycheck, and then it would start, after a little while, it would also start, some of it would also come out of your supervisor's paycheck, and so that was the part that bothered me because I was like, why should they have to pay for me being slow, you know, when yeah, that's just not fair to them. (L. Ainsworth, unpublished data)

Here, Lindsay describes incentive to work that is not based on getting paid a particular wage or simply attributable to her penchant for hard work. Rather, the responsibility of an individual to make choices and to do what is reasonable and ethical depends here on the *other*—to not make someone else suffer by your own hands. For a second it is possible to glimpse the crack in the assumption of the neo-liberal individual, humans not reduced to naive victims of neo-liberalism or the simplification of the "autonomous chooser" (Fitzsimons 2002). It is true that planters are workers, and their aims are entrepreneurial in nature. Yet such self-reflexivity as noted in Lindsay's narrative suggests a tension between personal choice and individual progress, on the one hand, and egalitarianism on the other. The presupposition of the value of humanism—personal happiness—is always situated in a particular landscape and historical period and with complex vernaculars and material relations; as I take up in later chapters, it is not such an easy simplification.

Elements of tree-planting work are set up to value the individual and the subjective choices he or she might make, since there is no technical minimum requirement of per-day planting, little oversight, and long swaths of unstructured time. Tree planting sets up for those who pursue it a particular narrative of individualism: freedom to make choices about when to work, how much to work, and whether to "cheat" the system. Tree-planting discourse sets up a particular narrative about humans: that each is an individual with the freedom to do as he or she wants, that each has a choice about whether to work hard, that those subjective choices are played out in an objective field. This is further instilled in planters' consciousness by their community-commonsense interpretation of silvicultural work as the "bottom of the totem pole" (G. Chappell, unpublished data), the "bottom of the industry" (S. Dyck, unpublished data), or the "bottom of the hill" (R. Boldt, unpublished data) of forestry work. In many ways, the narrative plays out as an underdog individualism, acceptedly self-branded—much like contemporary consumer trends—by "external disadvantage, and passion and determination" (Paharia et al. 2011, 775).

Yet this pride manifests itself in unusual ways, as James, a ten-year "veteran" planter, says: "You start to think of yourself, or you get either the reputation that comes first or you start to think of yourself that way or you think of yourself this way, and then it's a self-fulfilling prophecy. You think of yourself as a dirtbag, basically. I think dirtbag is the term most of us use to describe ourselves, fairly proudly, about living in a nonconventional way" (J. Simpson, unpublished data).

While James reflects on the pride of accepting an identity of a tree planter that embraces the unconventional, he uses the nonhuman vernacular *dirtbag* to describe such an identity—which could be substituted with a more common humanistic term such as *migrant worker*. The term usually means an "unkempt or slovenly person," yet such a reference is derived etymologically from "actual bags of dirt"—originally, sandbags or vacuum bags in the United Kingdom (Martin 2017). Planters embrace both ways of thinking; being a dirtbag is both living with unconventional employment rhythms and also getting comfortable with "just having dirt on you all the time" (R. Boldt, unpublished data). Such terminology saturates and disturbs the easy distinction between the human and the nonhuman and between economic and natural paces; as an article written about British Columbia's artist-dirtbags (Johnson 2016) hints, the two inform each other. As freelance illustrator and tree planter Max Brown explains, "Artistic people are attracted to planting because they need to pay their rent and student loans, and they likely aren't doing that by selling art." However, Brown simultaneously builds on this simplification, saying that "the [art] I'm doing now that uses repetition techniques is pretty much directly inspired by the way pieces of land are planted" (quoted in Johnson 2016). The dirtbag human is rife with possibilities: covered in organic matter, using movement and exposure to nonhuman elements to construct a self through interaction with what Jane Bennett (2010, xvi) might term *vibrant things*, moving agentive and persuasive capacity from the individual toward a collective of human and nonhuman.

### "Cream" vs. "Slash": Good and Bad Land

A common element within tree-planting vernacular is an assessment of the land workers plant on and that land's attribution of either "goodness" or "badness"—traits given to the land, but also properties that bleed into planters' assessments of their work, their feelings, their days, and what differentiates one from another. Here the attributes of "good" or "bad" are descriptive both topographically—qualities of landscape—and also evaluatively and affectively, how happy or unhappy the land makes the planter. That is, planters describe land in humanist terms that treat happiness as "the only good" and the desire for greater happiness as a primary motivation—whether it makes their job easy or difficult and thus whether they labor for more or less financial gain at the end of the day. In other words, they qualify the land based primarily on whether it makes their own lives better, with a few exceptions.

In terms of planting geography, "good land" "means it's a bit more environmentally decimated":

> Some logging companies will come in and will clear-cut most of the trees but will leave a lot of the, a lot of stuff standing, will leave bushes and alder bushes and trees and will leave all the logs on the land that they've cut that they don't want, which means that the land is able to come back to its natural state more easily but [also] means a lot more work for us. We're jumping over logs and climbing over things, and, especially if it's slippery, you're scrambling and falling and getting caught in alder bushes who knows how many times. Whereas other companies will come in and they will just clear-cut the whole thing, take everything, drag it into the center, and burn it, which means that it's a really nice piece of land for us to plant because there isn't all kinds of stuff to be climbing over. (E. Sawatzky, unpublished data)

All of the planters I interviewed differentiated between good and bad land by describing its characteristics in vernacular terms: "The name of good land is 'cream,' that's if you get 'creamy' land, that's the best. And so like, at least in the area we've planted, it's kind of different everywhere, but like, the definition of 'super creamy piece' would be if it was basically just dirt because a lot of what you're planting in is . . . like, it's been forested, right? And so there's stumps everywhere and then between the stumps there's sort of like—they call it 'slash'" (G. Chappell, unpublished data). All of the planters I spoke with made the distinction between good and bad land by tying it to both their progress and the preparedness of the land through machine-human intervention. As Ryan described, "There's just so many different variables, but in general soft land without any dried debris on top is good land, and hard, clayey baked land where there's tons of like little sticks . . . or if there's tons of fallen logs which you have to constantly step over and stuff like that, that's bad land. Basically, anything that slows you down is bad, and anything that allows you to go fast is good" (R. Boldt, unpublished data).

Although the fast=good and slow=bad equation sounds simple, the algebra involved was composed of complex descriptions of micro-sites that were created by machine preparation and dependent on soil type and topography. Planters were more than willing to describe land types based on preparation. Ryan further elaborated on three main types of cut blocks that determine a planters' experience of the land: prep blocks, direct blocks, and fill blocks. Prep blocks (another word for scarified land), noted overwhelmingly as the land most likely to be creamy, are those in which forested land is cleared by machine with little scrub or brush left in the way, either through digging large or small rowed trenches, scooping large holes in the earth and upending them into mounds on which planters plant their trees, or burning debris to provide cleared terrain and ashy soil (T. Kroeker, R. Boldt, L. Ainsworth, unpublished data). Direct blocks are those in which varying amounts of unusable debris ("slash") or significant layers of "duff"—"mossy, crumbly stuff that wasn't soil" (S. Friesen, unpublished data)—have been cleared, leaving debris either on the forest floor to decay or amassed in large piles (see figure 1.1). Fill blocks are those areas of deforested blocks that have been previously replanted but whose rates of growth are too slow and therefore they must be replanted, a kind of "failed block" for logging companies that seek to avoid penalty. Fill blocks are often the most challenging because planters are fighting through regrowth (R. Boldt, unpublished data).

Yet scarification was not the only factor in determining good land; planters determine land's goodness by its easiness to negotiate bodily, either in terrain attributes (flat vs. mountainous) or soil quality (organic vs. inorganic). Planters overwhelmingly described flat terrain as the best for planting (usually available in prairie provinces like Saskatchewan and Manitoba) and mountain planting (primarily in British Columbia or Alberta) as more challenging:

> You've got really steep topography or relief or whatever, and the forestry companies there had an idea that they needed to shelter the seedlings from the Chinook winds because they warm them up prematurely in winter, and they would leave them unexposed or something like that, so we had to, so we would have to plant them at a certain directional orientation relative to like an obstacle of some kind, like a chunk of wood or like a mound of dirt or whatever that just happened to be there, which is a huge headache, as you can imagine, and slowed you down considerably. It was

*Figure 1.1. Slash pile (Photo credit: Lindsay Ainsworth)*

> like you had to always shelter them from the southwest or something like that, I forget. Yeah, obviously really different because you're in the mountains, so it's like sometimes you're on, you know, I don't know, I probably a few times was on like a forty-five-degree angle, that would be pretty steep but that could happen sometimes. (T. Kroeker, unpublished data)

Georgia elaborated on the difficulty of mountain planting:

> You're in great shape if the slope you're planting on is the same direction you're supposed to be sheltering the trees—because if the slope is here and [the] tree is here [motions downhill] and then just the slope itself protects the trees, but I was planting on a very steep mountain that was also on the exact opposite direction I was supposed to shelter the trees from, so I had to find obstacles twice as big, and so I was basically like, it was just like rock in most places, rock with like a couple of inches of dirt on top of it so you couldn't tell where the rock was. And so, and there, there was no natural—there was no way to get your shovel deep enough to dig your trees in. So I was building little tipis for my trees to live behind. It was pouring rain, thunder storming all day. I was having a terrible time. (G. Chappell, unpublished data).

Topographic difficulty is compounded by soil type, as Nik, a three-season planter, described:

> Bad land is, well, we had lots of different kinds. So, swamp, I mean, that's just, the problem with that is just not a lot of good soil. A lot of what you can plant in is sphagnum moss, which is like, it's like a sponge basically, and you can plant in it, it's just, sometimes it's really thin, so you can't

squeeze a tree into something that['s] the depth of the pod, which is typically 2 to 3 inches, [it] won't fit into [the soil], or you'll fail your assessment. And other times with the swamp it's like, it'll look like it's solid, but it's not. So I used to wear rubber boots, but even once in a while you'd get a full leg in, and it's tough. It's just tough to get a good groove going. The best land is somewhere you can just, it's called "pounding," so you go, you know, head down, you just get into a good groove, you just, tree, tree, tree and you don't have to switch direction too much; you don't have to deal with too many obstacles. Some other bad land is rock top [cap], so it's just basically like an inch of soil with rock underneath, and that's just the worst 'cause you're slamming your shovel down, and you feel that come up your arm, hurts, and you just can't get trees in. So you're going around trying to squish little pieces of moss together; it's just futile.

In my second year, we dealt with this land called "chemical." So basically a plane flies overhead with a selective herbicide, and it kills everything, all the big leafy stuff, and then you go through and plant. But the problem is that it hasn't been mowed down, so I think mostly what they use it for is land that was clear-cut years ago but wasn't planted right away, so just random things, like natural forest, would regrow, but they're trying to have like an optimum spruce stand. So they go ahead and spray if after it's been growing for five to ten years, so you have [dead] trees that are like 6 feet tall, 4 feet tall, 2 feet tall, just a big mix, and planting through that stuff is just, the first time I hit that I was so choked, I was like, how am I supposed to [plant]. 'Cause you're just dodging trees, you're getting trees in the face, and you can't really, it just feels futile. There's all these dead trees, you're going through a dead forest, crazy. But yeah, there's all kinds of bad land. When it's all water, that's the worst though 'cause you're like, can I please not plant this? None of these trees are going to live anyway. (N. Friesen Hughes, unpublished data)

Thus the evaluation of land, its preparedness for planting, has little to do with how well the trees will fare, how optimal the land is for forest regrowth, or how ecologically viable it is. Instead, land is *schnarb* if it is difficult (T. MacInnins, unpublished data) and creamy if it is easy and allows a planter to move quickly and without fear of injury and, above all, if it allows a planter to "pound"—to get as many possible trees in the ground at the quickest possible rate. In this discourse, we see some accepted premises of the separation of nature from culture, whether in Nik's separation of "natural forest" from "optimum spruce stand" or Georgia's undisturbed mountainside contrasted with constructed tree tipis. No matter this reification of the nature/culture split, planters commonly see themselves—that is, humans—at the center of land evaluation; that is, land as an object is good or bad only in relation to the human subject planting on it.

Perhaps this is no more clearly evidenced in planting descriptions than when tree planters ascribe ownership to the planter, as Kailen does in the epigraph at the beginning of this chapter. All planters interviewed at one time or another described their work as working on "your piece" (G. Chappell, L. Ainsworth, R. Boldt, T. Bourlas, unpublished data)—that is, whether in statements like "I was out of land" (S. Dyck, unpublished data), "I had a good piece" (R. McCannell, unpublished data), or "everybody gets their land" (D. Cheater, unpublished data), planters view the land they are on as representing a kind of temporary ownership. This resonates with traditional notions of humanism and agency that place humans at the center of the narrative and, in this case, nature as exterior to it, as something that may be owned and transferred. Yet there is some complication in planters' evaluation of *their* land. Throughout their descriptions, we see the intersections of planters with *things*: machine mulchers, tractors and tows to create scarified rows (like bräcke mounders); planes filled with herbicide; shovels to *pound* with. We can't fully understand the geography of planting without also looking at the intersections of planters' relations with the nonhuman. Before I examine those relations, however, it is worth examining the intersections of humanism with rhetorics of efficiency built into the economy of tree planting, which depend on similar reasoning and logic.

### RHETORICS OF EFFICIENCY

There is a clear connection between the humanistic, happiness-seeking individual focused on the rationality of subjective choices promoted by planters' discursive choices and the rhetorics of efficiency, which are focused on an economic model of increased production as the definitive "good." As Thomas Princen (2005, 49) details, although we generally conceive of efficiency as a commonsense principle that has to do with a simple "calculation of output per unit of input," its relegation to a strictly economic notion of energy and outcome has been a modern revision from efficiency's classical roots. As Princen notes, the Aristotelian notion of efficiency had embedded within it principles of desire, planning, materials, and effectiveness and was concerned primarily with the fit, appropriateness, and effectiveness of the taskmaster and the task environment to the task—importantly, Princen (2005, 51) observes, *not with* the speed or cost of the labor involved in carrying out the task.

With the advance of mechanized industry, "effectiveness, goal achievement, the neat fit of means and ends slipped away as numbers were invoked to measure, indeed, define, efficiency . . . Efficient solutions to problems of production are [now] those that improve a benefit-to-cost ratio for producer or consumer. An economic efficiency lowers the cost per unit of output, without sacrifice of quality, in relation to the value or price of the finished article" (Princen 2005, 52).

Princen attributes Adam Smith's *Wealth of Nations* and the scientific rationality circulated by engineer Frederick Winslow Taylor as central to modernist underpinnings of the "economic man" and the rise of the corporation, which together successfully changed the meaning of *efficiency* from effectiveness to "nearly synonymous with 'productive,' or 'useful,' even 'good'" (Princen 2005, 50) and a singular notion of labor efficiency as "the shortest possible time for each job to be computed and fixed" (Princen 2005, 59). Yet Princen's work reminds us that this change has been a more than 200-year process in the making that has modified efficiency to not only a singular economic principle but also a social one—what it means to be a good and useful subject. In part, this was a result of the invention of an idealized "economic man," created by economists, a "hyperrational human who bases all decisions on perfect information to maximize personal gain" (Princen 2005, 55). In other words, a human who doesn't exist.

While this definition clearly resonates with the crux of the *anthropos*, in which there is no greater good, perhaps, than (hu)man maximizing personal gain, Princen also points out that the notions of personal gain and profit motives are modern ones by the standard of historical economists such as Robert Heilbroner (1953, 22), who notes that, although "ubiquitous," such a way of thinking is "as modern an invention as printing"—that is, it comes with a contextual and emergent history and may even be considered relatively young. Thus, while I attend to the ways tree-planting narratives similarly adhere to modern economic and social principles of efficiency, it is important to keep in mind two tenets of contemporary efficiency models that work to reify separations between nature and culture: (1) efficiency's imagined agent/actor as an impossible, perfectly informed, "hyper-rational," gain-seeking, pleasure-maximizing human; and (2) the purposeful construction of mechanical efficiency as created to separate skills from knowledge or "thinking from doing" (Haber 1964, 23–24). These separations are enabled by anthropocenic views of nature as a resource that hinder both dwelling perspectives (which denounce the split between mind and matter, thinking and doing) and human-nonhuman assemblages—"ad hoc groupings of diverse elements" (Bennett 2010, 23). As later chapters show, both of these hypotheses are patchy at best when viewed through an ambient perspective.

*The Money Function: Nature as a Resource, Trees as Capital*
In discussing the capitalistic values embedded in contemporary conceptions of environmental and ecological debates, David Harvey (1996, 150) argues that current views on nature (which he seeks to disrupt) rest similarly within economic thought: "It appeal[s] to the theory of markets, to the goals of maximizing utility, and to the centrality of money as the common means to measure heterogeneities of human desires, of use values and of elements and processes 'in nature.'" Importantly, Harvey (1996, 150–51) notes that this discursive approach to valuing nature is conducted almost exclusively through speaking in powerful and universal "money terms" in which a particular natural resource–cum-commodity is attributed a particular monetary value.

Planters certainly embrace the notion that nature can be measured and spoken through the language of money, which accompanied their discussion of good and bad land almost exclusively; as Sam noted, "usually, the standard reference is financial" (S. Dyck, unpublished data). Planting decorum at camp makes it poor form to discuss how many trees a person planted during a day; planters repeatedly noted to me that to disclose their tree-planting numbers on a given day is tantamount to tackiness, rudeness, and vulgarity. Yet planters had little difficulty talking in explicit numerical terms without prompting during the interviews. Contemporary notions of efficiency are concerned, as Mary Clark (1989, 275) argues, "only with what can be counted . . . How much? How big? How many? How fast? How long?" An interesting tension is thus revealed when a social injunction against talking about money is the standard of decorum in silvicultural work, yet planters are keenly aware of their numbers every single day they plant—pointing perhaps to the insidiousness of efficiency as an organizing logic of work, as a self-measure of the neo-liberal individual.

Planters would talk specifically about something they called tree price, which, despite the misleading name, means the money a planter makes per tree (not what a tree "costs" to either acquire or grow). Tree prices ranged from ten to twelve cents per tree on easy, scarified land (S. Dyck, L. Rempel, unpublished data), twelve to fifteen cents per tree on direct blocks (Boldt, unpublished data), and "twenty-five to fifty cents, something like that, depending on how hard the land is" (J. Simpson, unpublished data) in fill blocks, mountainous areas, and boggy land. As I spoke with Tamir, who mentioned during an interview that there were "summer" and "spring trees" (in my mind denoting tree type), he quickly clarified that "summer trees are, they're summer contracts, so, you know, you sort of bid on your spring trees, and they're sort of worth a certain amount, and many companies don't plant summer trees. Summer trees are generally in industry looked at as lesser paying, larger growth in the block . . . But the trees themselves are the same, but the contracts aren't as good . . . the tree is the same . . . It's sort of the name given to the contract" (T. Bourlas, unpublished data).

Tree price is the capital system by which all other numbers that interest planters are tallied; it denotes land price (i.e., "twelve-cent land") and even season (spring or summer). To this end, when planters talked about their experiences in numerical terms (a cornerstone of contemporary efficiency rhetorics), they did so with the underlying notion of tree price as the foundation of their narratives and a clear sense of the driving economy of the forest industry. As Jon articulated, "The government charges X-money per stump that the, it's called a stumpage fee, that the logging companies pay to cut in an area, but when combined, when you look at that stumpage fee versus the cost of growing the seedlings and paying the replanting, it's not balanced at all" (J. Sprohge, unpublished data).

Harvey (1996, 152) provides a detailed critique of valuing nature in this way, recognizing the constructed, volatile, and unreliable nature of the money system. He locates this critique in Marx's views on money as a social representation of "labor time and price" rather than a meaningful or steady representation of value, pointing out the unreliability of various money measures in world currencies and indicating the arbitrariness of assumptions that guide money terms. Harvey notes the problematic assumptions behind money prices being attached to *particular* things independent of their ecosystems (i.e., "we presume to value the fish, for example, independently of the water in which they swim") and notes that the linear, Newtonian temporal structure of valuation (i.e., discounting prices over time) does not fit with non-linear, idiosyncratic, and glacial natural paces (Harvey 1996, 153). This is particularly the case with tree planting, whose measure in cent-value per tree (as separate from the substrate that grows it) has nothing to do with the botanical timescale (the eighty years it will take for a pine tree to be harvestable). Such a skewed appeal to money-based valuations, Harvey (1996, 154) argues, "condemns us to a world view in which the ecosystem is viewed as an 'externality' to be internalized in human action only via some arbitrarily chosen and imposed price structure or regulatory regime," further entrenching the nature-culture divide by positing the external natural world as a resource (as in the case of a ten-cent tree and a twenty-five-cent tree *being exactly the same tree*). Even as planters keep track of their work by tree price, they also recognize the arbitrariness of the money system, whether by commenting on tree-planting companies' underbidding on challenging topographical contracts or logging companies' purposefully ignoring environmental protections rules by opting to "cut right to the bank and pay the fine" (J. Sprohge, unpublished data). Planters show an awareness of the preservationist-developmentalist divide as emerging from, as they contend, "the almighty dollar" (J. Sprohge, unpublished data). Despite this awareness to which many demonstrate a conflicted response, planters' commitment to economic and personal efficiency in their narratives, which I next take up, represents to some degree the restrictions posed by pervasive bifurcated views of nature that separate it from human ways of knowing and dwelling.

*Ghost Lines and Dead Walking: Economic Efficiency*

The history of modern economic models of efficiency logics originates in many ways from the work of mechanical engineer Frederick Winslow Taylor during the Progressive Era (1890s–1920s), who laid the groundwork for contemporary ideas about labor efficiency. Taylor is known for developing the human analysis of production, which he termed *scientific management*, by breaking down individual component machinist tasks into "elementary operations" and timing them with a stopwatch. Taylor broke labor down into quantity (tasks completed) and time, giving rise to the "differential piece rate" system in which workers were paid differentially, earning higher wages for working more efficiently and with higher production and earning less for lower levels of production and taking more time (Haber 1964, 2).

While today's minimum wage standards have virtually eradicated the differential piece rate system, it is important to notions of economic efficiency that planters describe, for a few reasons. The first is simple mimicking of taking a job apart by task "pieces," echoed throughout planters' language as a reference to a cut block of land. The second and more important infusion of Taylorism into planting practices is the elevation of quantified task and time that characterizes planters' relationship to their work, despite their assertions that "no one is going to make you plant." This is captured humorously in Kailen's introductory narrative realization: "I thought: 'oh my god you're supposed to be planting like fifty of these in a minute.' And I started panicking, 'I can't just stand here. Oh god, oh god!'"

Much like Kailen, each planter I interviewed described a typical day of planting in terms of how much, how many, how fast, and how long; planters also showed an awareness of the economy of movement ever present in their minds as they worked. Every planter I spoke to described trees numerically: "a box of 18 bundles, bundles of 15, so there's 270 trees total" (T. Bourlas, unpublished data). And although each planter described themselves as driven by financial gain, many spoke more about speed as their driving factor; as Tamir reiterated, "when you're planting you don't really think about money. You just want to plant more trees and cover your ground and cover ground efficiently." While the time needed to plant one box of trees differed by planter, the notion of efficiency—planting as many trees as possible in the fastest amount of time without sacrificing quality—was an overarching theme that emerged in discussions of the work. To plant efficiently, a planter first has to plant according to density amounts set by the reforestation company:

> What they do is they throw plots, have you heard of this? Okay, so checkers have plot cords; planters do too. They're these cords that . . . have a loop at one end, so they'll walk out into the land somewhere, plant their shovel, just like stick it in the ground, and put the loop over the shovel, and then they'll walk to the end of the cord and trace a circle around the shovel, and they'll count all of the trees that are inside there. So the first thing that they're checking is how many trees are in the plot, and that's how we determine the spacing of the entire area. So, at the start of the day, we'll be told, oh, we're planting tens today, which means if you are to do a plot, you would find ten trees in that circle, and they say if they find fourteen, that's too many; that means you're spacing too close and they'll tell you that. (D. Cheater, unpublished data)

Planters consistently described this process (i.e., planting sevens or planting eights) as the constraining force on efficiency and what separated "rookie" (first-season planters) from "veteran" planters, articulated well by Ryan, a thirteen-year veteran:

> Basically, [you're] doing the exact same thing thousands and thousands of times each day, so you're slowly refining your method; and since you're doing the same thing over and over again, you can shave even a fraction of a second off what you're doing, by the end of the day it really adds up, and you'll have made a lot more money, so working hard is really important, but also just being really efficient in what you do and not wasting any motions at the end of the day you'll be making a lot more money, so a rookie could absolutely kill themselves and work as hard as they possibly could and still make less money than a veteran who just seems to be lazily planting trees, simply for the fact that they've refined their methods so much over many, many seasons and hundreds and thousands of trees. So I would say, yeah, any veteran who's really planting consciously will have given a little thought to what they're doing and will have just refined their method over the years until they're very, very, very efficient and they're not wasting any time doing it. As soon as they put the tree in the ground,

they know just exactly how much effort they need to do to close the hole acceptably. They're not doing any extra unnecessary work. They've planted enough trees and gotten enough blocks passed that they're not paranoid about their quality. They know what they need to do to have a good tree, so, as I was saying before, riding the line between quality and speed is so important, so they don't spend extra time unnecessarily worrying about quality. They know exactly what they need to do to plant a good tree, and they don't do anything extra, and so as soon as they put the tree in the ground their head is up, and they're scanning for the next good spot in the area. Whereas when I think of rookies, I was actually the foreman for the rookie crew this past year, so I spent a lot of time around them. When I think of rookies the image that comes to my head is standing still and just looking around slowly, trying to get their bearings and figure out where to put the next tree. Whereas veterans are essentially never ever standing still. They're always moving; they, since they've done it so many times, they instantly know where the next tree needs to go and they're constantly in motion. (R. Boldt, unpublished data)

Each planter detailed the importance of not wasting time, giving specific details about how to plan and time an approach to planting a piece as calculating how many trees it would take for planters to get to and from their tree cache, which is where planters "bag up," or pack up boxes of trees they wear on their shoulders (or take water or food breaks, calculated into "bag-up times" [S. Friesen, unpublished data]). The object, planters described, was never to walk any land with an empty bag and to economize every step with planting in mind—each box taking between thirty and forty minutes to plant. As planters explained, the ideal economical, fluid motion of planting one tree—much like motion studies that study worker movement and time—would be a three-step process of opening a hole in the ground with a shovel, bending down and planting a tree, and stomping the hole closed with one stomp, "grabbing trees every two seconds or so" (R. Boldt, unpublished data)— the motion of Stephanie Clement's mantra *one, two, tree!* Any disruption to this process—extra stomps, an empty bag, thinking too long about the next location, difficult soil conditions, a water or food break—cuts into efficiency, so much so that planters developed a vernacular for inefficient planting, referring to "dead walking" and "ghost lines." As James outlined, "You're always planning out how far into the piece these trees are going to get you and how far back it's going to get you from dead walking from the way you planted your first tree to where your last tree is in the bag of the cache" (J. Simpson, unpublished data).

It is perhaps telling about the pervasive logic of efficiency that planters equate inefficiency with death, the end of human productive value. As planters relayed, the most efficient patterning of planting in a cut block would be to plant from the uncut tree-line border (or "back") of the block without cutting off any access to the cache planters need to return to periodically throughout the day. Planters thus plant in a grid, flagging seedlings with planting tape to know where they have planted and where they have not, and they never walk over any land without simultaneously planting a tree on it. As Ross put it, "You don't want to make . . . yourself do any dead walking is the term that they use, which is walking when you're not planting. Doing any movement when you're not planting trees as you go is stupid. You want to avoid it if you can" (R. McCannell, unpublished data). Georgia similarly described dead walking in temporal terms: "They call it 'dead walk' over planted trees—that you're kind of wasting time on what you could be planting, so it would be best that you could have a straight square you could always be planting so you're not having to walk over your trees and waste time or forget a little bubble because if you forget a little bubble, then you have to go back and plant it later and then nobody is happy with you because it wastes time" (G. Chappell, unpublished data). Any deviations from planting this "straight square"—that is, back and forth in a grid—are known as "ghost lines," lines that diverge from the standard back and forth of square grid planting and are thus tagged as "incredibly inefficient" (L. Ainsworth, unpublished data).

It is worth spending a moment with the metaphors of ghost lines and dead walking, which appear as vernacular for inefficiency coded within temporal and rhythmic situations of the cut block on the landscape. As I suggest in considering the role of affect in tree planters' descriptions of their work in chapter 3, the plantation-scape of the cut block is in itself a space of environmental loss, a place of confronting a variety of ghosts that force a different kind of reckoning with the land. This may take various affective shapes: the frustration of inefficiency, bad land, or spatial sense; the bewilderment of needing to gain one's bearings in a wasteland; the rookie moment it takes to grapple with the question *where the fuck am I supposed to put the tree*. Even these vernaculars that are the most depreciatory of inefficiency show an affectual attunement to the making of plantation spaces.

Yet it's true that tree planters' commitment to efficiency rhetorics was shown in many ways, most notably by readily available descriptions of their work in terms of numerical efficiency measures. Numerical details abound: what price per tree, how many trees per box, how many boxes per bag, how many trees per corded plot density, how many steps to plant a tree, and how much time it takes a planter to plant each box of trees. This, as Clark (1989, 275) maintains, is the epitome of the rhetoric:

"When efficiency takes over, 'goodness' is defined in numerical terms. Whatever is to have value must somehow be converted into a measurable quantity. What cannot be counted is 'of no account'; it is outside the system." While talking to planters, it's true that my interest was piqued far more by what they said that seems, in Clark's terms, to be "of no account"; however, before I attend to those accounts, it is important to look at the way efficiency has become a guiding principle in accounts of tree planting. Here, numerical "goodness" translates to planters' accounts of personal efficiency as not only an economic good but also a social one.

### Your "Personal Best": Accounts of Personal Efficiency

The insidiousness of efficiency is that it has become naturalized as an unquestionable good that has been written into the everyday of modern life, moving from the realm of "technical and managerial" to that of "social and political" (Princen 2005, 84). Today, "efficiency could be a personal attribute as readily as a professional technique" (Princen 2005, 75), writ so indelibly on the psyches of modern citizens as to appear natural and normal despite its ambiguous nature and ability to be manipulated and changed. This is perhaps in no way more apparent than in planters' descriptions of their accounts of financial success from year to year and their adaptation of such success into the rhetoric of personal efficiency—"hard work, thrift, willpower" (Princen 2005, 64)—that characterizes the standard unit by which planting success is measured: the "personal best," or PB.

When efficiency societies and magazines were having their heyday in the 1910s, the principles of efficiency were transformed into a social good, as Hays (1959, 125) cites from a 1913 engineering journal: "When humanity shall have learned to apply the common sense and scientific rules of efficiency to the care of body and mind and the labors of body and mind, then indeed we will be nearing the condition of perfect." Personal efficiency, then, was seen as the antithesis to laziness that promised both perfection and plenty through effort and hard work. This principle is described almost verbatim by planters who reflected on planting done during their first, rookie season:

> Your first day of planting trees pretty much across the board you make, you know, thirty bucks, forty bucks, for like a ten-hour day; and actually the first day isn't so bad, but the third day is horrible. The first day is kind of fun and exciting because you're learning a new thing and getting out there, but you know on your second or third day you start to realize how little money you are making and how hard you're trying . . . in the

beginning, you're terrible. And you make no money. You're not even making minimum wage . . . But then after a month, you like double the amount of trees that you're planting like every day almost, so you're getting better so, so, so fast and making money all the time, which is nice. But it's just so hard. (G. Chappell, unpublished data)

The first year, it's kind of tougher to make a ton of money because you're learning for half the season, and then the other half of the season you do make some money, but it's not as much as people hear about, so it doesn't really seem all that worth it. (S. Friesen, unpublished data)

The first two weeks of your planting career is [*sic*] the hardest of all 'cause it's just so frustrating. You're still, you're trying to learn how to do it, and from what I hear, you're steadily, you are pretty steadily improving all the way up to your fourth or fifth year, and then it's just a very, or third or fourth year, sorry, and then you're just a very, like I think you would still improve, getting more efficient at that point but not nearly as much as from your first to second year, second to third year. (L. Rempel, unpublished data)

Well, I can remember about halfway through the year just doing the simple math and figuring out that I had made nothing. If I encounter or took into account my flights out there and the camping equipment I bought and the money I spent just on our days off in terms of food and laundry and new clothes and whatever, then I had made nothing. (T. MacInnis, unpublished data)

My first day I think I made about negative two bucks; they charge you a camp fee of thirty dollars a day for food and transportation and all that stuff. And you obviously, as a competent tree planter, would make that amount back. But as an incompetent tree planter you very well might not. So I think I planted as a box, 270 trees, they were probably twelve cents each, so thirty-five bucks? So I made five dollars, apparently. You know, you know what? I bet I spent six bucks on beer, so negative one [dollar]. (J. Simpson, unpublished data)

Despite the fact that planting is tallied by tree price and infused with the promise of financial gain, it's clear that planters recognize that there is no direct correlation between input and output. Still, planters relay these narratives as evidence of their hard work and perseverance (making little financially but still sticking with the job).

Perhaps because of this inconsistency, planters give a great deal of credence to the idea of the PB, the highest number of trees they had personally ever planted in one day. Although PBs ranged from 2,000 to 5,000 trees planted in one day and are dependent on region, planters described their personal best days as some of the most memorable because it's "the only time you can talk about how many trees you've planted . . . that doesn't involve telling how many trees you've planted"

(G. Chappell, unpublished data). Here efficiency is concerned with numbers without numbers, invested instead on the personal value of hard work as a matter of pride:

> Particularly when you're starting to get good, then you become incredibly focused on numbers because that's the measure of your success, that's the measure of how well you're doing compared to other people, and it's a measure of personal achievement. And certainly, if you get a bigger number than you've had in the past, that's a matter of pride. (S. Dyck, unpublished data)

> I always looked at it like a game; for me, like I was just trying to be better than myself every day, which obviously you can't do every day, but like when I started it was a thousand trees, and then our camp boss wanted us to be really competitive, she wanted to form a competition just 'cause the more tree[s] you plant in a day, the more efficient the camp runs, so the more money the camp makes and the more money the planter makes, so, I mean, I know that I am benefiting them if I plant more, but I'm also benefiting myself. But I never looked at it like money. I just wanted to plant more trees, and I just took a lot of pride in that. So first I would try to go for 1,000, then I tried to push for two 2,000 and I finally got there, and then I tried to push for 3,000 and I got there. And that was like, that was the mark; once I hit 3,000 I was like, this is where I want to be at. And I hit 4,000 one day in my first year, which I was really happy about, and for days like that, I mean, you get efficient. (N. Friesen Hughes, unpublished data)

> One time I planted over nearly 4,000 trees one day, and it was very thrilling to sort of work my ass off and have a personal best for a day . . . Not much there really when you think about it, it's one tree after the next, but it's a very vivid memory and very exciting. I can remember putting my shovel in the ground, putting the tree in the ground, stomping on it, and doing that so quickly and being so efficient with my movement, and then getting back to the cache, emptying the box of trees, filling my bags up, crumpling the box up, putting it away, and nearly running back out to the block, sweat dripping down your face, adrenaline pumping, and then, yeah, at the end of the day being so exhausted, and, you know, I only made like 200 bucks more than I would any other day, but it was, that's very exciting. (T. Bourlas, unpublished data)

As Tamir notes, the financial reward for a PB is not hugely compelling; it is not the difference of thousands of dollars, it doesn't earn a planter a day off or a bonus. Instead, a PB is a way to indicate social status among planters and is couched as a measure of personal pride and individual hard work.

Here efficiency comes full circle, not only as a measure of success in an economic or a managerial realm but also in the realm of the social and the personal, cementing tree planting as a managerial act that constructs efficiency as what Princen (2005, 84) terms "a self-evident truth.

As individuals become ever more efficient, they, and the society they comprise, are better off." The implicit narrative of progress in these descriptions of tree capital, economy of motion, and numericalization of everything from bagging up to grid planting suggests that, indeed, those who plant are bound to think and act in ways that see nature as a market resource and culture as promoting its exploitation (even when they are giving numbers without numbers). We may wonder, then, if there is any room in the lifeworlds of anthropogenic plantation makers to move beyond these dualities. To answer in the affirmative, I draw my hope from Tsing's (2015a) notion of the *patchy* in the "patchy Anthropocene": that the Anthropocene, as *invented* through lifeworlds, is inconsistent, uneven, sporadic, irregular, or possibly, as she suggests, inadequate.

## DWELLING IN INCONSISTENCIES

In writing through the omnipresence of the nature-culture split through a delineation of its philosophical roots and transport to contemporary discourses that today overarchingly see nature as a resource, my aim has been to acknowledge the very real cultural and material impact such discourse has on human ways of thinking, knowing, and, in the case of industrial silviculture, working. Tree planters are not outside these pervasive ways of thinking about the world. However, the premises on which this divide rests are unstable, considering how often they are conflated with ideas of the hyper-rational human agent; the de-historicizing of contemporary economics, personal gain, and rampant individualism; the reification of the subject-object split for political or financial advantage; and the unchecked assumption of possibilities for unlimited growth. Erased from this discourse are infinite and real possibilities that have long been dismissed and disparaged by reason and rationality—the vernacular, the material, the parochial and the intensely local, the unreasonable, the perspectival, the sensorial, the illogical or nonsensical, the performative, the ambient.

To move from the discourses of the *anthropos* that close off possibilities by separating humans from lifeworlds, we must instead allow the limits of these seemingly commonsensical notions of humanism and efficiency to rise to the fore and recognize that dwelling perspectives have "to entail more than a *logic*" (Rickert 2013, 252) derived from the principle of exteriority. So where might we begin? First, by paying attention to the limits and gaps left to us by privileging humanism and efficiency as the only ways of knowing the world and instead turning deliberately to the particular, the temporal, the qualitative, and the heterogeneous; to turn from the ideal of Western individualism as having much explanatory potential and instead toward the living processes of landscapes as generated in movement, in relations, in affects. This work has to a large extent been done for us by those who take a dwelling perspective in their own work, whether by considering the vitality of matter, the posthuman condition, the porosity between interior and exterior, "cross-species interactions or disturbance-based ecologies" (Tsing 2015b, 15), or human-technosphere interaction.[21] Taken together as applied to the case of tree planting, I call this a new material environmental rhetoric. It means that rather than buy wholeheartedly into the evidence that industrial reforestation workers only see themselves as part of a resource chain anchored in personal profit and secured by promises of unending progress and increased ratios of output to input, our attention is drawn instead to the ways efficiency ratios are "neither self-evident nor is their increase unambiguously 'good'" (Princen 2005, 89). Our attention is drawn instead to the impossibility of the economic man, the nonsensicality of numbers without numbers, the affectual moments of panic and confusion and joy that are bound up in discourses of humanism and efficiency, the persuasive means gathered by nonhuman and inorganic actors. We look, then, to the ambiguous, to the inconsistent, to the planter who speaks in the same breath of efficiency, drain, and performance: "[The pressure to be a good planter is] emotionally draining a little bit because it's like ostensibly the only reason it matters how many trees you plant is because of how much money you make, but that's just not really true. And so, there's this . . . kind of like feeling that you really need to perform for this kind of vague reason you can't really put your finger on" (G. Chappell, unpublished data).

In other words, we look to the ambient as the place(s) within which meaning dwells, as the state of being that living in ruin compels, as an "entire way of life materialized in practices and *things*" (Rickert 2013, 253) that call for our attention when we view tree planting as more than a price per tree in exchange for a stumpage fee: in material human and nonhuman bodies in relation, in feelings and desires and dreams, in soldering lives to machines, all in contribution to inventing the fragmented Anthropocene.

### NOTES

1. "Bräcke" is short for "Bräcke mounds" created by a Bräcke mounder, a large machinic excavator equipped with two spades that mounds dirt into two rows, making land easier to plant.

2. See, for example, Harvey's (1996) discussion of "The Nature of the Environment" and Cronon's (1995) assertions in *Uncommon Ground*.
3. See Escobar 2008; Whatmore 2002; Lorimer 2012; Goldman and Schurman 2000; Maffi 2001; Pretty 2007 for representative samples of these arguments as taken up in their respective disciplines.
4. For a fuller discussion of deep ecology and spiritual essentialism, see Braidotti 2013, 86.
5. See also Oelshlaeger 1991.
6. Pilgrim and Pretty 2010, 1; Strathern 1980, 180.
7. For the sake of brevity, I have not included various responses to modernist conceptions of nature in the seventeenth through twentieth centuries; for a fuller discussion, see Oelschlaeger 1991.
8. See also Craig, Yung, and Borrie 2012 for an extensive historical overview of Glacier land claims.
9. For a nuanced discussion of this displacement as it pertains to American national parks, see Keller and Turek 1999.
10. For a discussion of how a "de-humanized nature" historically *and* contemporarily affects Indigenous landscapes of Amazonia, see Tavares 2016.
11. Tree planters also note this discrepant perspective in consideration of the sonic landscape created by logging roads, as discussed in chapter 4.
12. See Sandlands 2000, 177–79.
13. Natural Resources Canada 2016.
14. Comparable numbers in the United States are 1.4 percent of the GDP in agriculture, forestry, fishing, and hunting; 1.2 percent in mining; and 1.3 percent in the "utilities" sector (which includes the gas and power industries) (Bureau of Economic Analysis 2016).
15. See also Killingsworth and Palmer's (2012) discussion of Stephen Fox and his historic work on John Muir and the creation of Yosemite National Park.
16. For example, Winthrop 1972.
17. For further discussion of this tension, see Killingsworth and Palmer 2012, 24.
18. See also Descola 2013, xv-xvi.
19. For these discussions, see Gaonkar 1997; Grassi 2001; Althusser 2003; Mailloux 2012.
20. This stems from the "creed" of Robert Ingersoll (2009 [1900], 478), noted humanist and free thinker, who asserted: "Happiness is the only good. The place to be happy is here. The time to be happy is now."
21. See Bennett 2010; Braidotti 2013; Descola 2013; Haff 2013; Iovino and Opperman 2014; Tsing 2015b for detailed discussions of each of these topics.

# 2
## A NEW MATERIALIST ENVIRONMENTAL RHETORIC
*Rhetorical Bodies in Relation*

> *The grunt work penetrates. It gets inside us, one layer at a time, from our epithelial layers to the innermost connective tissue. In the beginning we collected blisters on our hands and feet. They filled with fluid, only to break and rub away. Now we're bruised on our hips from the weight of our bags, hairless on the thighs from the friction. The chapped lips, the broken fingernails. We fray along the edges. (Gill 2011, 44)*

> *You don't relate to people as well for a little bit, [it's] hard to cross the street. You lose your sense, that's the interesting thing . . . when you don't cross the street you lose your ability to time with the cars when you're walking 'cause you don't cross the street, like it's actually not as ingrained in you as you might think, so if you don't cross the street for a month, you're not sure when to walk. ~Tamir*

> *Well, the first thing is it changes your view of ground. You see ground differently as a planter 'cause you're looking for things, your brain is so used to looking for spots, you can, I can tell now just by looking at something, oh, that's a good place to plant. ~Dan*

As forest workers, tree planters are caught between environmentalist and developmentalist ideals, between nature and culture, in a locus from which experience is categorized in discourses of efficient labor practices and humanistic choice. They are not, after all, outside of contemporary notions of the Anthropocene that situate nature as primarily a resource for unrelenting human progress and development. Yet such a progressive narrative, as I've hinted, assumes an acceptance of modernism, a commitment to the mind-body (or nature-culture or human-animal) split, an unambiguous appeal to reason, a separation of

DOI: 10.7330/9781607328551.c002

subject from object, and a human notion of time scale. There is much, in other words, to qualify with a "but!" about. Here is where we can enter the chōra, invent other sides to what is perpetuated by Western thought—privileging the economic [hu]man above all else. In what follows, I suggest an intervention into the model of efficient humanism as captured in chapter 1, putting forward three alternate premises for what I call a new materialist environmental rhetoric, which I then use to begin to examine tree planting as a placemaking, ambient activity. I then look more closely at the bodies involved in tree planting—first planter-bodies, then animal bodies, and finally tree-bodies—to establish the ways planters' descriptive inconsistencies have the capacity to offer a richer model of natureculture (as opposed to nature-culture).[1]

Such descriptive inconsistencies offer us a glimpse of what is possible in acts of inventing the Anthropocene, hinging on the possibility that its invention is a choric one. If we entertain this possibility, that chōra is a place defined from within (as in animals grazing on a landscape) rather than from without (as on a boundaried map),[2] planter descriptions provide a particular vision that troubles the logics of efficiency and humanism, even if they do not wholeheartedly overturn them. They point our attention to body logics, which sometimes inhabit the world of efficiency and humanism (we cannot work if we cannot eat or rest, for example).

Yet these logics also extend out from the human body to other bodies, from efficient human work to the capacity for such efficiencies to stem from the capacity to affect and be affected. Such a turn suggests that the seeming constancy and un-mutability of humanism and efficiency are not the only available protocols at work on a landscape built from a sensorium.

To understand tree planting outside of these common narratives is a matter of invention, of tracing the relations that emerge through description, of instead accepting somewhat different premises, or what I'll call here *élucubrations—wild imaginings*.[3] These three premises together create a framework or approach to planter descriptions that I'm calling a new materialist environmental rhetoric, an approach that blends elements of ambient rhetoric, new materialism and material ecocriticism, and critical affect studies and that is resonant with postcolonial Indigenous research paradigms that value a relational ontology.[4] The first of these premises is that we entertain a notion of the rhetorical human that does not differentiate so clearly between the rational and non-rational, the communicative and the linguistic—beginning instead, as John Mucklebauer (2011, 99) suggests, from a "sociality of multiple forces and effects." The second is that we accept an "underivable rhetoricity" (Davis 2014, 536) of human bodies, plant bodies, animal bodies, and thing-bodies. The third is that we define a tree planter as one in a series of bodies whose affects we wish to trace among others in trying to give meaning to the phenomenon of tree planting. In accepting these élucubrations and focusing closer attention on planters' descriptive inconsistencies—patchiness—I argue that within the discursive space noted of efficiency and humanism, there are also the competing and messy recognitions of bodies that run right up against the edges of those discourses: injured forms that complicate efficiency, entwinenments of human bodies with animal bodies and with plant bodies that suggest relations that interrupt humanism as a binding or definitive worldview. These premises, which undergird the ability to see these descriptions through the lens of a new materialist environmental rhetoric, situate a plantation's vernaculars differently: not as hopeful per se—catastrophe is far beyond hope, as Anna Tsing (2015a) would tell us—but directing us instead to the ways human/animal/plant/thing heterogeneity assembles human livability as "a better way of confronting man": *man* who is slave to the human, slave to efficiency, slave to ruin.

## ÉLUCUBRATION 1, THE RHETORICAL HUMAN: NO DETOUR THROUGH LOGOS

One of the main tenets of contemporary humanism, as Steven Mailloux (2012, 136) asserts, is that it "always differentiate[s] humans from other beings," primarily on the onto-theological basis that "only the logical, rational word is valid and objective" (Grassi 1988, 144)—or in Jacques Derrida's (2008, 92) words, that only humans are "*able to do* 'I.'" While certainly contestable,[5] this not only makes it impossible to see humans as beings on the same plane as other organisms (such as animals or plants) and inorganic matter (rocks or machines), but it also makes central to human *being* the separation of the rational/communicative, on the one hand, from the mechanical/nonlinguistic on the other.[6] In such a model, there is a separation of reason from *unreasonable* forces: no room for instinct and the senses or for grunt work to penetrate, no possibility for rhetoricity as a necessary precondition for any kind of being, no room for bodies that do not behave as they should, no room for reactions that do not first take a "detour through logos" (Mucklebauer 2011, 96).

If we are to accept Thomas Rickert's (2013, 254) notion of persuasion as ambient, that is, "persuasion as a kind of attunement or listening to things and environs," we might recognize that we simply cannot accept such an idea without also acknowledging that there is room to refute the necessary detour through logic to get there. When we attune ourselves to an environs, when we listen, we don't hear only that which makes a stop through Station Logic. Instead, we are beset by things that don't make a whole lot of "sense"—by the ways our bodies feel in space despite how the space should make us feel; by the things we do that are not "good" for us; by dreams and memories that have come before; by decisions we make that seem "counterintuitive" (as though intuition also runs through logic before it hits us); by lust, ritual, and nonhuman interventions; by the way bodies respond to a variety of persuasive forces. It calls our attention to description that embraces bodies losing their sense, forgetting how to cross a street, seeing ground differently, breaking and rubbing away.

To grasp a patchy Anthropocene, then, one needs to make room for the inconsistent rhetorical human animal alongside *homo oeconomicus rationalis*. A great deal of what is emerging out of animal studies already makes this argument, and in far more sophisticated ways.[7] Yet I lean in toward the arguments John Mucklebauer (2011, 98) makes for rhetorical thinking, that it isn't either/or: "We are not faced with mechanical instincts on the one hand and free, rational actions on the other, but simply two different types of instincts, two different types of actions—one of which demands a 'mechanical' detour through logos, while the other does not."

In taking the contribution of those studying animal rhetorics seriously, Mucklebauer (not without skepticism) suggests that we enlarge our thinking about *being* out from the human, much in the way Scot Barnett and Casey Boyle (2017) do in arguing for a rhetorical ontology. To do so depends on problematizing the human/animal/thing divide, imagining communication models that move beyond "symbolic exchange," and, lastly, "loosening the stranglehold that communicative rationality still maintains on rhetoric's sense of the civic imaginary. Instead of beginning from a normative (human) ideal of the sociality of reason, we might begin from a nonhuman sociality of multiple forces and effects" (Mucklebauer 2011, 99).

While loosening such a stranglehold might take any number of forms, for Mucklebauer (2011, 99) the outcomes are substantial: "*The structure of how rhetorical scholarship enacts itself* (and not only what it writes about) would be at stake here," he says. This has been evident in the ways scholars are beginning to do this work; for example, how Tsing (2012, 141) takes up "fungal arguments," by the ways Donna Haraway (2003) theorizes companion species to detail interspecies relationships, through what Alex Parrish (2014) details as adaptive rhetoric, through what Jonathan Gray (2017) imagines as rhetorical-magical thinking, or through what Ehren Helmut Pflugfelder (2017) notes as kinesthetic rhetoric. It is alongside these thinkers that I argue for a new materialist environmental rhetoric, rhetorical scholarship that takes at the outset the inseparability of human from nonhuman, reason from unreason, and instead draws our attention to rhetorical energy, its forces and effects. A new materialist environmental rhetoric also suggests a move away from modernist notions of cognitive reason, aesthetic reason, or even reason that definitively answers the question, "how should I live"? In the time of the anthropocenic plantation, we cannot expect the pragmatic moral voice to correctly answer that question: perpetually living in ruin makes the question impossible to answer rationally, for the answer as we self-destruct is "not like this."

Thus as this chapter navigates the communicative non-rationality[8] of planters' lives that runs up against questions of reason and rationality, thinks through multiple exchanges between human and nonhuman bodies, and traverses logical and non-logical pathways for making meaning, it is my intention to call attention to the ways the ambient is an intervention into understanding the patchy and inconsistent Anthropocene—the way the landscape is understood to be made between *a sociality of multiple forces and effects* located within the interstices of both efficiency and inefficiency, humanism and animality, humanscapes and plantscapes. This understanding does not require a special type of magnifying glass or a PhD in ambience. Rather, it is the way human bodies—particularly those already attuned to ruin—make meaning of and in the world in relation to others.

### ÉLUCUBRATION 2, NEVER SIMPLY HUMAN: AN UNDERIVABLE RHETORICITY OF BODIES

Accepting that humans are not a wholly separate category from nonhumans has taken a great deal of work over a great deal of time by philosophers, scientists, and rhetoricians; although this is a recognizable commonplace in Indigenous knowledge,[9] the idea has only recently been recognized in settler epistemologies. In the space of one book, I cannot do justice to all of the work here or cover the historical span that would describe in a few pages the philosophies of Jakob von Uexküll, Martin Heidegger, Maurice Merleau-Ponty, and Jacques Derrida (among many others) as they pertain to the animal subject. Yet contemporary rhetoricians have taken up and qualified these philosophical arguments in ways useful to framing meaning making in the everyday and asserting rhetoric's relevance to making sense of the world. Debra Hawhee (2011) and Diane Davis (2017) note the "shockwaves" that emerged in rhetorical circles after George Kennedy presented his 1993 talk "A Hoot in the Dark," named after his 1992 *Philosophy and Rhetoric* article of the same name, which made the first case for an Aristotelian, nonhuman rhetoric. It could be said, then, that taking Western rhetoric into the realm of the nonhuman is barely twenty-five years old, although the questions contemporary rhetoricians struggle with in thinking about rhetoric and the nonhuman are thousands of years old, if the use of Aristotelian rhetoric to frame rhetoric among animals is any indication.[10] As rhetorical scholars have grappled with what interspecies or cross-species encounters might mean (or indeed if they could mean at all), they have come up against the same Cartesian dualisms that categorize nature-culture distinctions, whether in splitting mind-body or human-animal. As Davis (2014, 537) notes, for Descartes, "the specifically human part of the human animal—the thinking part—is not in *any* sense animal." Davis (2014, 537) takes us thoughtfully through arguments that try to separate out the thinking human as rhetorically apart from other living bodies, noting that historically the main distinction has been "the capacity for autoreferential self-distancing"—to not only have an "I" but to be able to self-referentially represent it.

Given the range of animal studies Davis cites, to say nothing of the early work Kennedy collected on crows and apes, as well as contemporary work on plant life[11] and increasing rhetorical scholarship on a range of nonhuman animals such as salmon, orcas, and vultures,[12] it is clear that the litmus test of being "able to do I" is less indicative of humaning than it used to be, depending less on an ontological "I" and often more on sense (for example, human sense in relation to plant sense [Chamovitz 2013, 6]).[13] Indeed, thinking widely—and not just humanistically—about persuasion widens its scope in innumerable ways. What Kennedy (1992, 3) called "rhetorical energy" or Rickert might call rhetorical attunement, we might find not only in human bodies the rhetorical sense of "I am." Instead, we might find such rhetoricity in what Mucklebauer (2017) suggests is visible in the everyday, as *relational* and *affectual* rhetorical forces located within action and motion. Such rhetorical forces may be found in animal bodies, as when animals grieve;[14] plant bodies, as when plants "remember past infections . . . and then modify their current physiology based on those memories" (Chamovitz 2013, 138); or thing-bodies, as when roads persuade us "to go some places rather than others" (Mucklebauer 2017, 37)—or in relations between bodies of all kinds. The focus here is not on the "I am" but rather on an "I" already located in the relation between self and other—*there is no "I am" that stands outside of relation.* This is well-represented by Shawn Wilson's (2001, 91) coining of the "self-as-relationship" (as opposed to "self-in-relation") Indigenous relational ontology in which the self is constituted by "relationships with all living things." Contemporary rhetorical theorists working at the intersection of rhetorical energies and adaptation are attuned to rhetorical bodies and forces and are aware of the complexity of rhetorical situations and the bodies that move to create them. Davis (2014, 536–37) calls this "the practically unfathomable scope and significance of rhetorical operations, which were never simply human. An underivable rhetoricity is the immaterial 'something' from which a presumption of self-knowledge arises . . . it's not an innate quality 'in man' but the already relational condition for *any* living being who presumes to recognize and refer to him- or herself."

I will add here to Davis's "underivable rhetoricity" of bodies and Smith's "self-as-relationship" Mucklebauer's (2017, 40) notion of a *heliotropic* vision for a new materialist environmental rhetoric, a framework that emerges in service of "flattening out the nature-culture distinction that is absolutely fundamental to the field" and moves us instead toward the belief that "plants turning toward the sun and audiences accepting an argument might well involve the same kind of action/motion." Again, this turns our attention (in our wild imagination) to the action of rhetorical forces, effects, movement, and relations on a multitude of bodies—a shared "irreducible rhetoricity" (Davis 2014, 537)—rather than to the split that separates human culture from nature.

### ÉLUCUBRATION 3, PLANTER-BODIES ARE SETS OF RELATIONS

If the imaginings of a new materialist environmental rhetoric have held to accept the inconsistently rational rhetorical human and an irreducible rhetoricity of bodies, then it is my hope that a turn to focus from a singularly human ability to be rhetorical to the relations among bodies in motion to reveal a rhetoricity of the everyday is not such a long shot. To that end, to imagine planter-bodies as a set of relations central to understanding tree planting as a phenomenon comes out of the work of Brett Buchanan (2008) and Jeffrey Nealon (2016), both of whom turn to Gilles Deleuze and Félix Guattari to frame their thinking on animal and plant bodies, respectively. Despite taking on very different subject matter,[15] both scholars frame the understanding of nonhuman meaning making with Deleuze and Guattari's (2003 [1987]) notion of *becoming*, or identifying the process by which different parts of an assemblage[16] change or move. Whether thinking through questions of relations between orchid and wasp, spider web and fly, octopus and water, or rhizomes and trees,[17] both scholars are compelled to view elements in an assemblage in terms of their variations, transitions, or movements—which give rise to both "individuation and environment" (Nealon 2016, 86) as opposed to a singular form. This same philosophy undergirds the discussion of circulating affect in chapter 3 and a consideration of the vitalism of thing-bodies in chapter 4.

While each scholar nuances arguments forwarded in Deleuze and Guattari's (2003 [1987]) body of work and uses them primarily to break down the distinction between human/animal, human/plant, and animal/plant, I'm particularly interested in their emphasis on affect,[18] drawn from Baruch Spinoza, which suggests that "affects are inseparable from their relations to bodies, where bodies are not considered in terms of their function or form, but in terms of how they can be affected, how they can undergo transitions, and, at bottom, how they define what a body can do" (Buchanan 2008, 158).

Here, attention moves from the mind/body split (an emphasis on form) to an understanding of things (human bodies, plant bodies, animal bodies, thing-bodies) through *their capacity to be affected*. In other words, while there may be no detour through logos, there is no avoiding the affective stop, a turn critical affect scholars take up. Thinking through planter bodies, then, means we understand them in terms of their relations with other bodies as well as how they engage in space and time. Rebekah Sheldon (2015, 217) offers a generative protocol for imagining such affective capacities by inviting a new lexicon: "*Composition* highlights the interrelations between parts; *movement* refers to the characteristic circuiting of energy through that form; *sound* to the layers or tonal stacks striating it; *rhythm* to the vibratory milieu created by it; and, finally, *gesture* looks to the capacities for connection and the production of potentialities. Together, these properties illustrate the internal workings of a form and its relations to the aesthetico-political milieu."

Thus, the remainder of this chapter (and indeed, chapters 3 and 4) will look at these affects and how they manifest through composition, movement, sound, rhythm, and gesture. Understanding tree planting through what a planter-body can do takes us into this next realm of when the forest beckons, to possibilities of plant selves and tree-bodies, black flies and crows that move up against communicative rationalism, which would suggest that a tree planter is simply an efficient profit-driven chooser. A new materialist environmental rhetoric re-understands the human as embroiled in lifeworlds that are always already caught up with other nonhumans in composition, sound, rhythm, and gesture and suggests the potential of the Anthropocene to not only be invented on the map but also reinvented from within. Bodies make and are made by the plantation-scape. Such an imagining has the potential to shift our focus from an apocalyptic Anthropocene, already predetermined, to other ontologies that shift focus to a different kind of equilibrium:

> A body can be anything; it can be an animal, a body of sounds, a mind or an idea; it can be a linguistic corpus, a social body, a collectivity. (Deleuze 1988 [1970], 127)

> Cloud, feather, rainbow, car, justice, spider-fly, a pack of rats. Each is a body. A body is the accumulation of relations that, at a certain state of equilibrium, is able to maintain itself without destroying itself as *this* consistency. (Buchanan 2008, 160)

Entertaining planter-bodies as sets of relations allows for messiness, for patchiness, for an examination of equilibrium and the rhetoricity of the everyday. The Cartesian split between mind and body (or culture and nature) has, so far, offered little complex explanatory potential to understand the experience of tree planting as an activity or, more broadly, to consider the role of affectual relations in constructing lifeworlds. I imagine a new materialist environmental rhetoric to be geared toward a much messier, richer view of the interrelation between mind and matter. Turning our attention to affect and bodies, we can entertain instances of persuasive bodies running up against destructive and productive affects, exchanges of actions and passions, and body compositions that move with and alongside efficiency and humanism in thinking through/with our environment. When we turn our attention to the messiness of human-nonhuman interactions and their non-logics, it is possible to see the contingent nature of the human that points to possible disruptions in thinking about both time scale (plant, human, road) and space-scale (ground, speed, movement order, disorder) that characterize the discourse of the Anthropocene.[19] Perhaps such messiness is what may allow a rethinking, not of the Anthropocene from without (as epochs of time suggest) or within (as metaphors of apocalypse encourage) but as a choric *through*, an ambient *with*. Planter-bodies and their interactions with land through pain, injury, and pleasure; planter-bodies moving with and against animal encounters; planter-bodies and affectual encounter with the rhetorical forces of tree-bodies—all of these encounters point to the ways a new materialist environmental rhetoric might closely attend to a way *through* using the human as a way *in*, a beginning.

## PLANTER-BODIES IN SPACE: RHETORICS OF EFFICIENCY AND HUMANISM IN RELATION

Maureen Johnson and her colleagues (2015) contend that recognizing the material body itself as a site of rhetorical power marks an allegiance to feminist rhetorical work that has been reduced in conventional scholarship because such scholarship minimizes focus on the body as a site of meaning making.[20] In turning to the human planter-body alongside animal and plant bodies, I am recognizing the contribution of both feminist rhetorical scholars who acknowledge the roles bodies play in ways of knowing as well as those working in feminist new materialism whose aims are to attune us to the relationality of natureculture.[21] In terms of understanding tree planting through the planter-body, I turn here to the idea that "bodies interact actively with discursive and linguistic rhetorical practices" (Johnson et al. 2015, 41) to make meaning. In doing so, I forward an understanding of tree planting as a relational phenomenon made from "not just forms and matters, but of the space that holds them both" (Sheldon 2015, 209). Thus a "planter-body" is not simply a human person who has a job planting trees but a human-shovel-tree-landscape assemblage that is constantly in motion. Reading planter-bodies (alongside animal, plant, and thing-bodies) as rhetorical sites of meaning of the not-*only*-human offers openings from which we might imagine invented landscapes, generated in motion and time, "through which subindividual matters, vibratory intensities, and affects might cross and be altered through that crossing" (Sheldon 2015, 212). Acknowledging the role of human and nonhuman bodies (and later, the vitality of thing-bodies) in planter descriptions in the next sections of this chapter, here I present descriptive moments read through a new materialist environmental rhetoric that complicate simplistic turns to efficiency by imagining it as also shaped through affectual choices, bodily sensation, and embodied interactions with nonhuman others. I represent such complication not as a simplistic explanatory model that conveys systemic resistance to the logics of efficiency—that is, I don't argue that such interruptions in efficiency discourses otherwise overturn traditional benefit-to-cost approaches. Instead, I see them in service of an intense rhetoric that works productively toward a new kind of rhetorical knowledge that is less intently focused on rigidity, logocentrism, and binary setups between growth and preservation that privilege only human agency. What such moments perhaps represent are messier notions of efficiency that resist teleological conceptions and are instead bound up with *desire* that originates from the material body, its affects and ability to be affected, its persuasive entanglement with nonhuman others, and its movement on the landscape over time.

### *Planter-Bodies, Injury, and Pain: Efficiency and the Sensorium*

Pain and pleasure are not natural opposites; neither are they always yoked to the physical body.[22] Yet here I wish to examine the ways planters invoke affects of pain (primarily through bodily injury) and pleasure (primarily through perceptions of pleasure/pain and bodily rest) as a way of complicating the seemingly commonsense rhetorics of efficiency that characterize planter discourses as discussed in chapter 1. In doing so, I am not suggesting that planters somehow necessarily escape or resist efficiency; instead, I draw attention to the ways embodied interactions of tree planting turn our attention toward an efficiency based on desire rather than only on speed or cost. While not wholeheartedly interrupting a singular discourse of efficiency—as planter descriptions tell us, the culture of tree planting is fused with money "logics"—traditional notions of efficiency cannot explain simply the ways persuasive affects not only make demands of the planter-body but also guide its decision-making.

Injury and pain in the planter-body was discussed by nearly every individual I spoke with. As Thomas Szasz (1957, 48) notes, pain is a "sensation [that] is our way of apprehending and describing a particular pattern of events." Pain is not inherently bad or destructive or un-useful (whether as a medium, message, or outcome), and recent work in neuroscience suggests that pain and suffering are located in completely different parts of the human brain.[23] For planters, pain—especially pain resulting in injury—in this case is taken to be a kinesthetic state invoked temporally by tree planting that is paradoxical, considering how highly tree planters value efficiency and output. As Thomas explained:

> People talk about it being good money, but when you think about it, in a way you're required to be at work 24/7 for the entire period of time that you're out there, so it's like you're sort of at work that whole time, and if you average out your money over all that time, it's not that great all of a sudden, so you have to like it for other reasons too in order for it to make sense, I think. Yeah, the worst parts are feeling like you're wasting your time or feeling really uncomfortable . . . This is a bit of a dead-end job because almost everybody gets some kind of injury eventually. (T. Kroeker, unpublished data)

Here, Thomas pits injury against the narrative of economic and personal efficiency that would place planters on the controlling end of labor time, if not tree price or market fluctuations. Thomas suggests that overall (total time divided by total money), the economic windfall promised by planting is a myth. He also draws a parallel between the undesirability of inefficiency ("wasting your time") and the bodily state of feeling uncomfortable, suggesting that because of the inevitability of injury (the state of the body breaking down and proving, finally, to be inefficient), the job itself is unsustainable—and indeed, by producing injury, rather inefficient.

Notably, the ways planters describe pain leading up to injury as commonplace seem to run up against the rational interpretation of pain as an affective and material descriptor of events that an individual generally listens to, which most of the time results in a "protective reaction"—the body's "withdrawal of the part involved or the emergent need to put the injured part at rest" (Szasz 1957, 60). Despite a handful of planters telling me that they did not continue to plant because of injury that prohibited them from doing the job in subsequent seasons, many of them also explained that pain acknowledgment (through pain complaint) was purposeless; as Georgia noted, "nobody really cares you had a hard day. Everyone else had a hard day, too, so nobody really wants to hear you whine about your hard day" (G. Chappell, unpublished data). Here pain is a message best left ignored, though spoken concretely through the body, through injury, as in these examples:

> Well, injury runs pretty rampant in the planting camp. I suffered from tendonitis in both my wrists and the top of my hand here, and I had an injury to my foot which is plantar fasciitis, which is a fallen arch, and not that I really cared at that point or really noticed it, but I have lower back issues, which, I'm a big guy which could be caused by that, but it really started when I was planting so I think it was from planting. And I guess how I dealt with it there was, sometimes you take a day off unless you can just plant through it, but really when you feel it is in the off-season, but somehow when you go planting all the pain goes away, maybe it's the blood flow or the, I don't know, like when you work out a lot you sort of don't feel your injuries. So I foolishly ignored those off-season signs and continued to plant through injury. And you can't really see this but that's it, doesn't really, I can't really open my hand much more than that, still. I haven't planted in six years. (T. Bourlas, unpublished data)

> And fast can take, actually isn't really great for your body because you're pushing so hard. I would much prefer the slower stuff, but the contracts we picked up further north for a mill there are a little slower and they're a little less, I think they're a little easier on your body. (S. Dyck, unpublished data)

> We worked a thirteen-day shift one time, like no breaks, thirteen days long, and it was just crazy, and we didn't know when we'd be stopping, they didn't tell us anything, they were just like "oh yeah, well, we'll plant another day tomorrow." And so things like that really turned me off of it because I was like I'm wrecking my body for this. (S. Friesen, unpublished data)

I did have a few bouts with tendonitis in my wrist and hand, which meant days off and, you know, treating it and stuff like that. And then I, this other injury I was talking about where I hurt my back in 2011, that kind of ended my season. Those are pretty much the injuries I had. Various other injuries happen to people like, as you would expect when people walk around a forest quickly, sometimes on slippery logs and things like that, people would fall and get like pierced by a branch or something like that or get like poked in the eye or things like that. (T. Kroeker, unpublished data)

I'm sure it's impacted my life in ways I don't realize, like I've experienced a little back problems [*sic*], I'm pretty sure planting is a source of that. When I'm doing front raises or weight lifting, then it's just this [left] hand 'cause I use my right hand for planting. This [right] side I can lift much easier than the left side, so 'cause that's the action of after you've planted a tree and you pull your shovel out of the ground, so I've done that thousands of times, but on this [left] side I haven't. (L. Rempel, unpublished data)

In northern Alberta or any of the northern areas in the rest of country where it's flatter, generally [you're] only planting one or two species and you're making a lot less per tree, so you have to plant a lot of trees in the day to make the kind of money I think that veteran tree planters expect to make. And there's more chance of repetitive stress injuries . . . I'm thirty-four now, and I just don't want to have to do that to my body really anymore; [there's] more chance of injury I think. (R. McCannell, unpublished data)

And there were also certain days where physically I would be in a lot of pain just because a box of trees weighs about fifty pounds, and you're carrying it around, and you're clambering over fallen logs and stuff like that. More importantly, you're bending over to plant the trees, so that puts a ton of strain on your back, and so physically you can really, really be in a lot of pain. Sometimes it's really hard, you'll just, unless you're careful, you'll strain various muscles. And also when I screefed, for example, I would kick the dirt from side to side, which is incredibly hard on your knees, and at the end of the season my knees were unbelievably sore. And I also held my shovel too tightly, so I ended up getting what we call "the claw" where basically the joints in your fingers seize up, and I remember when I woke up in the morning my hand would be basically clenched like I was holding a shovel, and I would actually have to use my other hand to straighten my fingers, and I could feel the joints releasing, and, yeah, I felt like I was turning into some weird subhuman tree-planting creature. (R. Boldt, unpublished data)

I've provided a range of descriptions by planters here both to illustrate how ubiquitous injury description (and even an invocation of suffering) among planters is and also to draw attention to the ways tree planting is constructed out of the intermeshing of form, sensation, and space. Here our attention is drawn to the planter-body as a form (hands, wrists, backs, knees, fingers, eyes); the discourses of pain, injury, and affect that run up against narratives of efficiency (suffering, pain, treatment, strain); and also the space between them out of which emerges planting as a phenomenon located in time, sensation, and relations between and among bodies (the "subhuman tree-planting creature" as perhaps a generative entanglement into *homo silvacultura*). The notion of a particular temporalizing is inherent in descriptions, whether through the acknowledgment that "fast" land is injurious land or the recognition that pain is connected to time spent working and time spent aging. The planter-body's marking of sensation and its intensities is spoken throughout—"wrecking" a body in one season; "screefing," or kicking the dirt to dislodge a top layer of un-plantable soil, resulting in knee injury; "the claw," or the locking up of finger joints from stenosing tenosynovitis. A sense of place (keeping in mind that each planter is amalgamating his or her seasons spent planting, if multiple, in a variety of places into one narrative) is put forward through dynamic sets of relations: the planter-body and the geospatial location (i.e., northern Alberta), the hand and the shovel, the foot and the land, the body and a box of trees, the branch and the eye. Throughout, there is a sense of movement inherent in these relations: of a body moving across topography, of a shovel pushed into the dirt, of a tree plucked from a bag to be planted, of a body bending over to plant the seedling in the hole in the ground, of the stomping closed of the opened hole. This movement, carved out of spoken sensation, temporalizing, and affective relations between the planter-body and other thing-bodies, constructs the space of tree planting. We are given hints of different times accorded to tree planting—a season, an off-season, a year of one's life, the time it takes a body to heal—that run up against quantified task time and money equations. Pain and injury become unquantifiable—the body an impossible measure of "How much? How big? How fast? How long?" (Clark 1989, 275). We are thrown by expectations that a human invested in the good life would ignore the protective reactions expected from a body in pain or experiencing bodily suffering—to stop working rather than "ignor[e] those off-season signs." In other words, there is no detour through logos. There may, however, be an accounting for desire.

Here the injured planter-body appears doubly inconsistent: (1) inconsistent in what planters privilege in terms of economic and personal efficiency and (2) inconsistent with outcomes usually following patterns of activity that result in pain sensation. Planters mediate pain and injury, but why? The answer, as Thomas first pointed out, is that you "have to like it for other reasons, too, in order for it to make sense"

(T. Kroeker, unpublished data). Ignoring for the moment that perhaps it doesn't "make sense," I'd like to examine the possibilities of pain sense alongside other co-felt intensities by planter-bodies that draw us more deeply into how affects shift and move, how desire, propagated through "liking it for other reasons" may better support an argument that planter-bodies are sets of relations, suspended in affect. All of these possibilities complicate the idea of the rational economic man and draw our attention to environments that are rhetorically sticky with elements of the sensorium.

### "And It Was Pretty Delicious": Planter-Bodies and Pleasure/Pain

Although I take up the meditative affects of planting and of "love-hate" feelings described by planters in chapter 3, here I turn to body pleasure senses described by planters that work alongside pain sense to invoke the rhetoricity of the planter-body as a persuasive means by which to keep tree planting appealing through more than just arguments of efficiency or economic gain. By "pleasure," I don't mean the simple absence of pain as a correlative to what I've just described; indeed, pleasure can be determined by its perception as a flow state, as the absence of pain, as meeting a bodily need, or as an experience (closer to a "mood") (Szasz 1957, 187–96). Here I'll speak to two notions of pleasure as they intermingle with pain senses. The first is the sense of pleasure as an emotional or physical "gain" (Szasz 1957, 215); the second is the pleasure of the body at rest.

Although the general evaluative association of pain with "badness" is common, planters don't totally agree. In fact, many posit that that a sense of pain—that is, to feel pain sensation in the body—is complementary to a sense of pleasure: that is, gaining something useful, delightful, or good. Thus it cannot be said without exception that a felt sense of pain will always simply motivate an intentional action (such as withdrawal of the pain-associated activity); as Tamir said, "I don't know if hard's bad. I mean, people don't die of hard work, although you do suffer long-term injuries . . . I guess it wasn't hard every day, maybe that's it. It was hard most days, but it was also really thrilling other days . . . it's like a sport. So, sometimes sports can be hard, sometimes they can be fun" (T. Bourlas, unpublished data).

Here Tamir, a planter who admittedly deals with long-term adverse physical effects from planting, is suggesting that pleasure (fun) is not the opposite of pain; rather, the relief that results from pleasure creates the desire to continue to plant despite the perceived pain of hard work and eventual injury. This mix of pleasure and pain creating something in-between was echoed by other planters as well. As Georgia put it, "And you wake up every morning and everything hurts . . . The thing that doubly sticks out is how much pain you're in, but you also feel like you're kind of invincible at the same time . . . Your body feels so like strong and good, at the same time you're feeling so broken and bad" (G. Chappell, unpublished data).

This sentiment is echoed nearly verbatim by Ryan (with the addition of details of motion): "I can still remember how incredibly tired my legs felt at the end of the fourth day. We had to walk back home to camp, I think it would have been maybe 2 kilometers or something and just feeling this incredible weariness of the likes of which I'd never experienced before, but it was combined with this strange elation. It just felt really good to push myself so much and to still be going and to still be feeling happy for the most part and to know that I'd been able to handle this very intense ordeal" (R. Boldt, unpublished data).

For planters, the stress of pushing a body into the realm of pain results not in motivation to quit or stop the pain but rather as a complement to pleasure: in feeling strong, happy, and elated by virtue of being pushed into a realm of physical intensity (which is taken up further in chapter 3). We might understand planting vernaculars as those that operate within planter-bodies, as those that consider this middle space of pleasure-pain as an emergent affect of tree planting. It is pleasure, and it is pain (and it is ruin, and it is regeneration). To that end, the pleasure might exist in the gainful knowing of such a middling affect; as James put it, "knowledge of my body is definitely a huge, huge reward . . . understanding what the limits of my body are, like how to safely and sensibly push those and how to completely disregard those limits and do really stupid things" (J. Simpson, unpublished data).

If the garnering of affect of nonsensical pleasure-pain is one marker of planter-bodies and their relations with others that similarly pushes up against contemporary rhetorics of efficiency (again, because pain and injury are not efficient), the other pleasure-sense that arose in the discussions about the physical difficulties of planting was the bodily enjoyment of rest, whether sanctioned (as in a night's sleep) or unsanctioned (as in a break from work). Important in planters' descriptions of pleasure-sense at scenes of rest is how they push at the edges of both rhetorics of efficiency and, by involving relations with other plant- or animal bodies, rhetorics of humanism. Many planters speak to feeling "different" while tree planting; however, they also speak to specific pleasure found in moments of rest that depend on the energies of the space:

I've had a long life struggle with insomnia; I never sleep. But I sleep at tree planting. And I don't know, partly because it's just I'm so tired at the end of the day. And you're falling asleep just like, you're listening to the little birds and the wind, and you just fall asleep just as the sun is setting, and you wake up and it's bright. It's just kind of like easier to get into that rhythm of like living without lights. (G. Chappell, unpublished data)

So we took a break, and we strolled through the forest, and we got to this little river bend, just in the middle of the forest. And so we were already like twenty-five minutes off from the main road, which was another ten minutes off from the highway, and we were just basically in the middle of the wilderness. And we were in this stream, and it was shallow, and we hopped in, and we rolled our legs up, and it was just like so amazing. I felt so connected with the earth. I was like, this is incredible. (N. Friesen Hughes, unpublished data)

I think one day I was, like the first year I was planting, I was having trouble with the motivation, you know, we'd been, I think we were twelve or fourteen days straight in the bush without a day off trying to get this cut, this contract finished, and we were already over schedule, and I think it had, probably was do with the fact that we had more new planters than veterans, so things were going slower than anticipated. And I just had a day that I didn't, I planted my camp cost, and then I sat under the silvicool [reflective shade tarp] the rest of the day; I just needed a day off. I wasn't productive, but that was kind of one of my happier days. (J. Sprohge, unpublished data)

One day was really just like such a beautiful day. It was, there's just so many beautiful elements in there, and it was in Alberta I think, and it was on this really high, rocky precipice, but it was overlooking this huge gorge, so I was planting there all day, just right up next to this gorge, and then there were just like mountains for as far as the eye could see all the way around me. It was sunny and gorgeous, and that day it was also strawberry season, so there's often wild strawberries all the way up your piece, so I'd be like planting a few trees and picking berries as I was going, and it was pretty delicious. And then I'd also try and, if I found cool things out there, if it was not such a hassle to bring them back, I would take them. Like often there were antlers or like jaws left from, you know, animals that had been through there, and so I found two sets of antlers that day, which was, or two antlers, not sets, and so that was pretty cool. (S. Friesen, unpublished data)

It's true that to guarantee labor efficiency in the long run, workers need breaks: the emergence of coffee and lunch breaks was prompted by threats to productivity in the forms of workplace accidents and illness based on worker fatigue. That is, breaks and the need to take them in and of themselves do not necessarily represent a threat to the overarching logics behind efficiency discourses because they prevent labor interruptions in the long run. Indeed, defining movements of economics have been rooted in the balancing of pleasure and pain.[24]

Yet even post-Enlightenment thinking recognized utility itself as "purely a relation between a thing and a person" and such balancing to be constantly in failure "of measuring directly the feelings of the human heart" (Jevons 1888, PS.25, I.17). These descriptions turn our attention to efficiency logics, a balancing of input and output, yes—but they also move us from a focus on only being given "fast" land, making a lot of money, or achieving a personal best toward matters of the heart and the body and the relation between human and thing. They are filled with walking slowly, sitting in the shade, planting a few trees while occupied with other, non-work tasks. They are filled with the sights, sounds, gestures, and rhythms of a composition of planting that depends on the nonhuman world and the specificities of motion and place: the birds and their song, the wind and its sound, the perception of light and dark, the feel of one's legs in a shallow stream (and thus, the water), the feel of shade under a silvicool tarp, the feel of sun on skin, the view of the mountains, the taste of the strawberries, the touch of antlers. While the notion of individual pleasure is certainly a mainstay of contemporary economics and humanism (in the Benthamite notion that humans seek to maximize pleasure and minimize pain), for each planter, not only is pain mixed with pleasure in complicated ways, but pleasure itself is not simply human.

Pleasure is not found alone. Rather, it is found in relation to and alongside animal, plant, and thing-bodies and their affects that give rise, to some degree, to a sense of a temporalized and felt landscape that rubs up against the commonsensical assumptions about the split between nature and culture. This is perhaps nowhere as evident as in planters' descriptions of multi-species encounters.

### RHETORICAL FORCES OF ANIMAL BODIES: TEMPORALITY, BODYTHINKING, "BUGGING OUT," AND ATTUNEMENTS TO NONHUMANS

It's true that despite their bleak and ruinous character, cut blocks constitute what Anna Tsing (2012, 141) might call a "multi-species landscape." Cut blocks are not independent and removed swaths of land, no matter how barren or aesthetically ugly they may seem. A cut block runs up against a tree line that may contain old-growth or replanted forests and may represent a corridor of human disturbance open to animal and plant inhabitants. Although I've characterized planters as deeply enmeshed in rhetorics of humanism that shape their perceptions of their work and construct a particular narrative of the human individual dictated by rational choice, here I turn to evidence that constructs tree-planting space as more distributed, more enmeshed in a nonhuman sensorium than simple individualized human interactions would suggest. In doing so, I draw not only on rhetorical work that examines cross-species encounters but also the scholarship of Jenny Edbauer (Rice) (2005) and Natasha Seegert (2014). In considering a new materialist environmental rhetoric, we would do well to consider Seegert's (2014, 160) definition of rhetoric—"rhetoric as the *relational* force of signals interacting with the world"—and Edbauer (Rice)'s (2005) emphatic focus on ecological rhetorical placemaking. Edbauer (Rice) (2005, 8, 10) suggests that any rhetorical situation is far more dynamic than the commonplace model of the elements "ethos-pathos-logos or rhetor-audience-constraints-exigence," arguing instead that we draw our attention to networked rhetorical motion and distribution, or "the interactions between." To do both requires an acceptance of the rhetoricity of *bodies*, what Diane Davis (2011, 89) calls "an affectability or persuadability that is due not to any creature's specific genetic makeup but to corporality more generally," and also an acceptance of Hawhee's (2011, 83, 85) invitation to "suspend the habituated emphasis on verbal language and consciousness" by considering what she calls "physical, bodily syllogizing," or "body thinking." Just as Seegert (2014, 160) invites us to learn "not just *about* the coyote but *from* the coyote" and Hawhee (2011, 85) suggests that animals are "expert in the bodily economies of perception and action," in considering animal bodies alongside planter-bodies, planter descriptions emerge that draw attention not only to the humanistic individual but also to the nonhuman, to body thinking, to the other-than-rational (Hawhee 2017, 7), and to interactions between bodies, to their composition, movement, forces, rhythms, effects, and gestures. Here tree planting emerges as a space in which insects determine seasons, in which planters not only talk to animals but are driven mad by them, in which animal bodies co-construct rhetorical situations in an ambient lifeworld.

*Animal Bodies as "Crucial Components of Rhetoric"*

We might enlarge rhetoric's purview if we understand it not as something relegated to special human circumstances in arguments, deliberations, and weddings but instead, as John Mucklebauer (2017, 36) contends, as "a practice in which everyone is engaged all the time." He argues that rhetoric consists of elements of the everyday, whether physical structures, sounds, sensations, nonhumans, or things. In embracing a rhetoric of the everyday and attuning ourselves to movement, process, and interaction as "crucial components of rhetoric," it is possible to note the ways relational bodies—in this case, the human and the animal—co-create tree-planting landscapes. Planters describe clear cases of this persuasiveness of the everyday in animal bodies, first recognizing how they display temporality; as Erin notes, "a planting season has three different seasons in itself. There's a cold season and then there's the mosquito season and then there's black fly season" (E. Sawatzky, unpublished data). Such temporalizing is echoed by Georgia, who suggests that perceptions of seasonality are dictated not only by insect bodies but also by how they converge; as she says, "there's this trifecta of black flies and mosquitoes and horse flies, and they all have different seasons slightly, but the seasons all overlap" (G. Chappell, unpublished data). Given that a planting "season" is geography-dependent,[25] planters' attunements to insect seasonality within a spring-summer period of time dictate the convergence of a calendar sense, a geographical sense, and a weather sense, as the hatch of insects such as black flies or mosquitoes is dependent on weather, rainfall, access to water, and latitude and longitude. An overarching connection that united all planter interviews was an emphasis on weather and animal (primarily insect) bodies, giving rise to a different temporality, a different rhythm: that of an animal-dependent season.

Insect bodies in particular persuasively construct planting spaces and interactions, shaping planters' attention not only to time but also to economies of movement (or their opposite, inefficiencies) as an ever-present nonhuman force that shapes decision-making in the everyday. In the following examples, I've chosen three such moments that illustrate this intermingling of planter-bodies and animal bodies, their forces and signals that engage and shape planter *being* in the world. The first, from Jon, suggests that animal bodies carry more persuasive energy than they are credited with:

> I remember once driving planters into a site, and we were in two multi-passenger vans. We drove into the site, we shut off the engines, and the van ahead of us was distorted in terms of looking through the windshield because of all the mosquitoes, and you could actually hear this "bzzzzzz" that vibrated the entire van. And we all sat there quietly, and it took me about forty minutes to convince the planters to get out of the vehicle. I told them about various methods that old-time loggers used to protect themselves against mosquitoes by actually jamming newspapers into your clothing, wearing multiple layers, people covering up their face with a T-shirt so only their eyes were visible, and your hands, we would take duct tape and tape all our fingers and hands, yeah, you know. And then you're covered up like that, and it's 35°C. (J. Sprohge, unpublished data)

Although Jon is reflecting on "difficult parts of the job," he describes a world in which planter-bodies are bound up with things (multi-passenger vans, duct tape), movement and sensations (driving the van, shutting off the engine, sitting quietly, the sound of mosquitoes buzzing, the silence from the absence of talk, the heat of the day, time passing), and insect-bodies (mosquitoes creating sound, vibration, and glass distortion). Despite both the efficiency of planting objectives (in which time equals money and all movement should be planting movement) and a rhetorically humanistic perspective that suggests that planters in the van should be intrinsically personally motivated to work, have the freedom to choose work rhythms, and overcome insect-sponsored adversity, here the insect bodies make a persuasive case against both ways of thinking. The promise of swarm, the *force* of thousands of mosquito-bodies feasting on human blood, rubs up directly against the *effects* of planter efficiency: for forty minutes (by planting math, at two seconds per tree, thirty trees per minute at 12 cents per tree, or $144), a group of planters could not be persuaded to exit the vehicle to work, no matter their motivation, personal identification (veteran or rookie), or work ethic. Here we are faced with a nonhuman intervention into the discourses of humanism and efficiency. In this case, cross-species body-thinking wins: the planter-body's reticence to get stung, the mosquito body's eventual success at getting a meal. Desire works both ways.

The notion of a rhetoricity of bodies is echoed in the next two excerpts, both of which frame planter-body injury in terms of animal bodies, bound up together in encounter:

> Some of the injuries I've got in my mind distinctly. I hit a moose. Well, I didn't hit a moose, my ex-girlfriend who was driving me out of camp hit a moose with the car while we were having an argument about her being my ex-girlfriend, and [she] decided to swerve to avoid the moose, and I, well, the moose came to the windshield and hit me in the forehead. That's a fairly intense memory. (J. Simpson, unpublished data)

> Wasps, on the other hand, yeah, I should talk about wasps because it's like you, hardly anyone goes without being stung throughout a season because just like last year I only got stung I think three times, but the year before I got stung nine times, and it's very common because you're planting so many trees, and you're doing lines that if there's a wasp nest on this piece, there's a good chance you're going to hit it or get really close to it. So I've had a number of times where I throw my shovel down, and I accidentally throw it into a wasp nest; they're hidden under the duff layer or just in the ground, and the wasps start streaming out, and you have to run away as quick as possible. And the beginner mistake is when you are shocked by the wasp is to run away and leave your shovel there, which happened a

couple times before I got used to it, 'cause then you have to go back and retrieve it. And all the wasps are now just buzzing around this nest, and so I got a number of stings trying to get through it, get back, get my shovel . . . Or even there's [a] time where I got stung on my eye, and my eye almost swelled shut, and I didn't even think to take a picture . . . I had a friend who actually, and I've seen it more than once where they've gotten stung on the eye or right underneath their eye, and their eye actually has swollen shut, so they have to plant without depth perception, and they tend to plant a lot less [sic] trees the next day. (L. Rempel, unpublished data)

These two descriptions portray moments of persuasive cross-species encounter along affective bodily intensities. In the first example, we have the material force of a moose-body (a 500–800-pound animal) coming up against the thing-body of car and windshield with the effect of both causing a physical injury to a planter-body and forcing the reaction of stopping an inter-human argument by an affective pain response. In the second, the planter-body exists as a broken machine (planting "a lot less the next day"), and the wasp-body dictates both response and reaction. The planter-body responds away from the notion of individual choice in the avoidance of shovel retrieval; the wasp-body reacts with territorial swarming and stinging. The planter-body reacts to a sting near an eye in a way that affects depth perception and interferes with productive output, thus embracing inefficiency. Such is the rhetorical force of the wasp-body up against the planter-body, bodily syllogizing on behalf of both planter-body (all wasp-bodies are pain, all stings come from wasp-body, all stings are pain) and wasp-body (all stings harm, all planters are sting, all planters are harm).

While we may consider these three examples to imagine rhetoric differently, it is true that they are examples in which animal bodies make claims on planter-bodies and intermix human and interpersonal knowledge with nonhuman demands and rhetoricity. The solutions to the rhetorical problems of bites, swarms, stings, and moose encounters cannot be simply had by making a different, more efficient human choice; as I next take up in the insect-prompted phenomenon of "bugging out," even when planter-bodies try their individual hardest to combat insect-bodies (as Jon suggests in relaying timeworn tricks of newspaper and duct tape), the cross-species encounter insists on a patchy efficiency at best, a humanism that is as responsive to being part black fly as it is determiner of "good" land.

### Black Flies, the Umwelt, and "Bugging Out"

If *Planting the Anthropocene* was to have an alternative title or subtitle, it no doubt would involve the black fly (*Diptera: Simuliidae*). There are over

2,000 species of *Simuliidae*, and over 100 of those species live in Canada (Brust 2006). Nonetheless, the black fly is well-known wherever it exists around the world for its biting and swarming behavior; as John Davies (2016), a medical anthropologist, says, "wherever they cause a nuisance they usually have a special name in the local language"—and true to form, the black fly was a topic raised by planters in every interview I conducted. In Canada, the black fly has given rise to its own dedicated folk song (Hemsworth's 1949 "The Black Fly Song") about surveying the woods of northern Ontario. The song locates the black fly's three major irritations: its numbers ("always the black fly, no matter where you go"), its non-biting, swarming behavior ("the flies swarmed heavy, it was hard to catch a breath"), and its bite, which is often painless or unnoticed because of the injection of anticoagulants and painkillers and which later causes a skin reaction of swelling, itching, and bleeding ("I'll die with the black fly a-picking my bones"). The female black fly is the only sex that bites, but the male black fly often swarms around females, making it impossible for a human to determine biting flies from non-biting flies; in addition, in species such as *Simulium johannseni* (found in the Canadian north), the females feed on birds but are curious about, and thus swarm, humans. Other Canadian *Simuliidae*, such as *Simulium bivittatum*, *Simulium griseum*, *Simulium hunteri*, *Simulium luggeri*, *Simulium vampirum*, and *Simulium decorum*, prey on mammals and are known to bite humans (as well as horses, ungulates, dogs, and other small mammals) (Currie 2014).

When considering the black fly as a nonhuman body, the details of its habits, proclivities, and responses to conditions are important not just for their explanatory potential of a multi-species landscape but also for imagining a profound rhetoricity of the nonhuman through which tree planting is to be understood (through a particular seasonality, topography, climate, and ecosystem). While I will not engage in anthropomorphizing the black fly (which determines the human to be the only kind of thinking body), it is useful here to consider its *Umwelt* (literally "aroundworld," meaning a kind of experiential lifeworld)—biologist Jakob von Uexküll's coinage for the organism-world that surrounds animal bodies and treats "the animal as a subject with its own experience" (cited in Buchanan 2008, 21). Important to the idea of the *Umwelt* and, as Brett Buchanan notes, "sharing affinity" with Martin Heidegger's notion of being-in-the-world (and thus Rickert's [2013, 248] notion of *dwelling*) is that we understand the animal together with its environment as inseparable: that is, "the animal and the *Umwelt* are not two distinct beings, but a unitary structure that must be considered holistically" (Buchanan 2008, 22).

The most famous example of examining the *Umwelt* is Uexküll's instance of the tick, which he suggests has three sensory cues—or affects—on which its *Umwelt* depends: the sense of the sun, the sense of the butyric acid coming from a warm mammal to feed on, and the ability to find a hairless spot on the mammal on which to feed (cited in Buchanan 2008, 24). The reason this group of cues constitutes the tick's *Umwelt* is that it focuses on the relational aspect of what is meaningful or significant for the tick (in a way that a sweaty mammal does not meaningfully signify for me in the same way it does for ticks). Anthropologist Eduardo Kohn (2013) extends the example of the tick to focus on the ways its *Umwelt* also designates what he calls an "iconic property" of confusion that characterizes the tick's sense of being in the world. For a tick (as for a black fly), Kohn (2013, 85) notes that "mammals are equivalent"—there is no distinction among a human body, a moose-body, or a dog-body; instead, a "general class" of beings emerges out of the tick's confusion, a confusion that characterizes a particular ontology.

If we consider the tick as having an *Umwelt* similar to that of the black fly, we might note that the planter-body and the blackfly-body (a relation constituted out of mammalian confusion) together constitute part of a black fly's *Umwelt*. Together, these bodies create particular affects, relations, and intensities; and the rhetorical force of the blackfly-body (and its collectivity, the swarm) houses the persuasive effects to induce particular responses and reactions from tree planters.

Before I take up those forces, it is important to note that such force is not a one-way (fly-to-human) street. It is a street composed of other kinds of insect-bodies, bodies of water, and life cycles of motion that convert species from water- to land-based, that involve the dissolution of organic matter, and that include the movement and change of carbon forms. Black fly hatches are dependent on unsullied, fast-flowing waterways; and large populations of black flies are an indication of healthy rivers and streams free of pollution (Eaton 2001). Although seen as a human nuisance, black flies "are keystone species in rivers and constitute an essential ecological resource. Black fly larvae are aquatic filter feeders and are able to capture material classified as 'dissolved organic matter' . . . This material is available to few other macroinvertebrates. As a result, this material becomes available to other macroinvertebrates and other organisms which feed either directly on the black flies or on their fecal pellets" (Brockhouse and Colbourne 2007, 2).

The other macroinvertebrates (i.e., caddisflies, mayflies, stoneflies, dragonflies) that feed on black flies are often used as scientific indicators of aquatic health and ecosystem diversity; further, dissolved organic matter is responsible for moving nutrients from the earth to water, as well as providing a locus of aquatic carbon respiration (Hood et al. 2005). In other words, large numbers of black flies not only story the health of an ecosystem but also contribute to carbon sequestration (removing $CO_2$ from the atmosphere) in the form of stored carbon. Thus the rhetorical force of collectives of black fly bodies is also one of human survival; to the extent that humans engage in carbon-sink and preservation-based activities (like reforestation), humans' rhetorical force is one of black fly survival.

The most telling of the rhetoricity of the blackfly-body on the planter-body, however, is in planter descriptions of what biologists term the "nuisance" of the black fly. As Ryan describes:

> Also, a real x-factor is whether or not the bugs are bad. They're this omnipresent reality out there, and sometimes they can really get to you. Mosquitoes are pretty bad, but the absolute worst where we plant are the black flies. There will be certain days where you will have a gigantic cloud of black flies following you around the entire day, biting you, and flying into your various orifices. For some reason they love going inside ears and nostrils and your mouth, and so you'll literally have a fly bouncing into some sensitive spot of your body every half-second for the entire eleven hours, and needless to say that can affect your quality of life and can be very, very unpleasant sometimes because both of your hands are occupied. One of your hands is permanently holding your shovel, and the other hand is grabbing trees every two seconds or so to plant, and so you don't really have much time to swat away the bugs, and even if you douse yourself with some crazy DEET-heavy thing, usually it doesn't work all that great on black flies. (R. Boldt, unpublished data)

Here we see that black flies induce not only a particular response—the swat or the application of DEET—but also a sensation of unpleasantness dictated by the pain of the bite and the movement of the swarm, resulting in blackfly-bodies "really get[ting] to you." This reaction, as a rhetorical moment of intensity brought on by the blackfly-body, is the one I want to take up. Described as a kind of "madness" (and not relegated to only dealing with the blackfly-body), planters term the inability to cope with the constant irritation of insects the phenomenon of "bugging out":

> And there's a thing, there's a term called "bugging out." So it's when you get, when you're so, and I didn't know what it was at first until it happened to me, and I was like, oh, that is bugging out. It's just when you're planting, and bugs are just constantly on you, and eventually it just gets to you and you like kind of lose it, and yeah, so it can get to a point where it's pretty frustrating. Also when you go back to your camp, often there's still bugs there, so it's like you can never escape them. (L. Rempel, unpublished data)

As a non-planter, it was hard for me to understand "bugging out" by this simple description; however, as I heard planters repeatedly describe the relation of intensity and "losing it," I began to see that what they were losing was a sense of themselves as rational beings:

> And yeah, lots of black flies, lots of mosquitoes, deer flies, lots of deer flies, and something called moose bees, which were never really a problem; they were just these huge, huge bees, and they would come and get you when you were in the water, so that's when you had to watch out for them, like a big horse fly. But the deer flies, I mean the black flies, they were brutal because they're so small, and they'd always try to fly into your eyes, and I just couldn't, I couldn't, I just couldn't, mentally that was one of the hardest things for me. The heat was fine. I could handle the heat and the mosquitoes, it was okay, but the black flies going into your eyes, I just lost it, I lost it. (N. Friesen Hughes, unpublished data)

> About eleven o'clock that day, deer flies came out. I don't know, have you heard much about deer flies from planters? No? Okay, well, deer flies are, well, similar to horse flies, these flies, they look kind of like bees, they're like yellow and black striped, and they're these flies that bite. They take big bites out of you, and your initial reaction if they bite you is to hit them, but if you hit them they attract more to the same spot. So a big spot for me is my shovel hand because it stays pretty level all day. They like to land on my hand, and I accidentally kill one without thinking, and then they would swarm my hand for the rest of the day or my face or wherever I'd hit them. And I think if you talk to especially Ontario planters, they deal a lot with black flies and deer flies, they will have the most, yeah, it really drives you insane. If you want to see someone at their worst, put them in a spot with deer flies all day. And you can't leave, right? It's not like the beach; if there's a horse fly, you just leave. You can't leave. You're stuck. So yeah, there was that on top of all that, deer flies, and then, yeah, I remember us going back and just, I think we both had separate moments of yelling really loudly and hitting things with our shovel and going crazy, basically. (D. Cheater, unpublished data)

> You go back to Slave Lake, and you're like slogging through brambles and like mud, and then there's like thousands of black flies, it's like this constant buzzing in your head, kind of like "bzzzz" but all day, and they're like crawling in your ears and in your eyes. You just kind of lose it a little bit after days and days of that. (G. Chappell, unpublished data)

> I remember on my third season the day that the black flies came out, and they were just absolutely incredible, and I had taken my shirt and like, one of my shirts, and wrapped it around my face so only my eyes were showing. Somehow they seemed to get caught in there, and I had dreadlocks at the time, and they were getting caught in the dreadlocks and buzzing and buzzing by my ears, and I couldn't get them to stop, and it was so, so hot, and I remember at one point I stood on a log to jump over it, and I fell off, and I fell on my back and my tree bags were so heavy with

trees that I just couldn't stand up, and it got to the point where I was like this day just sucks so much that it's funny, and I lay there and I laughed and laughed and laughed until I cried, and I took my bags off and went back to my cache and didn't plant another tree for the day. (E. Sawatzky, unpublished data)

Wasps and hornets, they have ground nests, and you'll come and walk by and put a tree right next to one and not notice until it's too late and you've been stung a few times. And so that's, I would prefer that to tons of black flies. I don't mind getting stung again compared to black fly madness. (R. McCannell, unpublished data)

There were just days that I remember the black flies and mosquitoes just being like insanity-inducing, like just, like there was nothing you could do to get away from them, and you were just covered in bites, and you start just like flailing your arms over your head every few seconds as you're trying to do your job and like sort of just ranting to these organisms, which have no, which you can't communicate with. (T. Kroeker, unpublished data)

In these reactions, we find compelling details that prove out distributed affects of bodies in relation to one another. We are given acknowledgment of temporality through both time and motion, of geographical and topographical space, of transitions of sensations told through dynamic and kinesthetic sounds, gestures, and moods. In each instance, there is not only the animal, as Deleuze and Guattari (1987, 263) would have it, but "the-animal-stalks-at-five-o'clock": "Climate, wind, season, hour are not of another nature than the things, animals, or people that populate them, follow them, sleep and awaken within them. This should be read without a pause: the animal-stalks-at-five-o'clock. The becoming-evening, becoming-night of an animal, blood nuptials. Five o'clock is this animal! This animal is this place! 'The thin dog is running in the road, this dog is the road,' cries Virginia Woolf. That is how we need to feel."

Here, the planter is as the fly; as Thomas notes, "they get in, and they just bite you behind your ear, and they inject some kind of anesthetic so you can't feel it at first, and then you just bleed as they bite you. And you have all these bites, and then later on they just swell up like crazy, so some people would get so bitten that at the end of the day their face[s] would swell, and they would be almost unrecognizable" (T. Kroeker, unpublished data). The planter-body is a place of confusion for the fly-body; the fly-body plays tricks on the planter-body so that the planter-body "loses it." There is a distinct human-nonhuman entwinement that results in non-logical pathways of making meaning. The deer fly bites at eleven o'clock. There are indeed blood nuptials here.

What I find compelling about "bugging out" is that it speaks captivatingly of the force of nonhuman bodies to disrupt the humanistic emphasis on both reason and happiness and to induce a reaction that planters themselves know is futile. As planter-bodies intermingle with fly-bodies (blackflies in eyes, nostrils, ears, hair, and clothing), again, the detour through logos is skipped. A wasp sting is preferred to a swarm of black flies. The sound of blackfly-bodies penetrates the skull. Planter-bodies are moved to speak, to yell, to hit things, to laugh, *but not to escape, not to remove the "maddening" stimulus.* Much like planter injuries that ignore the protective reactions of a body in pain, "bugging out" does not favor the humanistic scientific rationalism that would have planters basing their actions on reason rather than emotional response. In fact, blackfly-bodies often have the opposite effect: planters' reactions favor the bugs as they *stay* to plant, both providing a blood meal and ensuring the health of the black fly species, becoming together something else. Here the insect-body has a particular kind of agency, one planters notice across a variety of nonhuman actors.

### "They Say Crows Can Remember Faces": Resistance to Humanism and the Rhetoricity of Animal Bodies

Before moving on to consider the ways plant-bodies similarly make up the chōra of plantation spaces, a final word about planter-bodies seeking out communication strategies with animal bodies is necessary. Although the phenomenon of "bugging out" suggests that part of what make up planter experiences are the communicative moments accorded to insect-planter relations (i.e., yelling, ranting, waving hands), I turn here to the ways planters attribute recognition to nonhuman agency of other animal bodies. Throughout the interview corpus, planters described wildlife encounters, whether with sea life in coastal planting (orcas, dolphins) or with animals associated with the Canadian interior, rocky mountains, and prairies (moose, fox, wolves, wolverines, eagles, caribou, owls, deer, frogs and toads, cougars, and black, brown, and grizzly bears). In many cases, what linked descriptions of animal encounters were the ways the force of the presence of animal bodies provoked particular communicative responses in planters and the ways animal bodies responded in turn.

While planters recognize, to some extent, that animals are not human, they do not frame these encounters as only human (or human-dominated) ones: rather than greet animal bodies they encounter with silence or listening entirely to Thomas's rejoinder that there are nonhumans that "you can't communicate with," planters *do* communicate with nonhuman animals to try to shape events, emphasizing the idea that it's not that animal bodies cannot communicate (in fact, they do); rather, planter-bodies just haven't figured out the right appeals. Planter narratives are filled with a recognized nonhuman agency and descriptions of nonhuman sites of communicative encounters.

Tree planter Nik described various animal encounters, but his consideration of the crow stuck out as a scaffold for the ways other planters described their animal encounters. I chose the crow, too, to take up its continued rhetoricity as recognized by scholars like Kennedy (1992) and Seegert (2014, 164), both of whom point to the Corax (Greek for "crow") as "the 'inventor' of rhetoric." In this instance, Nik is relaying his multiple dealings with crows:

> I had a terrible, in my third year we had this crow that would wake us all up at 4:30 in the morning. They say crows remember faces, so I think somebody did something mean to one of them, and this crow kept trying, every morning this crow would wake us up. I couldn't stand this crow. But the worst was in my first year. I left my lunch on the road, which is pretty standard, and in a Ziploc bag, inside a bag that had a zipper, and I came back, and the bag was open, and the Ziploc bag was ripped open, and my lunch was gone. Like, three Rice Krispie squares, two sandwiches, two apples, I think there was like a piece of Rice Krispie square left, and I was like, who did this? I thought it was my crew boss or somebody, I was like, who would have eaten my lunch? This is ridiculous. My crew boss came by, and he said he saw these two fat ravens hopping down the road, and they opened my bag. And I looked at it, and my Ziploc had been pecked open, but they opened the zipper and ate my whole lunch, and they did it to other people's lunches too. They ate somebody else's stuff down the road too, like, I couldn't believe it. (N. Friesen Hughes, unpublished data)

This description includes two separate encounters with crows/ravens,[26] but the first informs the second. Although Nik might have attributed a crow's morning call simply to the ambient surrounds of a day beginning in any forested space (or indeed, as any of us who live around crows might assume, simply business as usual), he does not. Instead, he alludes to the intelligence of the animal and its scolding 4:30 a.m. call as an outcome not only of its intelligence but also of its memories of, and experience with, other humans and its communicative response. Nik's assertion that "crows remember faces," particularly those that have done them harm, has clear scientific backing. John Marzluff and colleagues (2010, 699) note that crows not only recognize threatening human faces, but they can remember such faces for at least 2.7 years, following and vocally "scolding" humans crows perceive as dangerous and communicating the threatening face to fellow crows who had not directly experienced the threat. Nik affirms what scientists have researched not only about crow intelligence but also what we might see as the affect of crow rhetoricity, the crow-scolding-at-4:30-a.m, a locus of time, sound, memory, relation, and effect. The crow is not just cawing to caw; the scold of the crow is a relational affect of crow-human interaction and bird memory.

The second encounter Nik relays is dependent on the first; in relaying the story of how his lunch was eaten, he is not only repeating evidence about crow intelligence but also describing the rhetorical force of the crow-body on the planter-body. While seemingly a humorous anecdote, the "raven stealing lunch" is a bit of a disaster for a planter-body. As Delia Roberts (2002, 566) describes in her research on the physiology and biochemistry of tree planters, even on a diet of 5,000 calories per day, planters lost 1.5 percent–1.7 percent of their overall body mass during a season and were known to be "borderline hypoglycemic throughout the planting day." The work of tree planting is often the work of slow starvation, and in this anecdote there is an extra-linguistic bodythinking that allows us to understand and map affects (whether responding to remembered threat or imagining blood chemistry) of both crow-bodies and planter-bodies. The experience of tree planting is one shaped greatly by both humans and nonhumans.

The way Nik takes as a given animal agency is echoed by planters' descriptions of animal encounters on planting sites. I offer two depictions of planters' communication strategies with animals here:

> One beautifully sunny morning, and I was planting along by myself, and I looked up, and I saw a beautiful orange fox. And I guess it looked up and saw me at the same time, and we both leaped about half a foot in the air and gave each other the biggest-eyed look, and the fox turned around on its tail and B-lined out of there . . . My least favorite encounter was during my first season of planting, and I was planting with a friend of mine together on a piece, and going on in the afternoon I looked up and saw a mama black bear and two cubs watching me plant, and I started yelling at them like "go away! I don't want you here!" and I never really realized up until that point how silly it feels to yell at bears . . . I knew that I should make them go away because they're dangerous, and I started yelling at them like "I don't know what to say! This feels really odd! I wish you would leave!" and they didn't go, and so I started kind of throwing sticks in their direction and banging things on my shovel and standing on stumps and waving my arms and trying to make myself look big, and they seemed to enjoy the show but didn't really do anything. And so I started yelling for my friend to come and join me, and he was way on the other side of the piece, and I just called to him "man, there's bears over here,

you need to help me come scare them away," and he's like "I don't see any bears," and I yelled back "well, of course you can't see them, you're too far away. Come over here," and he's like "I'll yell from here." And he yelled a little bit, which was utterly useless, and I yelled a bit more, and he was like "I'm going to go back to planting." So I stared at these bears for a while and was like I guess I'm going to go back to planting, too, and just kept on going, and every time I would pass that spot I would look up, and they'd be watching me, and I'd kind of say hello to them and kept going. (E. Sawatzky, unpublished data)

So I was planting. I didn't see this happen until I was right there, and then this owl started attacking me. This big, huge gray owl started dive-bombing me, and I was like whoa, what's going on? And then so the owl would perch on a really tall tree and then bomb me and then perch on another one and then perch on a really tall one, and then I looked, and I realized that 2 meters away from me there was this baby owl sitting on this little tree. And the baby owl's like this big [indicates 5 inches], and the baby owl's looking right at me. And I was like well, I got to plant through you, I got to fill this piece, and so I tried to speak to the mother owl, saying I'm not going to hurt the baby. And the baby didn't seem scared of me; the baby would just look right at me and like the baby didn't seem scared of me at all. And so I just planted by, and eventually the mother stopped dive-bombing me. (N. Friesen Hughes, unpublished data)

While surprise and curiosity are no doubt the registers on both sides of animal-human encounters, in these two descriptions the pressure of maintaining efficiency ("I got to fill this piece") is encroached upon by nonhuman agents. While Erin's description of the bear encounter and her response at first simply mimics best practices of bear safety (speaking to the bears, making noise, trying to appear physically intimidating), her later response, based on the bears' reaction (not moving) and the perceived uselessness of her first tactic, is quite different.

Knowing that calling it a day would be inefficient, Erin keeps an eye on the bears, notices them watching her, and says "hello"' repeatedly. Perceived danger of a bear attack is mitigated by both the aims of efficiency and the cross-species encounter. The perceived human logic of avoidance or abandonment of an area—particularly one with a mama bear and cubs, known to be territorial—would be the reasonable, rational response. Such responses are ignored, however, in the acknowledgment of relationality by both humans and nonhumans on a shared landscape. The bear-bodies' physicality energizes the landscape; in deeming the planters to be non-threatening, they engage in "body-thinking" that results in inaction (Hawhee 2011, 85).

Nik relays a similar reaction to the gray owl's response to his body on the landscape. Unlike the bear, the owl's bodythinking determines the planter-body to be threatening, and the owl responds with an aggressive attack. Yet the force of the owl-body's response is mitigated in its effects on the planter-body by a communicative linguistic response based in efficiency: "speak[ing] to the mother owl, saying I'm not going to hurt the baby." Here logic meets non-logic, the *homo oeconomicus rationalis* talking to owls. And yet, for the owl-body, not naturally territorial but protecting her kin, in this instance the rhetorical force of the planter-body has the effect of discontinuing the attack over time. While we cannot know exactly how each body is interpreting the other's sign—by presence, by linguistic cue—what we can see is a rhetoricity of bodies, a rhetorical energy, at work within the temporalized cut block that highlights the interrelation of bodies and their intensities: for the planter, the threat of pain by the owl-body's aerial dive; for the owl, the threat of kin in danger; and for both, threats mediated in the rhetorical energies between bodies.

Thus far, I've been making a case for planters' attentiveness to nonhuman details in the form of directing attention toward nonhuman animals. In the final section of this chapter, I turn away from what might be perceived thus far as "zoocentrism" (Hall 2011, 5) to the ways tree planting may be understood through human-animal-plant relations, focusing specifically on the tree as representing the prominent plantscape relationship of the cut block.

## RHETORICAL FORCES OF PLANT BODIES: J-ROOTS, RESURGENCE, TIME SCALE

In the prior example of the rhetorical interaction between the owl and the planter, what goes un-remarked but is as deserving of attunement to particular affects created in the encounter is the large tree lining the cut block, which enables the gray owl to attack, as well as the smaller tree in the tree line that houses the owlet. In such an example, the trees themselves are a central rhetorical being: Great Gray Owl populations are highly sensitive to forestry practices and are highly dependent on leaning timber for nest and roosting sites, as well as on small clear-cut sites next to tree lines, which create hunting perches (Duncan 1997). Without the trees, there are no owls, no aerial dives, no cut block, no tree line, no tree planter. Yet we often dismiss plant bodies as an integral part of being in the world. An exclusion of the plant-body from such an arrangement might be seen as "plant blindness,"[27] or what James Wandersee and Elisabeth Schussler (2001, 3) note as failing to notice plants in human life, seeing plants only as a "backdrop for animal life," and "failing to distinguish between differing time scales of plant and animal life." I next turn attention to the ways plant-bodies—specifically, the trees that planters plant—have affective, rhetorical capacities that relationally shape and are shaped by human (and, as in the owl example, nonhuman) encounters on the tree-planting landscape.

A number of recent studies in plant ecology, botany, and the contentious area of plant neurobiology have reached consensus on plant intelligence and "plant behaviour" (Trewavas 2009), noting that plants not only have senses—the ability to recognize touch, motion, and their environment—but that they also have memory and adaptivity, that they recognize kin, that they can discriminate between self and non-self, that they can communicate by way of chemical signaling,[28] and that they can anticipate "whens" and "wheres."[29] As noted by Matthew Hall (2011, 146), plants also show an ability to learn and a capacity for "basic decision making, problem solving, and reasoning." Recent thinking about plants in the biological sciences suggests that they are far less passive photosynthetic automatons and far more complex, communicative, agentive beings than once thought.[30] While I will not belabor this point here or engage in trying to imagine an "*experience* of planthood" (Fullarton 2014, 377) in the following planter descriptions (which rely on humanistic interpretations of events), it's relevant to note that in both the biosciences and the humanities, plant selves are taken seriously as beings, and their bodies may be models for attunement to environs by way of motion, memory, and vitality.[31]

In making the case for plant-bodies as having recognizable rhetoricity on the tree-planting landscape, it is my intention to point to the ways trees in particular manifest affects and transitions that cultivate in tree planters a way of plant seeing or *plant sense*, of attunement to noticing plant life and its time scales. I foreground such noticing as constitutive of planters' relationship with their work, their co-consideration of particular efficiencies, and the complexity of the space and time of the cut block.

### *J-Roots: The Rhetoricity of Gravitropism*

Plant-bodies are intrinsically bound up in the experience of tree planting by virtue of its very name; however, they are also rhetorical bodies that are caught up in, as well as shape, planters' notions of efficiency. As planters describe in chapter 1, they aim to plant trees as quickly as possible while still meeting quality control standards determined by "checking" staff, who are concerned with tree spacing and depth. While spacing may be measured with a plot cord, proper depth is checked by digging up a number of trees in a corded area (say, five trees) to make sure that soil plugs on seedlings are not too deep, too shallow, or misshapen (known as a "J-root"). Planters are allowed a slim percentage margin of error of J-roots to "pass" a particular piece. Anything more results in a planting company getting fined, and tree planters must replant without pay any area that fails this type of inspection. It is no wonder, then, that J-roots came up often in planters' descriptions of their work as a primary way of relating to tree-bodies:

> When you're not J-rooting the plug, which, I don't know if you know what that is, but when you plant and then the little plug of the seedling, this little plug of dirt, you want it to be sitting straight in the dirt, like straight up and down, but if you just jam it in carelessly, it's going every which way, and it's less likely to root successfully. (T. Kroeker, unpublished data)

> And so if either [quality or consistency] is bad, if you have what's called like J-roots, where your roots are curled up, or your holes aren't closed or your trees are planted crooked or they're too far apart or too close together, you might have to go back over your block and redo it. (T. MacInnis, unpublished data)

> The plug had to be all the way in the ground; it couldn't be sticking out of the ground, it had to be straight up and down, so if it was, you know, J-roots, where like if the root, if the plug was sort of curved up to look like a "J," then that was bad. If you planted the tree too deep or too shallow, those were equally bad. (L. Ainsworth, unpublished data)

> The trees come in little plugs of dirt, and the entire plug needs to be completely covered. If it's exposed, it will dry out, and the tree will die. Additionally, the plug needs to be straight down. If it's, a "J" root is when you just shove it and the plug of the tree forms a "J" . . . That's a bad thing, the tree won't grow as strongly as if it was straight down. (R. Boldt, unpublished data)

To a tree planter, J-roots represent a clear inefficiency: if they are found in too high a percentage of trees, a planter will have to replant an area without pay, thus wasting both time and money. A J root is an outcome of plant-body response to an environment.[32] In an immediate case, it may be a response to trauma (being "jammed" in the ground); within twenty–fifty minutes, it is a gravitropic response (response to gravity in the tree's root cap cells): the plant root stops growing downward in response to a physical obstacle and will instead grow horizontally or in other ways around that perceived obstacle (Massa and Gilroy 2003, 436). While planters agree that J-rooting is "bad," it does not necessarily mean the death of a tree, although it often makes seedlings "more susceptible to drought, disease, and insect attack" (MFA 2011). However, what is clear about J-roots, which are, after all, tree-bodies, is the way the gravitropic response to an environment (the "J") is a fundamentally rhetorical movement of the tree-body on the planting scene. By virtue of gravitropic movement, the tree-body persuades the planter to pay sufficient attention to the land, site preparation, and soil quality to be able to plant the tree with the correct depth and perpendicular alignment. A planter is persuaded into *plant seeing* by the threat of the J-root on labor efficiency; the tree benefits from a planter-body's careful attention by having greater chances of longevity. Yet the seedling—a monoculture produced for the plantation—is only one kind of tree-body on the planting landscape, and its failure to thrive marks a different possibility on the cut block.

*Trees and Time Scale: Plantations, Survival, and Disturbance/Resurgence*

Planter bodies are greatly impacted by tree-bodies every day: while carrying trees around and putting them in the ground by the thousands, planters simply cannot engage in plant blindness. Moreover, planters are very aware that the tree-bodies they carry are monoculture trees, grown in nurseries and shipped to cut block sites. They recognize that old-growth forests are made up of plant and ecosystem diversity and that planting one type of tree does not represent a commitment to environmentalism:

> One of the funniest things about planting, especially people who don't know that much about it, they're going like, "Good for you! You're saving the environment!" But it really doesn't feel that way because—so we're—I mean, if tree planters didn't exist, then it would be bad. It's good that they do it, but we're planting trees that are basically just like planting long-term gardens for the forestry companies to come back and cut down again. (G. Chappell, unpublished data)

> They've [loggers] cut them [trees] down for our use and then we're replanting them with, you know, a monoculture, and it's just these sort of tree plantations now, which is weird 'cause you, like you're basically ruining it, you're basically, they basically ruined the forest. I mean, you can say it's a necessary evil, and we're sort of, we're at least mitigating it somewhat by planting again, but the wildness is gone for sure. I mean, those animals and other organisms they come back and inhabit these trees, the forest that we're creating, but it's not the same. It's just gonna be a whole bunch of like black spruce or whatever. (T. Kroeker, unpublished data)

> We are in essence creating a monoculture, whereas in a natural setting you'd have diversity, diversity of conifers, hardwoods, deciduous, native

plants. In planting a monoculture, it's all the same species. A lot of them are either seed or tissue, cloned, tissue-generated . . . if you think of hundreds and hundreds of acres of one specific plant, one specific tree, and you have a disease or a pest that that's the host, that's their food line, it's a buffet. (J. Seniw, unpublished data)

In their awareness of monocultured plantation spaces, planters seemed familiar with the idea that planting a tree does not guarantee its survival. Some quoted a quality "pass" percentage of survival rates for seedlings, stating that "I think only 80 percent of them have to survive or else they have to go and replant them again later" (G. Chappell, unpublished data) or "we're planting thousands of small trees in the hope that 90 percent of them will grow" (D. Cheater, unpublished data). They also relayed stories of the problems of monoculture, such as "they had given us a lot of jack pine, which doesn't grow in high competition and doesn't grow in swampy ground, which is both of what we were doing [the planting] with, and so these trees were all going to die" (S. Dyck, unpublished data). In fact, the survival rates on plantations are far lower than the 80 percent–90 percent considered acceptable, which is usually 300 trees per acre. At densities typically averaging 400 to 700 seedlings per acre, survival rates of between 42 percent and 75 percent are considered non-failures, depending on planting density at the outset (Londo and Dicke 2006).

Yet the distinction between plant-bodies here is an arbitrary, humanistic one that does not account for the way failure of monoculture to grow in the cut block (that is, the inefficiency of monoculture, of the plantation) represents, in effect, successful establishment of a diversity of other plant bodies created out of human disturbance. While Anna Tsing (2015b) documents such a relationship in her work on matsutake mushrooms (which grow only in human-disturbed forests), research on biodiversity and silvicultural disturbance suggests that monocultural plantations are not necessarily "single-species, even-aged plantations" (Bell et al. 2014, 328). Instead, depending on a range of planting factors (particularly how often a block is replanted), forest layers are affected differently based on the reallocation of nutrient, light, and water resources. Overall plant species diversity is reduced in any managed forestry ecosystem that logs an established area, resulting in species simplification and openness to pests and disease. Yet while large, overstory trees may decrease on a cut block, understory layers like shrubs and herbs increase (although there is a marked reduction in bryophyte and lichen layers of the forest floor), and all forest layers are present on replanted spaces (Bell et al. 2014, 336). While I am not advocating for logging of forests here, my argument suggests that although plantations are not forests, they also do not block resurgence. Far from resulting in a single-species plantation, replanted blocks are nonetheless spaces of species resilience in the face of human disturbance. Yet the lesson from Haraway and Tsing, who focus on the dangers of plantations, is an important one; they urge us to think of ourselves in relation to multispecies resurgences. One of the ways we might do that is to note the ways the measured "success" or "failure" of plantation monoculture—the hallmark of tree-planting efficiencies—can be disrupted by plant-bodies themselves.

As Oliver Rackham (2015, 377) notes in his historical account of British forests and plantations, "A successful plantation is homogeneous and eliminates the patchiness that is an essential characteristic of ancient woodland." Tree-planter-bodies as forest workers are trained for success in plantation spaces, seeing the patchiness of biodiversity that comes in the form of seedling distress or death as a particularly inefficient failure. But interpreted another way, in which plant-bodies are instead territorial, adapting, remembering, learning, feral beings, the patchiness itself is the success rather than the failure. Such a reading throws the notion of efficiency (for whom?) on its head, questions the humanistic affect of care, reorganizes the anthropocenic response to logging, and turns our attention to the final vital notion of plant seeing: the importance of time scale.

It's clear from chapter 1 that planters are keenly aware of human-based time scale (down to the seconds), particularly as it equates to a money function and efficient human movement. Yet a key to plant sense is an awareness of the far slower time scale of plants, which, as biologists and ecologists note, "operate in weeks and months" (Trewavas 2003, 16). A pine tree can live between 100 and 1,000 years. Beyond a simple anthropological perception problem (i.e., the ignorance of plants because they don't seem to move on a human time scale), the slower time scales of plant-bodies represent a complication to investigating any plantscape. As Anthony Trewavas points out, time-lapse photography is beginning to shed light on this imperceptible world, but scientists are not yet using this technology in every study of plant biology. Thus it is clear that for humans, considering plant time scales is a matter of attunement rather than immediate observation and sheds light on the possibilities of attunement to time scale as part of what creates "thing power" (Bennett 2012) in any human-nonhuman relationship (see chapter 4).

Planters know they are engaging in plantation cultivation. Yet they are also interacting with living plant bodies every day in ways that temporalize their experience (and the experience of the plant-bodies in their charge). Jane, a four-season planter in the 1970s who later became an arborist, when asked what she might like people to know about tree planting that they don't already know, offered the proverb "the best time to plant a tree was twenty years ago" (J. Seniw, unpublished data). Similarly, when faced with the same question, Dan answered "that we're not planting trees that are 3 feet high . . . People would think we plant 10 trees a day, but we're planting 2,000, and they're this big [indicates 4 inches with his hand]" (D. Cheater, unpublished data). Planters gather knowledge of plant time scale from bodily knowledge, as in these three planter excerpts that describe navigating forest floors:

> Now poplars, in their first two years they grow into these spindly little bushes, and they're actually called "whips" because they're maybe like 4 millimeters in diameter each whip, and they get you everywhere and find a way to sneak under your safety glasses and poke you in the eye and all sorts of fun stuff, and you have to move through this dense thing carrying two big bags full of heavy trees, and then you have to plant them. (S. Dyck, unpublished data)

> We were planting in poplar trees that were higher than us, and there was grass everywhere, so you can't see your tiny little green seedling, they're like 6-inches-off-the-ground kind of thing. (S. Friesen, unpublished data)

> I think because coastal forest is so big and so majestic that maybe my opinion of it is emotional and kind of not really grounded in good reasoning. But logging that stuff it seems, it seems wrong. It really does. Those trees are so big and so beautiful and so old . . . It's just, it's something that really does make you emotional, especially the first time you see one of those stumps that is like, you know, we're sitting in a circle of chairs [gestures to interview room] that's probably 10, 12 feet across, that's your average size of stump out there; you can get your whole crew standing on the stump and have plenty of room to spare, and then you see **big** ones. That's not a big one, that's a normal-sized stump. So they're logging trees that must be, well, I don't know, you could probably look at the data on it, but it's just, it's pretty affecting. (J. Simpson, unpublished data)

For planters, size matters, both in terms of being able to locate planting spaces but also in terms of indicating the age of plant-bodies (the 1-year-old pine seedling, the 2-year poplar, the 250-year old-growth tree) and the affects they induce in planter-bodies (i.e., the "whips," the search for acceptable planting spaces, the emotion of irreplaceable old-growth trees). Too, planters realize that the efficacy of their work is at the mercy of both human and tree time scales. As Rackham (2015, 362) acknowledges, forestry management has become "obsessed" with fast-growing trees because "by the time the trees have grown, and the expense of establishing them has been forgotten, there is no telling whether a market for them will still exist . . . Difficulties mount up the longer the trees remain standing." Plantations depend on markets to be harvested again over time and are differentially "successful," as planters describe:

> You look at smaller countries in Europe where they do have, they still have problems with monoculture forest and that sort of thing, but they've been basically farming the same areas for 80-plus, 100 years or more, since prior to the first world war, and yet here in Canada, logging companies are always asking for more access to more virgin boreal forest, which grows at an incredibly slow rate in its natural way, and they don't take care really of the land that they've been given. (J. Sprohge, unpublished data)

> I remember being in the bus going up to the area that we were planting and passing this mountainside where the trees that we had planted were, because they're just little seedlings like they're not huge, there was this flush of green rows, and you knew that that was your effort 2 years before to see that and said, wow, we did something . . . I guess the downside was realizing that those trees weren't going to be there forever . . . Because you know in 20 years they're going to be harvested for pulp or paper or whatever it is. And that I don't know if they ever were. (J. Seniw, unpublished data)

> I don't think it's successful as far as reforesting Canada. I mean, I guess in 70, 80 years we'll see what happens (T. Bourlas, unpublished data).

> It's usually a mix of spruce and pine or spruce, pine, balsam, sometimes fir or larch, but by taking everything down and putting these saplings back in, you're not, we're definitely, we're not bringing anywhere near the natural diversity that occurred in that area, and then it'll come back yet, but it'll take a whole lot more time than just planting. (E. Sawatzky, unpublished data)

> You're not necessarily going out there to plant a forest that in 30 or 50 or 100 years you can go out to see and see there's a forest that you contributed to planting. (T. MacInnis, unpublished data)

> I definitely view the wilderness a little differently in that it seems more manufactured in a way because, or at least where we are, we're planting the trees, and they're just so perfectly aligned, all to be cut down again in 70 years. (L. Rempel, unpublished data)

Despite being mired in the day-to-day promise of time-money-movement efficiency, as planter-bodies negotiate tree-bodies' time scales, they recognize that plantation "success" is complicated and operates on a much longer time scale. Does success mean that in 2 years the planted monoculture has sustained 75 percent of itself? Does success mean the ability to re-harvest in 20 years? Does success mean mature,

80-year-old Canadian forests? Does success mean resurgence? As seasonal bodies relegated to a maximum of 100 years on earth, planters recognize the impossibility of answering those questions on a human time scale. But in coming into contact with tree- (and other plant-) bodies day after day, they are persuaded into seeing time differently, an efficiency flipped not only on the scale of the *anthropo* but also *in vivo*, in the processes that are taking place within living things and how long it takes for those processes to play out.

## EFFICIENCY AND HUMANISM IN KRISIS

It should be clear by now that tree planters don't escape the limits of the *anthropos* by participating (in part) in its making; that their participation in and acceptance of rhetorics of efficiency and humanism help perpetuate a particular kind of *krisis*, a particularized ongoing judgment of human activity in the environment of the cut block. Yet as I have shown here, the logic of efficiency and the logic of humanism are complicated in planter descriptions by a variety of nonhuman encounters. In a world in which dwelling perspectives take hold, the logos of efficiency is challenged when confronting the reality of the rhetoricity of a variety of bodies and the affects that circulate around them. When seen through the lens of a new materialist environmental rhetoric, in which efficiency must be viewed through nonhuman bodies that interact with one another to form rhetorical sites of meaning rather than the other way around, we are able to see in part the way both efficiency and humanism are shaped by nonhuman forces and affects. When inefficient planter-bodies prove more compelling than maximizing personal profit, when mosquitoes can delay a workday for forty minutes and wasps can impact depth perception, when crows are the difference between satiation and starvation and bears garner hellos, when a root's gravitopic response controls a day's output, when everyday time scales are challenged by the magnitude of understory resurgence—all of these kinds of attunements complicate simple calculations of output by unit of input. They not only call into question how valuable a rhetorical framework of efficiency is but suggest competing frameworks that change the notion of efficiency based on human time scale into a far messier prospect. Here we see rhetorical energies and forces at work that indicate connective relations *between* nature and culture that work together to create a complex argument about the environment that moves beyond individual humanistic choice. Planters are attuned to distributed rhythms of time and motion that range from the very small (the two-second "pound") to the geological. They are enmeshed in temporal systems indicated by plant and animal bodies, by earthly seasons, by imagined futures. Nonhuman interventions in easy conceptions of efficiency run rampant in planter descriptions, to the point where we must wonder if such a simple framework can apply. Instead, we may look at planting through the lens of the *underivable rhetoricity of bodies* and see that each body, each "accumulation of relations" (Buchanan 2008, 160), contributes to a way both of being and of making meaning of tree planting that is dependent on the affective capacities of each in relation to the other. I turn to some of these naturecultural interdependencies next as I focus on the particulars of emotions and how they shape bodies in service of an emergent new materialist environmental-rhetorical perspective.

## NOTES

1. I look more closely at thing-bodies in chapter 4.
2. For a larger discussion of how the chōra is used to conceptualize landscape, see Olwig 2011.
3. From the Latin *elucubrare*, to compose by lamplight; in English, *elucubration*, to produce by long effort. The French term, *élucubration*, instead denotes the opposite of reasonable thought, literally, "wild imagining."
4. Such an Indigenous relational ontology comes out of a recognition of the interrelationship between humans, nonhumans, and things, on the one hand, and seen and unseen worlds on the other (Wilson 2008; Fatnowna and Pickett 2002; Fitznor 1998) and of the sensorium as a way of making knowledge through being (Du Plessis and Raza 2004). However, because this book does not take power and settler-colonialism as a central point of critique, it cannot wholly be said to fit within a postcolonial Indigenous research methodology.
5. Grassi critiques this Heideggerian view of humanism, suggesting that Heidegger has misread Italian humanism as "onto-theological metaphysics" rather than non-Platonic humanism (Mailloux 2012, 137–38).
6. This is the main premise of Mucklebauer 2011, 96.
7. See, for example, Hawhee 2017; Seegert 2014; Parrish (2014).
8. Hawhee (2017, 11) suggests "positives" to non-rationality (which is framed in the negative): "energy, bodies, sensation, feeling, and imagination."
9. As Wilson (2008, 87) notes of his speaking with co-researcher and friend Jane Martin, "The only difference between human beings and four leggeds and plants is the shadow they cast."
10. For a further discussion about animality and classical rhetoric, see Hawhee 2017.
11. I'm thinking here of Nealon 2016; Doyle 2011; Hall 2011; Marder 2013b.
12. See the 2017 *Rhetoric Society Quarterly* special issue, *A Rhetorical Bestiary*, for coverage of these topics by Plec, Hughes, and Stalley; Gray; and Schutten and Burford.
13. Hawhee (2015, 3–4), describing rhetoric's sensorium, suggests that sense may be understood in terms of external senses (sound, light, touch, taste, smell) and internal senses ("pain; muscle, tendon, joint sense; equilibratory senses; hunger; thirst; sexual sense; fatigue; and . . . visceral organ senses")—what one might term bodysense.
14. See King 2013.

15. Here I'm purposefully circumventing biological arguments for leveling plant and animal sentience, which have been taken up by Nealon (2016, particularly his "coda") and notably by Wolfe (2012).
16. Heckman (2002) defines an assemblage as "any number of 'things' or pieces of 'things' gathered into a single context" that produces effects.
17. Buchanan (2008, 181) takes up the octopus, while Nealon (2016, 90) discusses the tree.
18. Deleuze(1988 [1970], 49) defines affect in terms of mode, effect, and transition states (feelings): "The *affectio* (affection) refers to a state of the affected body and implies the presence of the affecting body, whereas the *affectus* (affect) refers to the passage from one state to another, taking into account the correlative variation of the affecting bodies."
19. For a discussion of how temporal and spatial arguments shape Indigenous ontologies, see Smith (2012). For how they shape contemporary discourse of the Anthropocene, see Haraway et al. 2016.
20. The assumption is that conventional scholarship reiterates a mind/body, man/woman split in which the masculine mind knows and the feminine body does not.
21. See, for example, Sheldon 2015.
22. See Szasz 1957.
23. See Lee and Tracey 2010.
24. This approach has been taken most notably in the work of economist William Stanley Jevons (1888).
25. A planting season runs from May 1 to July 7 in Ontario, May 1 to July 15 in Manitoba, May 7 to August 7 in Alberta (Outland Reforestation 2017), and April 15 to July 30 in the British Columbia interior (Chisolm 2009).
26. While the crow is usually the American crow, *Corvus brachyrhynchos*, and the raven *Corvus corax*, most of the time the terms *crow* and *raven* are interchangeable to the layperson.
27. Although Wandersee and Schussler (2011) use the term *blindness* to describe the inability to see plants, the metaphor is non-inclusive at best. I take their use of the visual metaphor to mean something like "plant in-attunement," or a lack of plant sense.
28. See Callaway and Mahall 2007; Baluška, Lev-Yadun, and Mancuso 2010.
29. See Gagliano 2017.
30. See Garzón and Keijzer 2011.
31. Marder (2013a), Nealon (2016), and Chamovitz (2013) offer extended discussions of plant being.
32. Garzón and Keijzer (2011, 157) point out that "plants do not react tropistically to stimuli on a one-by-one basis (one stimulus, one directional response)"—that is, plants react to a multitude of factors in their environment.

## 3
# AFFECT AND INTENSE RHETORICS
*The Stickiness of Persuasive Entanglements*

> *Dreams were planting dreams. We planted trees all day and we planted trees all night. All of us, all the time. Even in the off-season; planting dreams were madly tenacious. Planting dreams—dreams about furrows that simply don't end. Dreams about wandering the woods while saddled with a bottomless set of planting bags. Dreams about planting things that aren't trees, about planting strange objects into paved streets. Dreams that wake you feverishly in the night because you need to plant the floor of your tent. Dreams about pockets of soil inside your sleeping bag, dreams about bundles of trees under the hood of your car. Dreams about stuffing trees into a grilled-cheese sandwich and eating it just to make them disappear.* ~Derkowski, Six Million Trees *(2016, 112)*

Thus far, the locus of persuasion away from efficiency and humanism in tree planters' discourse and its movement toward a messier rhetoric of natureculture has been emerging through descriptions of their relational entanglements with plant and animal bodies. I began chapter 2 by focusing on planter-bodies and the ways both injury and pleasure contribute to an inconsistent privileging of efficiency, as well as suggesting some of the ways tree planters are attuned to a kind of "body thinking" that involves a variety of nonhumans. Here I take a closer look at the affects generated by the movement and process of tree planting. By using work in contemporary theories of affect, I highlight what has so far risen to the fore in planter descriptions, what Gregory Seigworth and Melissa Gregg (2010, 3) call "forces and passages of intensity." In focusing on these intensities, I examine what affectual attunements tree-planter discourse can contribute to the placemaking of Canadian tree planting and to allowing a consideration of middle spaces among environmental loss, saviorism, and commodification.

Foregrounded in this approach to planter descriptions that I've labeled a new materialist environmental rhetoric are the rhythms and movement of tree planting that give rise to what Teresa Brennan (2004,

DOI: 10.7330/9781607328551.c003

3) might call a "transmission of affect"—the ways human and nonhuman bodies circulate energies, emotions, feelings. If chapter 2 could be said to capture a range of ways planter-, animal-, and plant-bodies entangle that indicate the shape contemporary tree planting takes (for now), this chapter turns more specifically to framing the affectual intensities that emerge out of the movement of the planter-body on the landscape. It looks at the way "affect is performed in practices and modulated within techniques, which exceed bounded individuated human bodies" (Blackman 2015, 25–26). It asks what arguments may be found in emotions, what kinds of effects they generate to help us understand this anthropocenic moment.

When I set out to interview tree planters, affect wasn't on my mind. If anything was on my mind, it was wondering what people who planted trees thought about their work, given the press tree planters receive in the national imagination that balances coming-of-age narratives with narratives of national identity, toughness, and worker exploitation.[1] What I found while listening to planters talk was instead a spoken focus on *intensity*, which they located primarily in the body—the "heightened experience," as Ross put it, "that comes from doing physical labor all the time" (R. McCannell, unpublished data). Surprisingly to me, given every planter's emphasis on individualism and economic and personal efficiency, was the fact that every tree planter's description was also filled with *feelings*—what feminist philosopher Teresa Brennan (2004, 5) defines as "sensations that have found the right match in words." Feelings, generally associated with non-rationality, are thus not usually associated with any type of efficiency; we are all familiar with the euphemism that feelings "get in the way." Yet feeling was manifested in planter discourse in a variety of ways: in determining that planters share a "love-hate" relationship with the work; in expressions of frustration, "bush-craziness," sadness, nervousness, or difficulty; in relaying dreams, memory places, or meditative states. In some ways, I wasn't prepared as a researcher to catalog or methodologize what I heard, since it didn't quite fit into larger schema: What do you *do* with emotions, after all? At the same time, I couldn't leave the mess of planters' feelings outside of an examination of what I considered more "meaningful" data, in order to see them through the lens of the ambient. I had to look instead at what those particular word matches were doing in insisting on a vitality, a life to planting that stood outside the national imagination or an assumed connection with wilderness or nature. Such feelings often ran up against narratives of freedom, money, and hard work. I instead needed to figure out what these word matches were trying to say; to, as Elspeth Probyn (2010, 74) suggests, "follow through on what different affects do, at different levels" and pay attention to the fact that "different affects make us feel write, think, and act in different ways." As planters repeatedly invoked emotions alongside bodysenses, they did so as a way to make meaning of their experiences that depended on both narrative content and an intensity of experience—of "belonging to a world of encounters" (Seigworth and Gregg 2010, 2) characterized by both non-rational ways of being and an underivable rhetoricity of human and nonhuman bodies.

Scholars in rhetoric and writing studies have increasingly engaged in what Patricia Ticineto Clough (2007) deems *the affective turn*, growing a body of work that investigates emotion, mood, and feeling. This body of work, in early iterations deemed "critical emotion studies" (Trainor 2006, 645), was later influenced by the work of scholars like Brian Massumi and Antonio Damasio (who worked to nuance the terminology of emotion and affect) and was later termed "critical affect studies," or CAS (Edbauer Rice 2008, 201).[2] As I handle the invented world of tree planting and its triptych of human body, tree-body, and shovel as it advances on the landscape, it is in the tradition of rhetorical and writing studies scholars working on the edges of CAS that I seek to continue by noting affect's "cyclical relationship with emotion" (Nelson 2016). Because many of the arguments that circulate within CAS are also those that have hinged on the nature-culture divide, I first take up a few key arguments in the literature before noting the ways affect circulates through the one primary commonality of tree planting: motion. I argue that the intensities of these circulating affects through moving planter-bodies, captured in planters' reportage of feeling, construct a particular meaning of what Catriona Mortimer-Sandilands (2010, 334) calls *devastated* landscapes. Understanding planter-bodies through this capacity to affect and be affected elides the simplistic view of a human-oriented environmentalism as critiqued by Nathaniel Rivers (2015), resting instead on the relations between and among planter-, animal-, plant-, and thing-bodies. It offers us a way to question uncomplicated thinking about the industry of tree planting as a simple outcome from equations of efficiency and humanism and instead encourages us to turn our attention to the ways all bodies, entangled, are altered by the site, motion, and emotion of the encounter.

### INSIDE OUT/OUTSIDE IN: STUDIES OF AFFECT

While Jenny Edbauer Rice (2008, 201) notes that "terms like 'emotion' and 'affect' are often conflated to the point of being nearly synonymous," their emergence within science and humanities scholarship has historically depended on a presupposition of the Cartesian split, caught up in trying to understand the relationship between cognition and feeling, the mind and the body. As Brennan (2004, 4) has it, much of our assumption about emotion and feelings and where they are located comes from Darwinian thought on the emotions and the James-Lange theory, which argued that "bodily responses give rise to affective states," thus separating the body from the mind. Located in this history, various scholars of affect have fallen into what we might think of as "inside-out" and "outside-in" schools of thought. "Inside-out" models locate the site of affect within, often as a biological or physiological state. "Outside-in" models give more credence to the realm of the social in shaping affective states. While this is an extreme simplification of a range of work that captures facets of everything from ontology and realism to evolutionary biology, my intention here is to give a nod to how much theories of affect are equally constrained by the nature-culture divide. As Edbauer Rice (2008, 206) indicates, "inside-out models" are those "where I express my internally felt emotions to those outside my own skin," and "outside-in" models "assume emotion resides in the social sphere and is later learned, or internalized, by an individual." This "difference in directionality," as Seigworth and Gregg (2010, 6) indicate, suggests either "affect as the prime 'interest' motivator that comes to put the drive in bodily drives (Tomkins); [or] affect as an entire, vital, and modulating field of myriad ways of becomings across human and nonhuman (Deleuze)."

While Seigworth and Gregg acknowledge a continuum of complexity that connects the poles of inside out and outside in, they attribute the split to exist primarily between the work of Silvan S. Tomkins, on the one hand, and Gilles Deleuze on the other. On one (in)side, there are scholars whose work draws or builds on that of Tomkins (1962–63): Paul Ekman (1995), Eve Sedgwick and Adam Frank (1995), and later, scholars in neuroscience such as Antonio Damasio (2003) and Arne Öhman (2006). These scholars attest that emotions are first registered by the brain and then experienced in the body—what Ruth Leys (2011, 439) calls the "Basic Emotions Paradigm"[3]—in other words, affects are experienced from the inside out. On the other (out)side, Seigworth and Gregg point to cultural critics taking up the work of Gilles Deleuze, Baruch Spinoza, and Henri Bergson (in CAS) such as Lawrence Grossberg (1992), Brian Massumi (2002), Patricia Ticineto Clough (2007), and Erin Manning (2010) (among others), who, as Lisa Blackman (2012) suggests, "refigur[e] our conceptions of bodies" and blur the distinction between body and environment—noting that affects are experienced from the outside in (and sometimes even blur the boundary of the human body, questioning what the inside/outside might be). Seigworth and Gregg (2010) note a variety of nuanced positions that run up against and among these poles;[4] similarly, Edbauer Rice notes the work of scholars like Sara Ahmed (2004), who claims for affect *emotions* and relationality, arguing that they are "the acts of orientation *between* bodies" (Edbauer Rice 2008, 206; emphasis added). Thus while theories of contemporary affect may be seen to struggle with the same duality of mind/body, feeling/emotion,[5] and nature/culture,[6] they also open up space in which to consider a nature-culture continuum (Massumi 2002, 11). Such a continuum can locate affect, or its "transmission," as Brennan (2004) has it, is a "process that is social in origin but biological and physical in effect." This has the potential to unite the mind and body by acknowledging that affect happens within as without (Brennan 2004, 11) and allows us to note, as material ecocritics do, that "there is no secure distinction between the 'individual' and the 'environment'" (Brennan 2004, 6).

## THE ENERGIES OF AFFECT: MOVEMENT, DURATION, MEMORY, AND PROCESS

Critical affect studies continues to wrestle with the imposed bifurcation between the biological and the social; however, a growing body of work suggests that "affects refer equally to the body and the mind" (Hardt 2007, ix), that they are represented through the language of feeling, and that they are energetic and relational, "generated in interactions among bodies" (Edbauer Rice 2008, 207). These are the premises that undergird a reading of circulated affects among planter-, animal-, plant-, and thing-bodies. To frame a new materialist environmental rhetoric, I work with a few useful premises from CAS. The first, taking mind and body together, I accept that affect is represented by intensities that rest or originate in the body but that through the language of feeling can reflect a particular "degree or duration" (Edbauer Rice 2008, 201) while acknowledging that "language describing emotion is necessarily less precise" (Öhman 2006, 35). Such a premise is supported by Julie Nelson's (2016) work that notes the complementarity of affect and emotion. She suggests that affect is bigger in its ability to hold symbolic expressions of emotion, while emotion is then "the most intense (most contracted) expression of that capture" (Massumi 2002, 28). Nelson (2016) notes the relational quality between emotion and affect, pointing out our dependence on the vocabulary of emotions to qualify and illuminate affect. I am less concerned, in other words, with the argument that tries to locate the time and space between bodily feeling and cognitive knowing or the separation of affect from emotion or affect from cognition.[7]

Second, unlike scholars working in the area of neuroscience, who argue that affect arises only from the body (Damasio 2003, 85), I instead embrace the view forwarded by Ahmed (2004, 7), who argues that affect can indeed shape and be shaped by objects. I shift the notion of "objects" here to "bodies," moving out from the work of scholars such as Brennan (2004, 8), who limit discussion of affect between and among human subjects, and including in such a shift the capacity for nonhuman bodies to also affect and be affected (Blackman 2012). To this end, the roles of both memory and the nonhuman body become key to the circulation of affect; as Ahmed (2010, 29) notes, "Affect is what sticks, or what sustains or preserves the connection between ideas, values, and objects." Ahmed (2010, 35) argues that such stickiness is also social, that objects "are already attributed as being good or bad, as being the cause of happiness or unhappiness"—or both, as I suggest in the case of tree planting.

Finally, I use as a framing insight a "focus on affective energies and creative motion [that] characterizes bodies in two ways: by movement and process" (Blackman 2012). By the first, I mean that planters' acknowledgment of feeling and emotion arises out of the affect generated by constant physical, bodily motion and entanglement on the tree-planting landscape, dictated through repetition and time primarily by *movement*. Deleuze (1991 [1966], 51) offers some insight into how such movement over time—unlike *kairos*, or rhetorical "right-timing," he suggests *durée*, or duration—is intricately connected to memory because it cultivates the "conservation and preservation of the past in the present." As much as an attunement to plant time scales is made from the planter-body's intimate contact with tree bodies, the physical repetitive act of bending over to put a tree in the ground, over and over, is also a continuous engagement of time, objects, and memory. As Deleuze (1991 [1966], 51–52) notes, "Duration is distinguished from a discontinuous series of instants repeated identically . . . two moments contract or condense into each other since one has not yet disappeared when another appears . . . the 'present' that endures divides at each 'instant' into two directions, one oriented and dilated toward the past, the other contracted, contracting toward the future."

Tree planting is always an act of memory caught in repetition over time, a reminder of what has come before caught in a moment preceding an imagined future action. Because planting movement on the landscape is produced in duration as an act of memory,[8] it lends itself to Ahmed's (2010) notion of sticky affect, as I take up in planters' descriptions of their love-hate relationship with it.

By *process*, I mean imagining planters' affective intensities as flows of vital processes emerging from their motion on the landscape and persuasive entanglements with nonhuman others. Such processes engage planter senses on the edges of the body: into dreams, meditations, and altered states of transformation toward "turning into some weird subhuman tree-planting creature" (R. Boldt, unpublished data). Taken together as part of what creates a new materialist environmental rhetoric, it is my intention that the turn to these affective intensities will show (1) how planters continually make and are made by place and (2) how their entanglements with nonhuman bodies shape their recognition of and relationship with the subject of anthropocenic loss in a way that does not fetishize wilderness or slip into "nature-nostalgia" (Mortimer-Sandilands 2010, 333). The potential of affective movement and process to give rise to a more complicated, intense environmental rhetoric offers one way we might observe and document the invention of the Anthropocene without succumbing to simple separations of nature from culture, body from mind, environmentalist from developer. Affective entanglements on plantation landscapes instead allow glimpses of what it might look like to argue nature's other as ourselves, to grieve the un-grievable, to imagine tree and other bodies as beings beyond resource capital, and to imagine ourselves as part of how the forest thinks.

## INTENSITY, MOTION, EMOTION: "THE UNFOLDING OF BODIES INTO WORLDS"

Although Brennan's (2004) work focuses primarily on the transmission of affect between human subjects, here I turn to the ways affect *moves* between bodies—specifically, human and nonhuman bodies that entangle on the planting landscape. Central to planters' descriptions is the centrality of physical motion or movement on the landscape (as discussed in chapter 1), which Ahmed (2010, 30) might call the "messiness of the experiential, the unfolding of bodies into worlds, and the drama of contingency, how we are touched by what we are near." Planter-bodies are caught up in being "constantly in motion" (R. Boldt, unpublished data); as Nik reminds us, "head down, you just get into a good groove, you just tree, tree, tree" (N. Friesen Hughes, unpublished data). As simple as planters make it sound, it is this motion, its duration, that consistently gave rise to their descriptions of emotions and feelings, sensation, memory, and recall. And it is the physical excess, the stress of the motion, the combination of body and land that underwrites warnings in tree-planting advice. As Jonathan Clark (2016b) writes in an online post meant to train new tree planters, "Anybody dealing with emotional stress should not go planting. If you have relationship hassles, depression, some kind of an existential crisis, or if you're in mourning, the bush is the worst possible place to deal with it." Despite this well-meaning advice, planters (who perhaps entered planting situations without "emotional stress") reflected back on their experience planting in emotional ways, often using the language of intensity:

> I think when you're doing any physical labor that's as strenuous as tree planting is day in and day out, there's an intensity from that alone. That's the main factor. You're also outdoors, of course, and subject to the elements, the heat, some days the rain, other days could be, or the cold on other days yet, and that all . . . lends it to being an intense experience and heightens your experience as well. (R. McCannell, unpublished data)

> Tree planting, it's either heaven or hell but it's very rarely anything in between. Life is almost always very, very, very intense out there, so it's almost never, you almost never get like this gray ennui that you often get in the city where you feel like you're just sleepwalking through life. While tree planting you're either, you're often either really, really happy or else you're really, really angry and upset and miserable, and there's almost no gray zone. So no matter what, you feel incredibly alive out there, and so as a result your memories are very, very vivid. (R. Boldt, unpublished data)

> There's the social intensity of like I, one year I ended up, there's usually a gender divide in camp. There's usually more guys than girls. You're in the bush for three months, you're in your mid-twenties or early twenties, you know, there's a lot of intense sexual competition, to put it mildly . . . So those romantic relationships can be really, really immediate and can be a role because your emotions are so roaring and you're kind of physically firing on all cylinders . . . Those intense, that kind of intensity. (J. Simpson, unpublished data)

As Ahmed (2004, 14) suggests, "Emotions might not have a referent, but naming an emotion has effects that we can describe as referential." While it's clear, for example, that what planters refer to as *intensity* does not directly and linguistically translate to what scholars of CAS mean by *intensity*, here planters' descriptions begin in the body and continue in what Seigworth and Gregg (2010, 1) call "intensities that pass body to body." These intensities are referential of physical motion of the planter-body on the landscape (which automatically implicates both tree and shovel)—from emotional states (feeling "really happy," "really angry and upset," or "incredibly alive") to temporal states ("sleepwalking," "really immediate") to other bodily intensities (i.e., sexual acuity). These intensities are characterized not only in terms of human bodies—that is, how "one person can feel another's feelings" or affects (Brennan 2004, 1); they are also characterized by the forest, trees, and the various nonhuman bodies planters encounter through daily motion. The unfolding of planter-bodies into worlds constitutes and is constituted by affects that stick not only to human bodies but also to plant bodies, animal bodies, and thing bodies. This stickiness generates a rhythm to the landscape and an attunement to a particular relationship with contemporary environmental management that stems primarily from bodily sensation. In other words, planters are touched by what they are near. Thus rather than divide their descriptions of experiences here by patterns of "basic emotions," instead I turn to the ways their affective experience is organized by what planters are near, in terms of how a particular landscape is carved out among bodily movements and processes.

### Movement and Landscape: A Love-Hate Relationship

As I turn to the ways affect shapes and is shaped by planter movement and the way it is "stuck" to human and other-than-human bodies, my intent is to do justice to chorography, to the invention of a particular landscape, which geographer Timothy Ingold (2000) suggests emphasizes both form and movement. Ingold (2000, 198) purports that landscapes "are generated in movement" and are living, temporal processes—thus a separation of what is meant by "movement" and "process" is perhaps somewhat conflated when it comes to inventing anthropocenic plantation spaces. Nonetheless, I take as my cue here first the ways affect is tangled up in human and nonhuman bodies through the movement of tree planting and then the ways "brain-body-world" (Blackman 2012) processes are similarly shaped by affective encounters (weather, water, sociality). Through a view of affective movement and process, it is my hope that a particular disturbance-based landscape is made present through the vernaculars of affect. Such vernaculars have the capacity to show these entanglements to be based in multi-species encounters as well as give rise to a generative potential middle ground—a new materialist environmental rhetoric—that sits between ecocentrism and anthropocentrism and resists a type of "nature nostalgia" (Mortimer-Sandilands 2010, 333) rooted in the environmentalist-developmentalist divide.

Prior chapters have provided descriptions of tree planting that make a clear case for bodies in motion and the action of planting a tree that is dependent on planter-body health, tree-body alignment, soil preparation, and shovel perspicacity. As Ross contends, successful planting is "a combination of memorizing where you've just been from visual identifiers—it's very difficult because cut blocks kind of all blur together—and intuition" (R. McCannell, unpublished data). Ross articulates Massumi's (2002, 180–82) notion of the "body topologic" here, which locates affect along a naturecultural continuum in which humans orient themselves on any landscape by both precognitive mapping ("memorization," "intuition") and visual orientation, using the two (inside and outside, if you will) together.

This topological movement of tree planting, located in planter-tree-shovel bodies, provides an umbrella for the intensities of affect that planters describe and thus deserves to be foregrounded as a particular unfolding of bodies in the world that affect "sticks" to in varied ways. The first is the way the motion itself construes a particular affect of meditation and peacefulness:

> There's something I think incredibly meditative about just the action of planting trees. You're step, step, step, step, plant; step, step, step, step, plant, and you get into the zone and just, I mean not always, but there are points when you can get into the zone and just go with it and be present to the moment, to your steps, to planting, and yeah, I found it quite a meditative activity. (E. Sawatzky, unpublished data)

> Some days I just felt like I was able to get into such a rhythm with this, it was sort of like I, people would probably disagree if I said it was like meditation, but it was sort of like just some sort of a thing where you're outside, you're doing this one thing, and you can kind of take your mind and your whole concentration off of that thing while still doing it. (S. Friesen, unpublished data)

> The thing I always loved about tree planting was you just, I always found it incredibly peaceful . . . You are by yourself, and I've always been a bit of a loner, so being by myself doing this job, this very repetitive job and letting my mind wander . . . I just found it very, very, very peaceful and very happy where, yeah, as I said before it kind of sends you into a trance, and I found it to usually be a pretty happy trance. (R. Boldt, unpublished data)

Note that the motion of planting, seemingly invisible, is tied to entanglements among planter, tree, shovel, and ground. Yet the motion itself appears to denote a kind of "happy object," in Ahmed's (2010) terms: the encounter with the movement on the landscape, the repetition, the ability both to be present in the moment and to let one's mind wander, to attach a particular happy orientation to the motion of planting. This repetition itself, as Deleuze (1991 [1966]) notes, with one foot in the past and one in the future, is always an act of duration and thus memory.

Motion-memory is located thus both in time and in bodies, and this might explain why planters project close to the opposite affect as well:

> Having the mental strength to keep on, just keep on doing it every day is probably the toughest thing. And my friend jokes, he's like "yeah, I don't even want to tree plant until halfway through the day." Like he says for the first half of the day he's just kind of going through the rhythms and then eventually he finally gets pumped up at around 12 o'clock. (L. Rempel, unpublished data)

> I've developed mental coping techniques. I'd say the biggest one for sure is the, I call it, me and my friends call it "infinite resignation" and basically just realizing you've got very little power over what's going to happen in your day and no power over what your block is going to be like, so basically just let it wash over you and know that there's going to be bad stuff some days and that other days will be good and just don't freak out over your total lack of control, and if something goes bad, just accept it and try to get through it, and don't let it bother you. And yeah, I would say with every single year I get better at that, and so I'd say with every single year I am happier and calmer because of these coping techniques. Whereas yeah, a lot of rookies, pretty much every single rookie I think, cries at some point in their rookie year. (R. Boldt, unpublished data)

> It was just slogging through a bog all day, your feet were soaking wet, you're mucked up to your knees, your hands are, though covered in duct tape, they still get like dish-wash hands, and that was just a tough, tough day. And one of my good friends, she, the checker came and didn't like her quality, and she ended up having to replant all of her trees, and she sat there and cried for so long, and I had to comfort her a bit. It was just such a, that was a tough, tough day. (J. Sprohge, unpublished data)

Here the same repetitive motion imbued with meditative and peaceful qualities is also imbued with negative affect: a recalcitrant rhythm, a slog that requires a coping mechanism of "infinite resignation" to try to overcome a sense of powerlessness or worse, the inevitable cry of disappointment and the frustration of exhaustion. As Sam says of the constant motion, "Just making yourself do that thing, that same exact thing . . . some days is kind of meditative but some days is just the worst; I just can't imagine planting another tree" (S. Friesen, unpublished data). The Janus face of two-way feeling about tree planting is perhaps the primary characterization of the work; as Jon summed up in his interview, "it's kind of a love-hate relationship with planting. Sometimes you hate it when you're there, and you miss it when you're not there" (J. Sprohge, unpublished data). It's this complex both-ness that I want to unpack in terms of the bodies involved in tree-planting movement, the ways the forest, the trees, the animals, the shovels, and the planters create an affective landscape with particular rhetorical force and effect;

the way the forest thinks through bodies.[9] What bodies cultivate happiness, love, sadness, and hate; and what meaning might be made from the effects of affect? I'll begin with the where, the way affects gather in the forest.

*Planters in Motion: The Stickiness of Forest Bodies*

For tree planters, the forest (or, more accurately, forests) is/are more than a setting or a backdrop for work. On the one hand, forests are separated from cut blocks (blocks "blur together," as Ross suggested); on the other, planters describe both forests and cut blocks and their locations as differentially significant, being able to speak at length about the differences between planting in the Rockies of British Columbia or the muskeg of the prairies. Still other planters have forests and blocks emblazoned in their memories:

> It's crazy how I can still picture the blocks that I've planted on and what each, or a lot of the pieces, were shaped like. And like if you brought me back, I would know because they're generally not just a rectangle. Because of the way it's clear-cut, it tends to be a weird shape, and you may have to go, or you will probably have to go around corners, and yeah, if I were to draw it on a bird's-eye-view map, it would look like in some weird way, and there's sometimes contours like rivers and things going through. So it's crazy how there's moments or how I can really remember how these blocks looked. (L. Rempel, unpublished data)

> What you actually remember planting, because I can remember not all of them but enough of them in fairly good detail, a lot of the land that I've planted. I can tell you roughly where it is, I could probably find it on a sufficiently detailed aerial photo, and I can sort of describe what it was like, what that day was like, stuff like that. (S. Dyck, unpublished data)

> I just truly love being out in the forest. (J. Sprohge, unpublished data)

> And also the destruction, [I] saw a lot of the clear-cut stuff that was, it was disheartening some days. Your foreman would bring you to an area, and you just drive through the depth of the woods, just seeing trees that are enormous swaying like 200 feet above you, and then you just get to this hole and it's just where you know that big machinery has just tackled everything and big piles that were just pushed together that are eventually going to be burned. And it just, it's, I don't know, I love the forest, I love feeling like I'm part of the forest, and then when you get to these clear-cuts, it . . . just sometimes felt like you were on a different planet. (T. MacInnis, unpublished data)

> Just spending hours and hours and hours every single summer outdoors, unfortunately you're usually planting in a cut block, and the forest is

usually beckoning to you off in the distance when you're so hot and sweaty, but you're not allowed to go in there because that would mean you're shirking and not working, but just being, there are still animals, and there are still birds, and you still see the trees off in the distance, and on days off you still get to walk through forest. (R. Boldt, unpublished data)

What we know from excerpts like these is that the forest is not a simple or a foundational place; it is both old growth and cut block, filled and empty, dynamic with movements of sweaty humans and flying nonhumans, a place of *being*. Cut blocks are only given a shape by tree lines creating negative space. Some planters, like Jon, make no distinction between forest and block as a site of love. Others, like Thayer, distinguish living forests from the "different planets" of clear-cuts.

Some of the first denotative bodies on these landscapes are trees. Planters like Ryan see the "trees off in the distance" as those who beckon rather than the forty-pound bags of seedlings he carries across the block. There are tree-bodies of the cut block, many of which have been mentioned in prior chapters (seedlings, whips, snarb, stumps), and tree-bodies of the forest (mature trees that line the block). Without tree-bodies, there is no distinguishing shape of the block, no forest beckoning. Here planters imagine the forest as a place of also *being-with*, shown in their affective investment in the stickiness of forest-bodies and the way they talk in affective terms about tree-bodies.

While trees, on the one hand, signify a commodity (as designated by the tree price system described in chapter 1), on the other they are sites of affective stickiness, cultivating in planters a sense of care and nurturing—for example, Georgia building tipis for trees to live behind. Conversely, as James remarked about the denigration of old-growth forest in chapter 2, sadness and futility are also affects that stick. Trees are bodies with which planters are entangled every day as they move on the landscape. They are not simple objects, as the rhetoricity of J-roots and plant time scales suggests. They are nonhuman bodies that planters are affected by as much as planter-bodies affect seedling success:

> There's a typical sort of three steps to planting a tree where you cut open the hole, you put in your tree, and then you stomp it closed. And usually, I did the first two just fine, but then when I was stomping it closed, I would sort of really baby the tree. I would do maybe three or four soft stomps and then just readjust the soil around it to make it more ideal for the tree. (T. MacInnis, unpublished data)

> I'd spend more time making sure the tree was good than just sort of trusting that it was good and moving on, you know, so I was quite slow. (L. Ainsworth, unpublished data)

If you're in a position where you are nurturing a live thing, be it animal or plant, in order for you to do a good job, you have to have a connection to that . . . These trees have, they're all living beings. (J. Seniw, unpublished data)

Here the affect gets in the way of efficiency: planters want to plant a "good" tree to avoid having to replant, but they do so from a place of connection and care. In the motion of planting, planters "baby" trees, actively making sure trees are properly planted, noting that a "good job" is represented not only by getting a seedling in the ground but also in having a connection to a living being and caring about its livelihood. A planter-body is made up of human-tree-shovel-land entanglements. It is perhaps because of these generative entanglements that planters are led to see what they are doing as futile, as Nik suggested in his articulation of chemically prepped land in chapter 1: "So they go ahead and spray if after it's been growing for five to ten years, so you have [dead] trees that are like 6 feet tall, 4 feet tall, 2 feet tall, just a big mix, and planting through that stuff is just, the first time I hit that I was so choked, I was like how am I supposed to [plant]. 'Cause you're just dodging trees, you're getting trees in the face, and you can't really, it just feels futile. There's all these dead trees, you're going through a dead forest, crazy" (N. Friesen Hughes, unpublished data). Sam echoes this futility in a description of stillness: "And some days I would just sit on a log and look out at everything I had planted already and everything that I still needed to plant, and it was just like one of the most depressing things, I'm like can I even go on right now" (S. Friesen, unpublished data).

Trees emerge as complex sticky bodies. Here, the feeling states associated with trees are imbued with caring—connection, trust, "baby"ing—as well as hopelessness and futility. The planter-body is bound up with the tree-body in each case, whether in readjusting the soil, dodging dead trees, or sitting on a logged stump; in each case the planter-body is recalling a particular memory of affect that moves beyond trees as capital-producing objects. Tree planting is more than simple movement. It is an *encounter*, and planters' descriptions of their feelings solidify it as such.

Such affectual buildup is not relegated to tree bodies, as is evidenced in no small way by planters' encounters with insects captured in chapter 2. Animal bodies are bound up in planters' associational feelings, and it is often their physical manifestation (that is, animal bodies on the landscape within a planter's sensorium) that generates powerful and mixed affects:

> So there's something about breathing fresh air every single day and hearing birds singing and feeling the wind and the sun on your skin for hours every single day which I think just makes me feel calm and happy in a way that is difficult for me to duplicate in the city. (R. Boldt, unpublished data)

> Just, there's days when you're in land where it doesn't, it's so difficult, like there's so many obstacles to actually planting good trees [that] it's very frustrating. And then on top of it, maybe it starts raining, and then it starts hailing, and then there's a bear over there, and it's just like why am I doing this to myself? (D. Cheater, unpublished data)

> One time I was planting on Crown land, which to my understanding is that we were replanting it, and it was not going to be reforested, or, yeah, it wasn't going to be touched again. We were trying to restore it back to its natural state. So we were all on the fringes of some protected land, and during my day I just looked up, and I hear this "frrp-frrp" sound, and I look up and there's a herd of caribou running through my piece, and it was just like, I just stood there, and I just started crying. (S. Friesen, unpublished data)

> My friend J [who] I was planting with found an orphaned baby deer one day, and it was really cute. It was really sad. She really followed us around for a while, and we didn't think we should touch her first because we'd think her mom would go back to get her. But then yeah, she was following us around, and we had been in a similar area the day before, and my friend S had found a baby deer that was following him around all day, so we assumed it must have been the same one. And I kind of fell in love with her and I really wanted to take her back to camp, but then I realized it was probably impractical. (G. Chappell, unpublished data)

Of course, generated affects that circulate around animal bodies are memory-dependent; what one planter may recall as a sense of calm generated by birds singing in the sun, another will recall in terms of rain and the scare of a potential bear or coyote attack. Too, affects stick to both animal bodies and land types; Sam differentiates Crown land (land that will not be designated for logging, for now) from average plantation landscapes as she describes crying among the caribou. Georgia recognizes the impossibility of the wild in wild creatures and the sadness and love it cultivates within her: the baby deer that no doubt will die without a mother, the impracticality of a human mother on the plantation landscape. In each encounter, it is not the planter-body alone on the landscape feeling a particular sensation that begins in the body. Instead, each describes the ways animal bodies generated a particular affect, whether happiness, frustration, sadness, or love. Although not reflected in great depth in these snapshot moments, crucial to these descriptions is the active vitality of the animal bodies in the multi-species encounter:

the bird who sings, the bear who waits, the caribou who gather to run, the deer who follows. Each description captures a moment of movement, not only of the planter on the landscape but of the animal as well.

Perhaps the most unnoticed relation on this landscape that is peppered with nonhuman beings, invisible in most descriptions but always present in hand (indeed, in every use of the verb "to plant"), are the ways planter and tree are entangled with the constant movement of the shovel. This thing-body, invisible in some accounts, is as present in others for its capacity to circulate affective effects:

> But you have no idea what a cut block looks like, and you have no idea how—like you kind of know—okay, you use a shovel, a lot of people assume you're digging a hole with a shovel, you know? And there's kind of no way to describe to somebody the emotional and the mental, like the mental and emotional state you get into several months into it. (G. Chappell, unpublished data)

> There were a lot of times for my first few years when I would just get so angry, and I would just like, something would just boil over, my frustration, I would just throw my shovel like into the woods and like yell and be so, so frustrated. Of course, nobody was around me, so it was just me raging impotently by myself, and then, of course, it's just worse 'cause you have to walk and go get it and go back and just keep on doing what you're doing. (T. Kroeker, unpublished data)

> I remember one time I had just an awful day, and the bugs were terrible, and I was not planting as many trees as I wanted, and I was just frustrated with people in camp, and a stump got in my way, and I accidentally stepped on it and tripped, and I just lost it, and I took my shovel and I destroyed that stump and looked back and said wow, Erin, I didn't know you had that in you. (E. Sawatzky, unpublished data)

Here the shovel is another being on the landscape, one linked to exhausting physical and mental states, as well as a conduit for feelings of rage and frustration. The shovel does not meet our expectations. It doesn't dig as we might expect, as Georgia says. The shovel pries into the earth only as much as is needed, the tool that enables a planter-body to *be* a planter-body and not just a human body. Yet this action repeated over time, in constant motion—duration—is what allows Georgia to make the immediate segue from shovels that don't dig to the emotional and mental toll tree planting takes on planters over time. This toll is echoed in Thomas's and Erin's excerpts in which shovels are an extension of affect: the tool that creates the planter-body is also a vessel of frustration and impotence, shoved into stumps or thrown into the forest, perhaps to reduce the planter momentarily back to human. Here planter-bodies—always in motion with tree bodies, shovel bodies, animal bodies—draw out of this kinesis a series of affects: sadness, frustration, happiness, love, depression, care, peace, anger. It is true that in talking during interviews, these are but moments of memory and recall. Yet what they have in common are the connections between word and motion that emerge out of bodily affect and intensity, not only individualism and efficiency. These connections—demonstrated in chapter 4 using Ehren Helmut Pflugfelder's (2017) notion of *kinesthetic rhetoric*—are similarly present in the ways planters talk through their entanglement with other vital things and processes that are sticky with affect.

### BEING-WITH PROCESSES: PERSUASIVE ENTANGLEMENTS OF WEATHER, WATER, SOCIALITY

Admittedly, what separates water-body from, say, tree-body is artificial if we are to embrace the Deleuzian notion that bodies are known through interactions, through their "capacity for affecting and being affected" (Deleuze 1992, 625). I've chosen to examine the affects that move among planters and weather, the way water generates particular affect,[10] and the ways the sociality generated between planter-bodies produces affective capacity as dynamic processes that move up against planter kinesis—taking as a starting place that such kinesis is born out of duration, the planter-tree-shovel movement on the landscape. It's true that the weather as a body cannot truly be affected by one tree planter (although in the age of global climate change, perhaps this is not such a stretch). However, as I argue later in this chapter, the ways planter-bodies are affected by elements like weather or water contribute to a larger schema, a suasive landscape rich with sociality, a change of mind, an anthropocenic moment that works its way through planter-bodies by the way those bodies are affected. However, as readers will note from the following excerpts, each element bleeds into the other, is tangled up with other bodies.

Planters clearly identified weather as a fundamental aspect of what constitutes a good or bad day or as what can increase topographic difficulty, as when Georgia described the difficulties of mountain planting in chapter 1, building tipis for her trees while "it was pouring rain, thunder storming all day," leading her to assert that she "was having a terrible time" (G. Chappell, unpublished data). In many planter descriptions, weather directly affects bodies, feelings, and mood, with the condition of each interdependent, as Sam notes: "There are sort of other conditions, so how you felt mentally the whole time is significant, how you felt or other things, the weather, the weather can be a huge part. If it's really hot, that's a terrible day, that's going to be a terrible day. If it's really cold, probably also not that good; if it's raining, that's usually not a good sign either" (S. Dyck, unpublished data).

For bodies that move on temporal landscapes—whether in terms of clock time (*chronos*), duration (*durée*), or the right moment to act (*kairos*)—the weather is no small thing. As John Durham Peters (2015, 244) notes in his study of media as both a natural and a cultural phenomenon, weather and time are dependent semantic fields, whether in ancient Greek terminology for right-timing *kairos* or in contemporary Greeks' use of *kairos* to mean weather: "In Latin, *tempus* means weather and time, giving English such words as *temporal* and *tempest*, and French *le temps* and Spanish *el tiempo*, both of which mean both time and weather; the Spanish *el tiempo* means both 'in season' (of fruits) or 'at room temperature' (of drinks). Terms such as *temperature, tempering, tempo*, and *temperament* show shared semantic fields across heat, harmony, rhythm, and mood."

"The weather, with its intermittent reinforcement of irregular patterns of blessing and bane," Peters (2015, 244) sums up, "behaves like gods and parents—one reason why we are so emotionally attached to it." We might rephrase Peters to say that we are affectually attached to the weather; that is, such attachments are in between material body spaces and cognitive knowing- or feeling-places. As Tamir says: "It was just so weird. You know, your first year it's like you're in a bit of a dream or something. It doesn't quite, a bad dream even, but it doesn't quite, you don't understand what's going on around you. You have no control. Everyone's telling you to go places, do this, and I, I guess in May I had some doubts on whether I was going to be successful or not. And cold. Spring plant is wet and cold, that's for sure" (T. Bourlas, unpublished data).

Here Tamir links the planting experience in a cold spring to a "bad dream" that constructs a weird-scape. The time—May—and the weather—wet and cold—combine in a baneful pattern in his first season. Ambient temperatures during a Canadian "spring" (the months of April and May) range from about 26ºF to 57ºF, depending on provincial location, and planting in snow is not unusual early in the season. Similarly, conditions in late summer can include temperatures in the 50s to the 100s; although planters more commonly complain of rain and cold, they are as quick to assert that a hot day is equally uncomfortable, given the fact that clothing is what hinders many biting insects. Weather emerges as sticky for planters' affects: indicative of mood, spurring bodies to action.

Perhaps the most lighthearted but significant description of the way weather's stickiness moves through planter-bodies is Sam's depiction of a day spent entangled with rain:

> I was planting by myself. We were planting in like poplar trees that were higher than us, and there was grass everywhere, so you can't see your tiny little green seedling, they're like 6-inches-off-the-ground kind of thing, and so I was lost, I didn't know where I was going, it was raining all day, my feet were soaked, and they hadn't dried out for days because we had been working for so long my boots never got a chance to dry out. There's water all over me because it's coming off of the trees that are beside me, I'm cold, I'm grumpy, I've nobody to plant with because my planting partner was sick that day, and I was so miserable I didn't even, I didn't even want to go to the bathroom properly, so I just like, I was like, okay this is the most dire thing, I'm just gonna pee myself, that's just what's gonna happen today, and I'm gonna be fine with it. And I didn't realize I wasn't completely, entirely soaked until I did that, and I'm like oh crap, well, there we go. And then, you know, I was even more miserable walking around all day after that . . . If it was sunny out or even if there were, even if it was cloudy and it was just warm and pleasant to be outside, then you could get through it, or I felt like I could get through it, but when it was, when you're soaking for days and your boots were just squishing up at you and you also had to like smash into rocks trying to find places to put trees, those were the, there were a few days like that, and they were just terrible. (S. Friesen, unpublished data)

Here the weather, "rai[n] all day," has its attendant processual impact: gathering on poplars and boots and skin, manifesting emotion and mood (misery, grumpiness), and culminating in a physical, bodily decision ("I'm just gonna pee myself"). Sam's description proves Ahmed's (2010, 37) observations about "feeling the atmosphere": "Having read the atmosphere," she says, "one can become tense, which in turn affects what happens, how things move along." In Sam's description, she reads the atmosphere (wet, lost), registers emotion (lonely, miserable), and reacts with a bodily response (dire). The physical gesture of urinating compounds the misery of the rain; much like Delsartean[11] philosophies applied to acting, the physical gesture then articulates the emotion and in so doing, brings it into being (Warhol 2003, 19). Reflecting on how the weather influences planters, Sam then connects weather to its sticky affects: sun and warmth allow the positive mental capacity to "get through it"; days wet with rain and compounded with difficult terrain create days that are "just terrible." Sam's example represents both the circulation of affects and the entanglement of bodies (can the rain be separated from the way water gathers on the poplars? On planter's skin?), the change weather-bodies induce on planter-bodies, the relational rhetorical forces at work in the everyday—in another sense, how Sam is persuaded by the rain.

The second descriptive moment that depicts affectual links among weather, planters, and social relations is one Nik relayed about his second year spent planting:

> We had, my second year I was learning how to plant unscarified, so you have to look for your trees and space off them whereas before it was just you would run the rows, and it snowed, and it snowed for the first two weeks, and it was just freezing cold. I just remember, even at night I put all my clothes and all my laundry on top of myself in my tent and just curled up, and I couldn't get anything dry because it was always like raining and snowing. And trying to spot the new trees, it was really, it was really, what's the word I'm looking for, it was defeating, it was a struggle. And we had a friend that came with us for her first season in our second year, and she was having a really rough time the first few weeks with all the snow and everything. 'Cause every year a few people quit, like it's really not for everybody, I think some people just don't like being in their head all day kind of thing, which is totally understandable, and it's really physically tough. And she kind of had a breakdown, and she, well, we had to deal with her, and it was just tough at the end of the day trying to support her when it was just a hard time for everybody. And she actually ran away one morning, and we didn't know where she was, so we had to follow these footprints in the snow, and we did find her, and yeah, it was crazy, like I don't know what you call it when somebody goes into, it's like she turned into a different person. She eventually got air-lifted back to Hearst [Ontario]. (N Friesen Hughes, unpublished data)

Here Nik describes moving bodies in proximity, the ways weather (in the form of rain, snow, and low temperatures) creates a specific kind of right-timing (a *kairos kairos*) for his own physical discomfort and feelings of defeat as he tries to navigate unscarified land for the first time. He also portrays the way such defeat traveled to other planter-bodies: a friend who experienced such a difficult mix of weather and physical duress that she had to be air-lifted out of camp to the nearest town. It is also the story of the way circulating affects have effects—the difficulty snow, rain, and cold create in planter-bodies as they navigate and move on the landscape (which extends to slipperiness of terrain, soil compaction and shovel resistance, and physical comfort)—and the ways those difficulties are in turn felt by other planters: a transmission of affect, as Teresa Brennan (2004) would have it, that sticks not only to the weather but also to the shovel, to the damp clothes, to planter-bodies, to planter actions (running away), to planter emotions ("a breakdown"), to planter transformation (turning into "a different person").

Affects circulate, in other words, and our senses of happiness or unhappiness are associated with or stuck to thing-bodies like weather, which persuade us into action. They also move from body to body (i.e. shovel to planter) and move among and between human groups: the atmospheres planter-bodies "feel" are often similar and shared. Affect has emerged thus in the literature as both contagious (in this excerpt, both Nik and his friend experience defeat born from the weather and physical stress) and contingent (Nik stays and indeed plants for a third year; his friend quits planting entirely).[12] Despite the fact that "bodies can catch feelings as easily as [they can] catch fire" (Gibbs 2001), we might say that in this case, only some bodies burn. Such catchable feelings are bound up with an attunement to situations, yes, but situations (particularly when they involve elemental bodies) are often not conveniently parsed into knowable units or un-packable as separate—particularly as they generate affects, as Ross points out:

> You get, camp life is intense, so for a lot of people they might have something going on in camp where they have a conflict with somebody else in camp, or what's going on romantically for them in camp could be souring or going poorly, or they might have a conflict with their foreman, just, I mean, tensions can run high when you're doing work that's that intense and living with people that intensely, you might have some kind of, something happening in your social life that's affecting your work, certainly . . . And so the difficulty of the planting and the difficulty of what you have going on and the dehydration that's making you crazy because you are never consuming enough water and the weather and the bugs can all weigh on you to let you have a terrible day. (R. McCannell, unpublished data)

It's impossible to separate into pieces what "terrible" is stuck to here: the intensity of camp life and social relations (whether romantic or industrial), the bodily difficulty of planting on "bad" land (terrain, slope, soil, preparation), the difficulty of a bad mood ("what you have going on"), the difficulty of the condition of physical dehydration and its emotional correlation ("making you crazy"), weather, bugs. It is difficult, to echo Brennan's (2004, 6) terms, to find a "secure distinction between the 'individual' and the 'environment.'"

Yet the function of "terrible"—stuck to all variety of humans, nonhumans, and things—works in particular social ways not only to somehow give rise to love of the forest, as Jon states, but also to create an "atmosphere where people are very, very supportive and very loving" (R. Boldt, unpublished data). Inasmuch as each planter relayed his or her "rookie cry," for example—and each one did—they also talked about the ways the shared physical difficulty of planting and its emotional intensities gave rise to happiness:

Since you've spent so much time alone, everyone is usually pretty happy to see each other. So even though everyone is so exhausted, there's usually a lot of very animated, passionate conversations and a lot of laughter. It really seems like since tree planting is so difficult, people, as a survival mechanism, really are looking for any possible chance to make a joke or laugh, and so there's a lot of, for people who have just been doing brutally difficult physical labor for eleven hours, there's a surprising amount of joking and laughter and happiness. It's a really, really nice time usually, and everyone's all together in the mess tent so you really feel like a community at that point. Yeah, just I think there's something about knowing that everyone has gone through the same ordeal and the same difficult experience that breaks down boundaries and makes you feel close to other people, knowing that you've had this shared experience, and so I personally am, maybe I feel like I can be a little bit of a, I guess, not a super-warm person necessarily. I like to do my own thing and keep my distance, but I find that tree planting makes me feel warm and open toward people in a way that I rarely experience. In the city, for example, I'm a lot more neurotic and standoffish. (R. Boldt, unpublished data)

Here we might see the motion of planting embodying an entirely different process of sociality that is both collective and contagious (happiness in camp life that sticks to difficulty of planting-bodies in motion and emotion) and contingent upon discrete human responses ("warm and open" as opposed to "neurotic and standoffish"). Out of memories of difficulty, planters refer to their time spent planting as "transformative" (N. Friesen Hughes, unpublished data), whether in feeling "alive" or in relaying a sense of calm and good health, as Erin did: "I deal with some mental illness in my life, with anxiety and depression, [and] what I find the most rewarding about tree planting is that that's the place where I've felt the most healthy in the last few years" (E. Sawatzky, unpublished data). Out of bodies in motion washes a wellspring of conflicted affects, a "perpetual becoming" of bodies formed through "forces of encounter" (Seigworth and Gregg 2010, 3)—whether with humans, nonhumans, or things. Yet out of this love and hate the question that still emerges, put to readers who study affect theory, is "how does a body, marked in its duration by these various encounters with mixed forces, come to shift its affections (its being affected) into action (capacity to affect)?" (Seigworth and Gregg 2010, 3). It is this question, built on the accumulation of affects I've thus far discussed, that I next try to answer.

## THE ARGUMENTS OF AFFECT: DREAM REALITIES, GRIEVABLE OBJECTS, AND INTENSE RHETORICS

Thus far I've shown the ways planters speak about affective links in their entanglements with the motion of planting and its attendant forest bodies, the ways dynamic processes like weather and sociality flow through their everyday encounters, the way body and mind join in affective relation, the way the forest bleeds and sticks. Such dynamism isn't relegated to the immediacy of the material world, as Ryan suggests:

> Even though I felt like I was pretty happy during the day, I remember at night, almost every single night, I would have planting nightmares where I would be planting trees all day and basically all night I would have nightmares about planting. I would often be planting inside of my tent over and over and over again, and every time I finished I would have to do it again, and there would always be something wrong. I would always be worried about something going wrong, and I would often have pretty bad sleeps because of it. (R. Boldt, unpublished data).

Ryan's anecdote about bad dreams, like Kristel Derkowski's opening description from her memoir of planting, *Six Million Trees* (2016), suggests that the forest is by no means a place emptied of affect—it is a place of rhythm, where out of "step, step, step, plant" emerges complex tree dreaming bound by motion, repetition, worry. On the one hand, we might view this circulation of affect into dream worlds as nothing more than worry about work, the same way many teachers dream of showing up to class naked. On the other hand, we might consider, as anthropologist Eduardo Kohn (2013, 13) does when he deliberates on human and nonhuman entanglements, that "dreams too are part of the empirical, and they are a kind of real." We might note what the function of bypassing logos really *does*. There is much to worry about when it comes to tree planting. Tree planting as an endeavor, the attunement to the cultivation of a plantation space, is constantly about something going wrong. Tree-planting dreams are a kind of real.

In covering a variety of affects that circulate through bodies in motion, I have so far focused primarily on how planter-bodies are affected as they move and converge with other bodies on the landscape. Yet just as dreams are a kind of real, giving us a sense that planter-bodies "have worked themselves into a state of heightened receptivity" (Massumi 2002, 55) born from physical intensity, it is possible that planters are also building through this heightened state a kind of action, a kind of capacity to affect, that relies on affect's capacity to move between forest bodies. This shift, I argue, is reflective of what Mortimer-Sandilands (2010, 333) would call an "active negotiation of environmental mourning" that recognizes "nonhuman beings, natural environments, and ecological processes as appropriate objects for genuine grief."

Mortimer-Sandilands (2010) suggests that in this anthropocenic moment, human beings are bound in their reactions to environmental loss by the forces of contemporary capitalism, represented by the rift between nature and culture. Such a rift is located in the primary invitation for human-nature relationships to objectify nature as resource capital (see chapter 1). As Mortimer-Sandilands (2010, 333) attests, human reactions are bound by a "core of grief" that exists around environmental destruction, but such grief is "psychically un-grievable" because the objects of loss—nonhuman beings, natural environments, and ecological processes—*as* nonhuman, cannot be fully recognized. She suggests that without full recognition of these un-grievable objects, loss is displaced and becomes a form of "melancholy nature," or "nature-nostalgia," because "the object that cannot be lost also cannot be let go" (Mortimer-Sandilands 2010, 333). Such a position, reflected by contemporary environmentalist messages of saving the earth or mourning the "loss of the pristine," for Mortimer-Sandilands (2010, 348, 354) represents a holding pattern that simplifies this loss into new, commodity-based endeavors such as ecotourism and environmental campaigns that urge us to "transfer attention to a new relationship/commodity."[13]

Conversely, Mortimer-Sandilands (2010, 333) contrasts melancholy nature with contemporary work in queer scholarship, particularly that stemming from the AIDS epidemic (focusing on the work of Jan Zita Grover and Derek Jarman), which, in her terms, centers "exactly on the condition of grieving the ungrievable":

> How does one mourn in the midst of a culture that finds it almost impossible to recognize the value of what has been lost? As this scholarship has pointed out, melancholia is not only a denial of the loss of a beloved object but also a potentially politicized way of preserving that object in the midst of a culture that fails to recognize its significance. Melancholia, here, is not a failed or inadequate mourning. Rather, it is a form of socially located embodied memory in which the loss of the beloved constitutes the self, the persistence of which identification acts as an ongoing psychic reminder of the fact of death in the midst of creation. In a context in which there are no adequate cultural relations to acknowledge death, melancholia is a form of preservation of life—a life, unlike the one offered for sale in ecotourist spectacle, that is already gone, but whose ghost propels a *changed* understanding of the present.

Mortimer-Sandilands indicates that writers Grover and Jarman politicize environmental melancholy by their public recognition of both the loss of nature and the way that loss is synecdochically recognized as representative of their ongoing relationships with the environment. This appears in their work through an acknowledgment of the way they are transformed by environmental loss and the way they find beauty and community in unlikely places: "wrecks, barrens, cutovers, nuclear power plants[, and] landfills and clear-cuts." She suggests that their attunement to these incongruous spaces helps recognize "the simultaneity of death and life in these landscapes" (Mortimer-Sandilands 2010, 343–48).

Mortimer-Sandilands argues that "embodied memory in which the loss of the beloved constitutes the self" is what moves queer melancholy from the realm of spectacle into thoughtful and ethical remembering. This queering of melancholy moves outward from Tim Morton's (2011, 176) notion of melancholia in object-oriented ontology, which suggests an "operationally closed mood," and toward Nathaniel Rivers's (2015, 431) idea of "deep ambivalence," of feeling both ways in "oscillation." Here I take from Mortimer-Sandilands's queering of melancholia to build on such a deep ambivalence in constructing a new materialist environmental rhetoric. It is not a hard leap to make, perhaps, from the realm of embodied remembering that is touched by life, death, and loss in the wake of AIDS to the embodied affect of planting a tree seedling in a devastated landscape. As bodies tangle and engage in becoming planter-tree-shovel body, the human body, as I have been suggesting, is remade into the planter-body on the landscape, which is constantly bound up in life and death while moving across the plantation. As I've shown through planters' descriptions, such movement marks planter-bodies and evidences their being affected, whether in physical sensations arising out of frustration (or happiness), multi-species encounters giving rise to sadness or elation, or nonhuman interactions with shovels or rain or cold. Yet such rhythms also give rise to a changed creature; they shift planters' thinking and their capacity *to affect*. They are evidence of Probyn's (2010, 76) characterization of such an embodied capacity: "We work ideas through our bodies," she says.

Thus when I think about the ways planters may be "transformed by environmental loss," I am reminded of Thayer's sentiment in the introduction, his assertion that "particularly earlier on in the season, I spent a lot of time thinking about myself planting a forest, and by the end of the year actually my perspective was altogether different. I was planting a crop, and it took me a while to reassess that" (T. MacInnis, unpublished data). This sentiment, moving over time from nature-nostalgia to the acknowledgment of contributing to a plantation landscape, appeared in every planter interview. It constructs both plantation landscapes and embodied action by the working of ideas *through* planter-bodies. The capacity to affect is a rhythmic process that is working through planter-bodies constantly amidst the embodied experience of being with nonhuman others. Being-with, being affected, allows a recognition of the un-grievable object; it acknowledges nonhuman beings (and thing-bodies), natural environment, and ecological processes as appropriate objects for genuine grief, as Georgia's except suggests:

> And then it's emotionally challenging because it's really hard. And there's days where it's pouring rain and you're so tired you can't think, and you forgot to, you know, pack a lunch just because you couldn't get your shit together, and then you're on horrible land and you can't figure out what you're doing and you haven't seen anyone in six hours and you're just— I've definitely just sat down in the middle of like this weird cut-down forest you're planting in and I just had a little cry sometimes. Because it's just hard, that's kind of the only word I can . . . describe it with. (G. Chappell, unpublished data)

Here, a range of body-mind affects in a planting day—weather, hunger, isolation—combined with the weirdness of the plantation-scape allows a place to grieve that is unencumbered by an insistence on saving the environment, a moment among ghosts. As Georgia moves on from the description of crying, she does not offer a simplified happy focus on planting a tree, personal achievement, progress, romanticized nature, or environmental preservation:

> We're kind of like, our companies we work for are contracted out by lumber companies and so you're very much "working for the man," as they say. Your money is directly coming from lumber companies, and you know your money is coming directly from lumber companies and planters are definitely like the bottom of the totem pole, that whole kind of like lumber-forestry chain, and so it all happens to make it easier to cut down the trees later. Like it's not, they're all monocultured trees, it's all one kind of tree that you plant everywhere, and so it's not like it's been done in a particularly any sustainable way; like ecosystem-wise, they're just planting one kind of tree to make plywood or whatever they make . . . I guess, of course, it's necessary, but a clear-cut forest is pretty like decimated-looking, it's pretty gross. It's like, you know, there'll be forest everywhere, then this sort of like, it just looks like it has been, it looks like it has been ravaged by machines, which there's stumps everywhere and mulch and like crap. And it's very sad. And so, yeah, it's a little bit depressing in that way, but I mean there's the way the world is now, there's not much of another option, so it's at least good there's planters coming in and replanting, but I don't know if I necessarily believe if anybody's, you know, saving the forests by planting trees necessarily. (G. Chappell, unpublished data)

Georgia's conclusion borders on relativism ("there's the way the world is now"); yet taken with other planter descriptions in terms of a patterned reaction to planting spaces, it still suggests that planter-tree-shovel bodies work critically through simplistic ideas about pristine nature as somehow suddenly lost.[14] Instead, such a description shows the chōra, a constantly unfolding and intentionally "gross" world-space available for plantation critique: as Georgia suggests, "it all happens to make it easier to cut down the trees later." This critique, one human way to story destruction and resurgence, is what the forest thinks through tree-planter–bodies again and again, from planters like Ryan:

> Some people, when they hear that you're tree planting, they instantly say "oh, good for you, you're healing the planet and saving the world," and I would like to believe that that's what I'm doing. But I think that the objective fact is that you are part of the forestry industry. If it wasn't for you, these logging companies would not be allowed to cut the forest down in the first place. And I think there's probably no way that a regenerated forest that you've planted yourself, it's going to take a long time for it to be as healthy as original old-growth forest was. So the environment is still being degraded. It's definitely better that the trees are being planted and that clear-cuts aren't just being left as is, but you are doing a job in the forestry industry for money, and you are part of a system that cuts down original forest and degrades the environment. So I would like to believe that I'm doing this noble thing, but I unfortunately don't think that's really the case. So that's a bit of a conflict for me. But at the end of the day I guess that lumber is a necessary resource if we want to have the society that we have today, and it is good that trees are being replanted rather than the cut blocks are just being left as is. And also at the end of the day it feels better to put the trees in the ground than to cut them down I'm sure, just at an immediate psychological level. (R. Boldt, unpublished data)

Also from planters like Jon:

> The realization that there's less and less of [the] wild and that most of it has been set aside not for protection, but it's been set aside for basically corporate money making, whether that's mineral extraction or forestry extraction, it's not set aside to protect it. Like the Boreal Forest is an incredibly important ecosystem for the planet in terms of carbon absorption and oxygen generation and just the biodiversity of plants and animals; it is the largest forest on the planet, and we seem to just allow it to be stripped of its natural being and then try to make excuses to say, well, we'll replant, but it's not the same. We're, as humans we're molding our planet and we're taking more and more of the wild out of the wild. You can drive from the south of the province to, you know, almost to the top, and everywhere, like if you've ever flown over Canada, you can see the amount of roads and cuts and it gets bigger and bigger every time. (J. Sprohge, unpublished data)

And from planters like Sam:

> I'd go into these places where it's all clear-cut, and like some of the areas we go into, we've gone into year after year after year and just replanted different portions because they're cutting different sections at different times. And they're replanting, but the animals don't come back in the same way that they did, and they, like you look out over the forest, and

they're all in perfect lines and grids and everything, and it just doesn't look natural, and so I think that, I think that I think a lot more about, I don't know, it's hard to think about like exactly what the resource is that you're drawing from sometimes. (S. Friesen, unpublished data)

In these three excerpts we see a melancholic attachment, a relationship to the wild that perhaps would qualify as positing an implicitly pristine, untouched, preexisting mythic nature that existed before culture began, as Jon says, "taking more wild out of the wild." Yet these descriptions are mired in a melancholy nature only if we view them outside of their already affective commitments: in Ryan's acknowledgment of "happy trances," "infinite resignation," "forest beckoning," or recognition of self-"neurosis" through the process of planting; of Jon's "slogging through a bog," comforting a sad colleague, or his love, hate, and missing of the forest; of Sam's planting-as-meditation, crying at caribous' "frrp-frrp," wetting herself in the rain. Taken together, these descriptions represent what Rivers (2015, 431) might call a "deep ambivalence," a feeling that both possibilities may apply. Yet circulating affect stemming from these rhythmic entanglements does more than reproduce what can be critiqued as an impotent melancholy or a slide into contingency or relativism. These entanglements give humans a way to be, yes, but they also allow new ideas to emerge through their bodies in motion: as acts of a new materialist environmental rhetoric, they allow an acknowledgment of human devastation on the landscape as a process, an acknowledgment of what must be remembered. Instead of an un-grievable object of melancholy that forces the imperative to "move on," planter-bodies on the landscape are caught up in a remembering that allows both love and loss, sadness and happiness, anger and elation; it allows planters to, in Grover's words, "pull from it what beauties remain" (quoted in Mortimer-Sandilands 2010, 347). Like Mortimer-Sandilands's (2010, 349) assertion of a queer melancholia, tree planters are caught up in "a dialectics of loss that recognizes dying, and also beginning that is born . . . from death."

Instead of losing touch with a beloved object, tree planters are in constant contact with the very real object/bodies of loss: dead trees killed by chemical preparation, planting trees in rows on scarified landscape, piles of slash generated by machines, the way the cut block stands out in stark relief from a 200-foot tree line, and thousands upon thousands of seedlings to plant. This affective experience moves beyond the pristine nature-fantasy, instead creating a naturecultural middle ground, a reflection on dwelling, a deep ambivalence, a new, intense rhetoric. In this regard, two planter descriptions stand out the most in refusing the bifurcation of untouched nature/destructive culture:

I was, last year in Saskatchewan, as we were leaving I was talking with the maintenance guy at the site we were staying at, and he had planted in various places including in Ontario, and he was saying "yeah, it's just not as scenic there." It's a cut block, it's not supposed to be scenic, but yeah, I think that, I forget sometimes that people, whenever they see cut blocks, are always a little taken aback because it is in some ways a sparse environment . . . I mean, I've seen a lot of them so I kind of regard them as benign, but there is, I don't think, they're a little less dead than people foresee, so there's all these things that, I mean, you'll [see] some sort of initial low shrub growth or things like ferns that have, maybe not so much ferns but sort of other plants that have moved in to take advantage of the sunlight, and then there are lots of, and they still do leave standing trees because, at least in Ontario, they are required to by law to leave a certain number of standing trees and then leave these residual patches, but there are a decent number of particularly birds that will nest in cut blocks, which is interesting because they don't like you wandering around, and they will dive-bomb you and get mad, but that's on the side. So cut blocks are, I think, a very interesting thing, and I think there's, I've learned to appreciate them as less desolate while not being, while still understanding the problems of industrial logging. (S. Dyck, unpublished data)

But a cut block is not exactly a natural environment; well, it's not a natural environment. It's a very unique environment. I mean, the forest has been leveled; everything has been cut down. It's really unique. I don't necessarily mind it, but it's different than walking around the forest. It's a different thing altogether. It's a different environment altogether. So you're not, you know, you're not hiking through the forest. You're hiking through a cut block and putting trees in the ground . . . The heart, that's lost when you get in to northern Alberta. It's now, you know, there's a part of me that enjoys a degree of the austere and harsh beauty of northern Alberta forest, but I'm also horrified by it and find it revolting . . . Nature is at its full challenge there, I think, in terms of being a little bit gross and horrifying and literally eating you. It's eating away at you all the time, so that's harder . . . You are out in the elements. You're still out in the weather. It's just you're not under a canopy of trees, and it still can be, I find cut blocks beautiful in another sense aesthetically, all the sharp edges of stumps and all the slash that's left on the block, you know, I think a lot of the images that the photographers that I've planted with have captured of the cut block are beautiful, and a combination of cut block and then the tree line and the forest captured in one frame [is] really beautiful, and that's what you're seeing all the time. (R. McCannell, unpublished data)

Both of these planters recognize the grievable loss that exists in a plantation space; neither would deny Georgia's feeling of a "weird cut-down forest" that prompts "a little cry sometimes"—a "heart that's lost," as Ross puts it. Both descriptions recognize that cut blocks are dead spaces, leveled spaces, desolate spaces, sparse spaces. Yet each description is also acknowledging patchy *living* spaces that aren't "supposed to be scenic" but yet have a sense of aesthetic beauty. These are descriptions of cut blocks and forests in motion, constantly growing and resurging, constantly filled with the rhythms of plant time scales, dive-bombing creatures, media captivity. These are the descriptions of a patchy Anthropocene, a moment of a storied *now* of being in the middle of destruction—perhaps even participating in it—and also being destroyed, a nature that is "literally eating you." These are not the simple stories of saving the planet, of an over-privileging of human control to either destroy or renew. These descriptions remark on nature's agency as much as they remark on planters' ways of being-with in the world, not a simple even-or of nature or culture, body or mind, love or hate: these, I argue, are new materialist environmental rhetorics, *intense rhetorics*, as Rivers (2015, 422) defines them, reflecting deep ambivalence shaped by both the human and the nonhuman.

## MORE THAN "FEELING GOOD": ATTUNEMENT TO PLANTATION-SCAPES

As I've examined affects' effects, I've argued that tree planters' entanglements with nonhuman and thing-bodies is what situates them within a naturecultural landscape, one that imagines humans to be always dwelling in a world of encounter. While I've taken as my unit of interpretation the human—that is, planters' descriptions of their experiences—these descriptions are also a way to "bear witness," in Jane Bennett's (2010, x) call, "to the vital materialities that flow through and around us," composed of all manner of beings, bodies, things, and energies. As I've traced the role affect plays in descriptions of tree-planting practices, I have also traced its stickiness: affect is what intimately connects human, tree, shovel and landscape into a moving "planter-body"; it is affect's effects on human bodies that allows them, in turn, a particular capacity to affect.

What we might expect from tree planters as workers who give high credence to individualism and the importance of personal and economic efficiency is an unconflicted stance toward environmental management, more along the lines of "plant a tree, save the planet" humanistic environmentalism. As Ariel Ducey (2007) points out, there is now more than ever the expectation that the wage labor people undertake needs to be saturated with meaning, with "feeling good." It would be easy enough for tree planters to echo a humanistic environmentalism about their work, to reflect an uncomplicated stance toward carbon offsets and their role in producing them, giving rise to greater degree of personal satisfaction—who doesn't want to be a savior of the environment? Instead, we see revealed the ways their registered bodily intensity, fostered out of movement on the landscape, enlists a host of entanglements that makes that perspective impossible. The affect generated by physical movement and encounters with other forest bodies—of care, frustration, anger, sadness, love—gives them an altogether different, perhaps unexpected, stance. Affect's effects here are persuasive: they give rise to deep consideration of the ways planters themselves are implicated in industrial forestry, in questionable stewardship of the land, in a constant acknowledgment of life in the middle of death, of the ways planters mark and are themselves marked by forest bodies. Perhaps the ways affects circulate on plantation-scapes such as the ones on which tree planters labor draw our attention more closely to the ethical import of such practices, where bodies can be persuaded by feelings to take more complex stances in which "the loss of the beloved" (nature) is also "the loss of the self" because, well, nature is "literally eating you." Here, attunements to the energies and affect between bodies make for a real recognition of ongoing loss, of a nature that "resists human mastery" (Rivers 2015, 424), that blurs the line between nature and culture because it recognizes that "the wild" is made up of both human and nonhuman bodies. Planter-bodies' acknowledgment of these persuasive entanglements produces a degree of attunement, of dwelling, of awareness of the way physical sensations call forth a range of ways of being-with that place humans firmly within environments rather than outside them and facilitate an understanding that environments are not "a code that can be read, mastered, and controlled" (Rivers 2015, 428). If the forest can be said to think, then one of the ways it does so is through bodies. And if, as Probyn suggests, we work ideas through our bodies, affect is one of the ways the forest works its way through us. This is perhaps nowhere as evident as on a plantation space, a different planet infused with vitality. It is this vitality to which I turn next in tracing the role thing-bodies play on the plantation landscape.

## NOTES

1. For examples of these treatments, see Cowell 1982; Rankin 2005; Luke 2014; Walker 2015.
2. Though interdisciplinary, Edbauer Rice notes that critical affect studies is united by its use of primary studies of affect by Deleuze and Guattari, Henri Bergson, and Baruch Spinoza (2008, 212). We might view contributors to developing this interdisciplinary body of work as, for example, Antonio Damasio (1994, 2000, 2003), Brian Massumi (1995, 2002), Eve Kosofsky Sedgwick and Adam Frank (1995),

Sara Ahmed (2004), Teresa Brennan (2004), Denise Riley (2005), Daniel Gross (2006), Ann Cvetkovich (2007), Kathleen Stewart (2007), Patricia Ticineto Clough (2007), Ben Anderson (2009), Lauren Berlant (2009), Melissa Gregg and Gregory Seigworth (2010), and Lisa Blackman (2012), among others. The extension of the use of CAS scholarship has been notably taken up in the field of rhetoric and writing studies by leaders of scholarly institutes (Rhetoric Society of America's "Rhetoric's Affect/Affect's Rhetoric," led by Joshua Gunn and Jenny Rice), conference presentations on affectivity in public life (Greenwalt 2016), haptic rhetorics (Loe 2016), rhetoric and emotional suppression (Ortega 2016), affect and social activism (Toomey 2016), writing pedagogy (Sherman 2016; Luther 2017), archival methodology (McNely 2017; Bratta 2017), and sonic rhetorics (Hammer 2017), as well as publications about writing pedagogy and writing program administration (Micciche 2002, 2007; Lindquist 2004; Robillard 2007; Mills 2011; Stenberg 2011; Davies 2014; Davis et al. 2014; Nelson 2016) and a growing body of work that uses ambient rhetorical approaches to frame a variety of objects of study.

3. This paradigm suggests that there are "'affect programs' located subcortically in the brain and defined in evolutionary terms as universal or pancultural categories or 'natural kinds,' basic emotions which minimally include the emotions of fear, anger, disgust, joy, sadness, and surprise, [and] are viewed as genetically hardwired" (Leys 2011, 438).
4. Arguably, a few of the scholars mentioned here could straddle this divide.
5. Damasio (2003, 7) contends that "emotion and related reactions are aligned with the body, feelings with the mind."
6. An excellent critique of Massumi's use of the neurosciences in affect studies can be found in Leys (2011, 468), in which she argues that even the most materially minded scholars of affect "privileg[e] the 'body' and its affects over the 'mind' in straightforwardly dualist terms."
7. Affect scholars have been drawn to "the assumption that there is a half-second delay between affect and cognition" (Blackman 2015, 34; see also Thrift 2007; Massumi 2002; Leys 2011).
8. For an extended look into how memory and affect relate, see Cvetkovich 2003.
9. For a semiotic reading of how forests think, see Kohn 2013.
10. For an in-depth approach to water using a new materialist lens, see Chen, MacLeod, and Neimanis 2013.
11. For further reading on the thinking of François Delsarte, see Ruyter 1999.
12. Ahmed (2010, 36) provides a detailed synopsis of both the contagion model, as put forward by Brennan (2004) and others, and her suggestion of contingency, or situation-dependent contagion of affect.
13. A quick search for "environmental projects" revealed top-hit links for relationships with TD Bank (#TDCommonGroundProject, "connecting people with nature"), geo-tourism destinations (Evergreen Brick Works), an overview of Global Service Trips with the Foundation for Sustainable Development, and environmental construction and remediation engineering firms.
14. Mortimer-Sandilands (2010, 337) suggests that this simplistic form of environmentalism fetishizes a "mythic, idyllic" nature as a commodity.

# 4
## PERSUASIVE MOVEMENT
### The Rhetoricity of Things

*The first day of our heli show, our gear was slung in before us, we waited in anticipation for the chopper to return but it seemed strange that it was taking so long. After what seemed like an hour we finally heard that the helicopter sling had malfunctioned and the chopper was picking us all up to comb the forest for it, as they didn't know how scattered the gear was. So we all spread out along a kilometer or so of road and started walking, eventually it was found mostly in one spot sunk into the sphagnum moss a few feet. Almost everyone had something that was crushed, work and/or personal gear. After all the gear was reunited with it's [sic] owner we went back out to the road to get flown back to camp. Instead we were informed that the chopper had to leave and we had to walk the 3 h[ou]rs back to camp. ~Layla (in Martin 2017)*

*I remember my watch beeping at 6:00 PM. I had a hard day, and was completely spent. I waited at the road for awhile before red flags started appearing in my mind. I took a look around and realized I was the only person left on the block and it hit me, I had been forgotten. Trying to stay calm, I occupied my mind for awhile by first building Inukshuks,[1] then brainstorming and planning how I could start a fire/survive the night in case I was going to be stuck until morning. It was almost two hours back to camp driving in the van, so I knew my best bet was to wait and stay hopeful. After a long while I eventually decided I may as well continue planting until it was dark as the best way to pass the time. Hopefully soon somebody would notice I was missing. Near the end of my bag out I heard the honking from a truck as my crew boss and supervisor picked me up. They had a big container for me full of the dinner I had missed as we rolled back to camp in the darkness, several hours later. ~Arron (in Martin 2017)*

While my attention in focusing on a framework for a new materialist environmental rhetoric has often coalesced around organic bodies and their material, discursive, and affective effects—moose, wasps, owls, roots, seedlings, poplars—so far, the space that thing-bodies have

DOI: 10.7330/9781607328551.c004

taken up in discussions of efficiency, humanism, and affects has been relatively minor. It has been relegated to the investment planters make in things while describing other events (for example, the invisible shoulder bag that carries the trees, the neurotoxin of DEET that undergirds planting experiences) or to a brief consideration of things and affect in discussing shovels, weather, and water in chapter 3. Up to this point I've examined tree planting through these affective connections and meanings; here I draw on the ways these human and nonhuman assemblages also gesture outward toward the sociopolitical arena and note how they are, in Jane Bennett's (2010, 94) words, participants in "political ecologies"—intense rhetorics that similarly make up contemporary silviculture. Much like other scholars interested in new materialism, I choose to focus on thing-bodies here not because I see a distinct line between organic and inorganic matter[2] but rather to give a more nuanced focus to the rhetorical power of thing-bodies as they arise, move, and wane, thus co-inventing the planting landscape. Scholarship on what I'm calling "thing-bodies" here recognizes their shape in many other terms: objects, agents, actors, artifacts, actants, matter, material, tools. Ultimately, my argument is not to toil in the distinctions between this object or that material, this thing or that thing-body; instead, to gain an understanding of the rhetoricity of bodies, their affective stickiness, the importance of an examination of forces and effects, and circulations of affect, my attention is turned toward the persuasive work of thing-bodies and their contribution to a new materialist environmental rhetoric. This assertion is similarly echoed by Scot Barnett and Casey Boyle (2017, 2), who call for attention to rhetoric's materiality, forwarding their vision of a *rhetorical ontology*, a rhetorical way of being in the world.

Thinking through what such a rhetorical way of being might mean—whether through notions of attunement, ambience, being-with, or dwelling—suggests accepting the idea that as "vibrant actors," things affectively provoke us, often in ways that "exceed (and are sometimes in direct conflict with) human agency and intentionality" (Barnett and Boyle 2017, 1). In Layla's opening story of crushed gear and helicopter expectations, every planter-body caught up in the search for lost things is bound up in a thing-world that impacts everything from dinnertime to getting back to camp.

Roads, watches, trees, bags, Inukshuks, vans, trucks—all agents in the opening stories—are evidence of the ways planter-bodies are grounded in material relations with things, relations that emerge in co-constitutive ways through interactions and circulations between and among "people, objects, and everyday practices" (McNely 2016, 143).

We have already been engaging such a rhetorical-ontological worldview in recalling examples of Sam and the rain in chapter 3 or J-roots' impact on efficiency in chapter 2. Attention to thing-bodies and their role in rhetorical work, as Thomas Rickert (2013, 263) contends when examining the case of EV1, the first electric car, "disrupts a humanist rhetorical framework by foregrounding our constitutive involvement in a larger ecology, or in how we dwell." This may be similarly seen in Indigenous research practices that revolve around the inclusion of things—for example, spoons or baskets as central beings to the activity of a focus group (Chilisa 2012, 281).

Barnett and Boyle (2017, 6) recognize that an attunement to nonhumans and things may move us outward from a humanist frame—a posthuman turn—yet they also point out that "it need not be an *anti*human one." This is well represented in Bennett's (2010, viii) oft-cited work on vital materialism, which she defines as "the capacity of things—edibles, commodities, storms, metals—not only to impede or block the will and designs of humans but also to act as quasi agents or forces with trajectories, propensities, or tendencies of their own"—to have a degree of liveliness or vitality in force and energy. Bennett (2010) takes up different examples of these vital materialist tendencies in her examination of the 2003 US Northeast blackout (with a focus on electricity and power grids), food and obesity (with a focus on metabolic processes, moods, and morals), metals (with a focus on Prometheus's adamantine chains and polycrystalline grains), culture-of-life advocacy (with a focus on human stem cells), and political publics (with a focus on worms and human-nonhuman assemblages). The work done to focus on the vibrancy of matter and of thing-bodies does not do away with the human; instead, it presents human agency as already bound up in a world of things—"an assemblage of microbes, animals, plants, metals, chemicals, word-sounds, and the like" (Bennett 2010, 120–21)—and points our attention to the ways human situations (whether they be blackouts, obesity, or culture-of-life politics) are intimately connected with the nonhuman.

Scholars who call for our critical attention to things perhaps overlook, as I did, the ways our attention is already on them. Listening to tree planters describe their relationships with things[3]—and here I'll recall the way the tree-planting shovel both creates a planter-body out of a human body and modifies the body by creating the "claw," or an injury known as stenosing tenosynovitis, that develops in one's hand as a result of holding it—made it impossible to ignore what Bennett (2010, 20) calls "thing-power." Why is such power an important scaffold through which to position contemporary silviculture? Because, as Bennett (2010, 112) argues, "materiality is a rubric that tends to horizontalize the relations between humans, biota, and abiota." In drawing our attention to human-nonhuman entanglements, Bennett suggests, the prominence of man's hubristic agency is reduced. This is concentrated by the attention given to the ways human bodies themselves are made up of "*an array of bodies*, many different kinds of them in a nested set of microbiomes," and it disrupts common assumptions about nature as either "a purposive, harmonious process" or a "blind mechanism" (Bennett 2010, 113). In disrupting this dualistic view of nature, Bennett (2010, 115) also disrupts, too, the idea that culture is somehow "of our own making, infused as it is by biological, geological, and climatic forces." Attention to thing-bodies also cultivates attention to disrupting the rigid script that separates nature from culture.

Take, for example, a revisitation of Jon's description of his forty minutes spent trying to convince a group of planters to begin their day from chapter 2:

> I remember once driving planters into a site, and we were in two multi-passenger vans. We drove into the site, we shut off the engines, and the van ahead of us was distorted in terms of looking through the windshield because of all the mosquitoes, and you could actually hear this "bzzzzzz" that vibrated the entire van. And we all sat there quietly, and it took me about forty minutes to convince the planters to get out of the vehicle. I told them about various methods that old-time loggers used to protect themselves against mosquitoes by actually jamming newspapers into your clothing, wearing multiple layers, people covering up their face with a T-shirt so only their eyes were visible, and your hands, we would take duct tape and tape all our fingers and hands, yeah, you know. And then you're covered up like that, and it's 35°C. (J. Sprohge, unpublished data).

I've discussed to some degree the ways this example represents human-nonhuman entanglement, particularly with an eye toward the persuasiveness of insect bodies. In its simplest humanistic terms, this is a description of a man trying to convince a group of people to begin their workday with his words. As I argued in chapter 2, it is also a description of mosquito swarms' convincing agency to prevent a workday from beginning. It is a material-discursive event. As an act of new materialist environmental rhetoric, we could also examine for a moment the ways rhetorical agency is spread throughout both human and thing here, that is, the way rhetorical energy travels throughout this example. Rather than view rhetorical agency in this anecdote as what Jodie Nicotra (2016, 190) calls "unidirectional and single-pointed"—a human agent acting on a group of other humans, a group of insect bodies acting on a group of humans—instead we begin to see an opening up of what is meant by agency because we can think through this example in a variety of other ways. We might think through the van as a thing-body that provides a more suasive force in protecting planter-bodies than does the human trying to convince them otherwise—at least for forty minutes. We might view the way mosquito-bodies create distortion of the troposphere through the way their vibration—*rhythm*—on the van's metal body becomes a rhetorical force that acts on planter-bodies. We might acknowledge the intensity of the weather and a day's heat (everything from temperature to humidity to barometric pressure) as exerting force on a van full of human bodies, persuading them eventually that the company of insect bodies is preferable to the interior of the vehicle. In Nicotra's (2016, 190) words, as in this re-casting of Jon's anecdote, "Change emerges as one result of an interaction of a multitude of material and discursive things." Nature, in this example, is neither purposive (the weather and insects do not conspire against human bodies) nor blind (the planet heats; the mosquitoes swarm). Culture—the humans, the warming van and still engine on the landscape, the clothing, the windshield—is not uniquely human. As Rickert (2013, 268) suggests about attuning ourselves to things, "Performing rhetoric in an ambient key is less a matter of *adding them back in* than reattuning ourselves to their station, and to what their station may yet be, in our struggle to find better, more sustainable practices." Thus this chapter is an attempt to (re)examine the station of things as they exist in a new materialist environmental rhetoric—particularly automobiles, roads, and helicopters—relevant to the silvicultural landscape for the ways they invent the plantation-scape, the ways they perpetuate particular discourses, and the ways they imagine possible futures.

In focusing primarily on a few infrastructural thing-bodies to the exclusion of many others that co-construct tree-planting worlds, a few points must be addressed. The first is the practical matter of *which* thing-bodies deserve explicit attention over others. Planters' descriptions are filled with relevant matter of the everyday that shapes and is shaped by their experience: the high wax-content boxes that carry seedlings (which are highly flammable) and planters' interactions with them, primarily around the sociality of fire; the colored flagging tape planters use to help them maintain direction and boundaries and to show safety hazards; pesticides, fungicides, and herbicides that are applied to harvested land to deter pests and fungi from growing on monocultured plantation trees or to kill other plant competition; hydrogen sulfide, or sour gas, poisonous to humans, which generally arises near oil and gas infrastructure; the variety of machines that prepare land for planting: discers, ripper plows, Bräcke mounders, scarifiers, skidders, bulldozers, excavators, backhoes—each with implications for micro-environments like soil temperature, moisture, aeration, and porosity (Haeussler 1989). Each of these is an example of vibrant matter in its own right, circulating with other affective bodies. However, I've chosen to focus here on infrastructural thing-bodies for two reasons. The first is that planters are affectively "near" to these bodies in ways they are not as near to things like machines or herbicides used to prepare land (which is done before tree planting ever takes place). The second is because of sheer numbers: individual planter interviews acknowledge these infrastructural thing-bodies with some degree of development and care. Taken as a whole— "many views from many places, over time" (Marcus, Love, and Best 2016, 9)—these descriptive patterns provide a convincing case to look more closely at these thing-bodies (rather than others that may only get a brief mention, such as sour gas). Finally, these thing-bodies overtly hint at larger anthropogenic issues on the Canadian landscape that involve both the fossil-fuel industry[4] and Indigenous land claims. Because of the ways these thing-bodies interact on a larger scale and their relation to the anthropocenic moment, I've chosen to focus on them to the degree that such entanglements, as Bennett (2012, 268–69) suggests, "shed light on the role that a not-quite-human form of effectivity might be playing in maintaining an over-consumptive, ecologically disastrous society that I inhabit."

In so doing, I need to make clear that unfortunately, this focus is not one that will successfully question the "power of infrastructure" or completely challenge "the fundamental precepts of automobility" (Rickert 2013, 265). Instead, it offers a window into the way human and nonhuman "entanglements-for-now" (McNely 2016, 143) help sustain contemporary discourses of efficiency, on the one hand, and interrupt the nature-culture divide, on the other. In offering these discrepant practices, I point to the *patchy* of the Anthropocene, the ways nonhuman agents suasively participate in political ecologies and help perpetuate naturecultural tensions.

### THE PROMISES OF AUTOMOBILITY

The culture of automobility is one in which we are all embroiled, and it dictates everyday lives from the ground up, suggesting the planning of human cities and the development of our spaces—from driveways to interstates—as well as denoting and controlling access to our public places. Of course, the automobile and its reliance on fossil fuels, and our contemporary addiction to it in a time of rapid global climate change, also presents a clear environmental problem.

Thomas Princen (2005) suggests that we have trouble seeing automobility as a cultural form because it is so ubiquitous. In addition, efforts to address the increasing problems of automobility—traffic congestion, vehicle safety, greenhouse gas emissions, increased consumption, land development—often take a productive approach by redesigning roads and signals or redesigning cars with greater safety features or lower emissions. These solutions do not, as Princen (2005, 317) argues, adjust "underlying structural and behavioral causes of ever-increasing auto use." Instead, they reify our dependence on automobility, which Princen (2005, 292) defines as an unfettered sense of access, mobility, expansion, speed, convenience, and personal freedom—the ability to drive where one wants, whenever one wants, for as far and as long as one wants. It assumes that all roadways are public and that humans have the freedom to live without proximate access to where they "need" to go—to work, to school, to find food. This dependence also, as Princen (2005, 324) notes, raises mobility itself to an unquestionable good while promoting the nature of the individual by endorsing "speed, time-saving, comfort": in short, the model of rational, humanistic choice and personal efficiency.

Princen (2005) takes as one case the study of Toronto Island, a car-less settlement in Lake Ontario across the water from the city of Toronto, and examines the conflict created in the 1950s between the city government and island residents by the suggestion that the island become accessible to the mainland by bridge or tunnel (and thus require the development of automobile infrastructure). Princen (2005, 163) argues that citizens' successful lobbying to keep Toronto Island car-free was a turn to sufficiency—a recognition of and confrontation with "natural constraints"—rather than efficiency (what would make Toronto Island a greater economic success). However, Rickert (2013, 260) extends the case of Toronto Island by examining it from an ambient perspective and argues that the islanders, to continue their successful argument to live car-free, must create not "resistance to automobility, but a new relation to it, one that takes on the full affective import of the auto as a co-actant in a larger ecology." Rickert (2013, 258) argues that automobiles "attune us materially and socially"—one might say, persuasively—and that to become more aware of that attunement, it is important to resist a superficial evaluation of things for "use-values" that only reify a logic of efficiency and personal choice.

Much like the Toronto Island case, the case of tree planting similarly depends on automobiles as co-actants on the landscape that enable and constrain particular possibilities.

The translation of automobility as a cultural form among tree planters takes place by way of the thing-bodies with which planters come into daily contact. Thus it is my aim to suggest that these thing-bodies—buses, trucks, quads, "mules," ATVs—interrupt some of the tenets of mobility-as-a-good, primarily in the ways they counter the efficiency-based "goods" associated with automobility as noted by Princen: speed, time saving, comfort, and access. In doing so, I turn attention to the rhetorical capacity such material thing-bodies have—not to suggest that vehicular consideration somehow challenges the cultural form of automobility (indeed, by their very bodies, vehicles are a clear contributor to it) but instead to look closely at the ways such an assumption of use-value can foreclose some of the very real relations of humans to things, of human-nonhuman being-in-the-world. I agree with Rickert and Princen in their common claim that thing-bodies such as automobiles "fatefully prescribe essential aspects of how we build and dwell" (Rickert 2013, 260)—we cannot remove, for example, the manufacturing process from the appearance of a vehicular thing-body on the landscape or its dependence on oil and gas infrastructure. Yet vehicular bodies persuasively co-construct planters' sense of time, mobility, and access to spaces, which is fundamentally different from considerations of automobility in city and rural spaces.

To understand this difference, it's important to understand the setup of tree-planting camps. There are three types, and although some of the planters I talked to experienced more than one kind of camp, all planters were primarily drawing from their experience in "bush" (also called "isolation" or "tent") camps. The other two kinds of camps—logging camps and hotel-based camps—use existing infrastructure of towns or existing buildings and count among their amenities flushing toilets, running water, heated buildings, and cell phone service. In the case of logging camps (which are growing increasingly rare), tree planters stay in permanent or semi-permanent logging trailers on land owned by forestry companies that are in close proximity to well-maintained, usually private roads. In the case of a hotel-based or town-based accommodation camp, tree planters live out of existing developments in hotel or motels or take up spaces in town community halls, arenas, and public green space (for tent camping). In the latter two types of camps, planters drive to planting sites each day and return "home" to these rural areas after work.[5]

In bush camps, all infrastructure—including generators, propane tanks, water barrels, and trees— is brought in, either driven by truck (if areas are accessible by road) or flown in by helicopter.[6] Tree planters sleep in self-provided tents, dig latrines, set up gray-water systems, and connect water lines for showers from existing water bodies. Infrastructure is set up only as long as a contract lasts—a few weeks to a couple of months—and main components are a mess tent or cook trailer (where meals are prepared and eaten), a first aid tent, a fuel depot (which stores gasoline for vehicles), a shower tent or trailer, outhouses, and a dry tent (which is kept heated by a kerosene heater) to dry planters' clothing overnight. Bush camps are designed to be taken down in a matter of hours and moved to new spaces. The majority of other planting infrastructure in bush camps constitutes the variety of vehicles required for the job: "reefers," or refrigerated trucks (that transport trees, which must be kept cool); ETVs (emergency transport vehicles, or "crummys"); crew trucks; vans; quads (small four-wheel all-terrain vehicles, which often transport people and small amounts of trees); and occasionally and depending on the season, Hägglunds (Swedish military vehicles used to transport people over swampy terrain)[7] or Rolligons (large all-terrain amphibious trucks that have balloon-like floatation tires). Access to planting sites from bush camps is varied; some cut block sites are walkable (a few miles or less), some are driveable if they are in proximity to roads of some kind (anywhere from forty minutes to two hours), and some are accessible only by helicopter (there are either no roads or they have been deactivated or reclaimed). As Arron's story in the epigraph to this chapter suggests, planters' days and often their lives depend on vehicular accountability. Workdays are largely determined by the vehicles they have around them and the infrastructure to support those vehicles; while it may be said that human bodies on planting landscapes exist without vehicular bodies, there is often no planter-body without its corresponding transportation thing-body.

*Thing-Power and Persuasive Movement*
One of the ways things exert thing-power, according to Bennett (2012, 252), is the "'speed' of the thing, the relative slowness of its rate of change," which, she contends, has a "comparative advantage over human flesh when it comes to endurance, patience, waiting it out." We can perhaps see this thing-power play out in the ways tree planters are attuned to plant timescales, as chapter 2 suggests. Bennett (2012, 252) argues that thing-power is in part a "power of slowness . . . in part a

function of its exemplary patience, stability, duration." While Bennett is talking specifically about things people hoard—rocks, let's say, or videocassettes—it is interesting to see how the idea of the slowness of thing-power plays out in co-constructing the planting landscape in the case not only of the trees planters plant but also through their descriptions of camp vehicles. On the one hand, the very materiality of any vehicle—its construction of metal and glass and plastic—is a substantiation of Bennett's claims of slowness, as anyone who has ever passed a junkyard, replete with slumping metal bodies, also knows. On the other hand, and unlike plants, vehicles as a function of automobility are associated with both speed (they are designed to move people at a faster rate than they can walk or run) and time saving (if a person can drive somewhere, he or she can get to that destination faster than can human-based modes of transportation, such as walking or running). If a vehicle cannot be fast and efficient, in other words, it is destined to a life of slowness and greater visibility in its decay. Yet rather than emerge as a ghost, instead it garners thing-power.

It is the idea that planters are entangled with and show an attunement to camp vehicles and their attendant rhetorical thing-power that I wish to address next. Because of the ways their bodies are intimately entangled with vehicular thing-bodies, tree planters cultivate an awareness of the contradiction of the slowness of thing-bodies as well as the pressure of the culture of automobility, which privileges speed and time saving. Judith Donath (2011, 156) reflects on automobiles being seen in both of these ways in a piece on evocative objects, in this case a 1964 Ford Falcon: "When a car works perfectly, doing exactly what it's supposed to do," she writes, "we experience it as pure machine. But when it acts imperfectly, choosing to do some things and not others, it becomes an almost autonomous agent." Applied to the case of the thing-power of vehicles, we might imagine that when a vehicle is doing what it is supposed to do—saving us time, moving us (or us moving it) speedily across landscapes—we don't notice it as having much thing-power because it can exist as an unproblematic, "pure" machine. However, when a vehicle stops doing what it is supposed to do—takes time, breaks down, gets stuck, moves slowly—we perceive its thing-power more pointedly and its agency in more distributed, affective ways. It does things to us—makes us late, frustrates us, costs us money, requires more material to fix. Thus a vehicle's thing-body is already rhetorically sticky by virtue of its ability to move seamlessly or glitchily on the landscape; vehicular bodies and their connections to movement and time in particular create meaning that often runs up against human agency, intentionality, and the wish for efficiency.

Such stickiness is taken up in technical communications scholar Ehren Helmut Pflugfelder's (2017) case for persuasive transportation using an actor–network theory approach to a range of automobile case studies in transportation history and design. Pflugfelder's (2017, 7) work turns to the interconnectedness of humans and nonhumans in cases of automobility, arguing that "automobiles are more than the material forms they take, but the social connections and protocols of movement they constrain and enable." He calls our attention to the idea of *kinesthetic rhetoric*, or persuasive movement, noting that "transportation activities throughout the world—as enacted by the coordination of people and technologies—are forms of persuasion . . . These kind[s] of movement-oriented persuasions are never merely the intervention of people into situations, nor the application of meaning to cold, dispassionate objects, but a process that occurs whenever we move, with various technologies, things, and affordances" (Pflugfelder 2017, 17, 15).

As I turn my attention to the ways automobiles are tangled up with planter-bodies, it is my aim to acknowledge the ways vehicle bodies engage in persuasive movement, attuning planter-bodies in specific ways on the landscape and generating particular affects as they do so.

### *Vehicular Time: Waiting Bodies*

As the description of bush camp life and the opening narratives suggest, tree planters are beholden to motorized transport to get them into remote planting areas that have already been logged, just as tree-bodies are similarly dependent on refrigerated trucks to keep them alive.[8] While this view might certainly suggest an uncritical stance toward thing-bodies for their human uses or functionality in human life,[9] a less superficial look into the ways thing-bodies co-construct planter worlds indicates that vehicular thing-bodies are far more engaged in everyday acts of persuasion than a view based solely on use-value would suggest. From the formation of crews to the structure of a day, vehicle bodies are constantly entangled agentively with planter-bodies. As Luke indicates, "There are generally six-pack crews or twelve-man crews, which means, it's just, it's six or twelve because that's how many seats there are on the truck" (L. Rempel, unpublished data). The primary setup of who will be working and how many humans make up a particular crew is preemptively determined by the truck-body: a seven- or thirteen-person crew is an impossibility on the planting landscape.

Similarly, tree planters talk about their planting day in terms of both time and distance enabled or constrained by vehicles:

Usually, by 6[:00 a.m.] everyone would be more or less ready to go, except sometimes we'd have a meeting there in camp, sometimes we'd wait until we got closer to the work site. We'd hop in trucks; drives range from ten minutes to two hours, and then sometimes we'll have walking components, rarely, but sometimes we have walks in there too . . . repeat that until usually about 5:30 [p.m.], and then I'll get back into a truck, drive back to the camp. (S. Dyck, unpublished data)

We'd have to be on the bus before 7[:00 a.m.], and then we would drive to the block, so either we'd all take one bus or we'd split into two different groups, like we had two crews, and sometimes a different bus would go somewhere different. So typically the ride would be about half an hour to an hour, and then we'd get to the site. And once we got to the site, we'd usually walk out to our piece, which is usually anywhere from five minutes to an hour and a half away, and then you start planting. (N. Friesen Hughes, unpublished data)

Trucks and stuff, breakfast didn't start 'till 6[:00 a.m.], and trucks didn't leave until 6:30, 7[:00] . . . Loading up the trucks usually took fifteen to twenty minutes. We'd grab, at some of our camps we would have a big refrigeration trailer, and that had all the seedlings inside, and so we would drive our trucks up to this bigger trailer, and we'd take out whatever trees we were planting that day . . . Everybody would load into the trucks, and we would drive off to wherever we were driving, and sometimes it was a really short drive, maybe ten minutes; other times, and often, it was, you know, an hour or so. (S. Friesen, unpublished data)

You would hop into your big, we had a Suburban, other people had a Ford Explorer I believe is the name, the really big SUVs, and then we all head out to the block. Once you got to the block it was about ten hours you typically spend planting, and then at a set time again you usually meet at your muster point, or your foreman comes around and collects you with the truck or the quad and gets everyone together, and then you head back to camp, maybe about an hour, thirty minutes before dinner. (T. MacInnis, unpublished data)

You're getting in trucks that drive you on logging roads to the block, and the drive can be anywhere from twenty minutes to two hours depending on how far away from camp you're working. And then you get [out] of the trucks, and your foreman pulls a bunch of trees out of the back of a truck, and you bag up. (R. McCannell, unpublished data)

Vehicles are a constant reminder of time. On the planting landscape, with its unpredictable road access, vehicle condition, and questionable GPS coordinate mapping to arrive at a block location, they function as time keepers: drives are ten minutes, twenty minutes, half an hour, an hour and a half, two hours. Pflugfelder (2017, 11) notes that some who study transportation often struggle with the idea, as Juliet Jain and Glenn Lyons (2008) put forward in studies of vacation travel, that "travel time is 'wasted time'"; the perception of time itself can often be enabled or constrained by its perceived "speediness" through space. As Mark Dery (2006, 228) remarks, "At a time when cell phones, laptops, and the wiring of the world have made a mockery of time and geography, the car is a nagging reminder that we still haven't figured out how to zap our Darwinian luggage—the body—from here to there, in *Star Trek*'s transporter." Part of a thing's thing-power, then, lies in its reminder of human materiality and affective expectation. On the planting landscape, truck-bodies, disappointingly, never measure distance: planters don't denote kilometers or miles as they describe their routinized planting schedules. And for good reason: as I discuss in the later section on roads and forest infrastructure, a planting site may be geographically "close" in distance, but because of lack of access, it may take an inordinate amount of time to get to.

Distance, in other words, does not equal time in ways that have become ubiquitous in thinking about transportation in cities (we might say that we live 2 miles, or a fifteen-minute drive, from work, and both are acceptable ways of measuring the distance) or in contemporary mediated life. Unlike Paul Virilio's (2007, 100) assertion that because of networked media and globalization we now have to account for a collapse in distance and time, the automobile-body on the planting landscape is instead the last holdout against the *dromosphere*,[10] the "Everything! Right Now! hypercentre of temporal compression." For Virilio, such a time-space collapse unmoors us, disorients us, because, as James Brown summarizes Virilio's view, "nothing is tied to a locality." Vehicle-bodies on the planting landscape are uniquely positioned against such unmooring, precisely because of their rhetorically sticky bodies, because of the ways they often resist human agency and human wishes for *Star-Trek*–like efficiencies. Instead, the terrain, working with (or against) vehicle bodies and makeshift roads as they transport planter and tree bodies, *all entangled*, is the determiner of time. Vehicle-bodies drag us, rather uncomfortably, back to our locality, back to our own bodies, to the "parochial, perspective, and performative" (Tsing 2015a).

*Hurry Up and Wait: Everything Breaks*
Bennett (2010, 59) points to the "metallic vitality" that operates at the atomic level of all metals. As I was talking about this chapter with a close friend who is schooled as a jewelry maker and a metalsmith, he elucidated Bennett's coverage of science history by referring to "metal

memory"—the ability of a metal's polycrystalline structures to "remember" the degree to which they have been heated and changed before they reach a structurally rigid point and break—easily observed by bending a paperclip back and forth until it snaps. It was useful to keep the life of metal in mind when listening to tree-planting descriptions of being with vehicular bodies, made primarily of metal shells and chassis and rubber tires. One of the primary ways vehicular bodies create a kinesthetic rhetoric, as I've mentioned, is in their ability to move efficiently on the landscape; when they slow, glitch, or break, they reveal a thing-power that is at once more visible, durable, and patient than human bodies, despite the frustrating effects. Planters depend on vehicles for a sense of efficiency, whether to get them to and from planting sites, to enable checkers and foremen to get from site to site, or to enable (when possible) runs to town during days off. Yet their descriptions are filled with the inefficiency of things that break, get damaged, and require human fixes, as Sam contends:

> This was two years ago in Saskatchewan, one of sort of the company's second-in-command drove a truck into a washout he figured he could get through. He didn't. He swamped the truck, and so he walked back and got another truck, I think he walked like 5 or 6 k [kilometers] to get this other truck with a winch to pull it out, and he got that truck stuck too. Same day we also broke four quads, which was, and so we were stuck ... out [there] for a good solid few extra hours waiting for, they got, this is just a rural Saskatchewan anecdote, they called the garage in town, in the nearby town, and he [the second-in-command] says "okay, we need a tow on this road, can you come pick us up?" and he [the garage owner] says "oh, okay, well, I have the tow truck, but I also have this monster truck," and so he brought this literally small monster truck with tires probably 4 feet high and driving down the road, and as we were waiting to get picked up he drove down the road just holding a can of beer in his hand down this logging road driving this big truck, and he pulled the two trucks out simultaneously, cost the company thousands of dollars for all those repairs, and that was just sort of very much the sort of the things sometimes go really bad, and you have to deal with it, and you just have to kind of live with it and try and just kind of be ambivalent about the whole thing. (S. Dyck, unpublished data)

Trucks especially, as demonstrated in Sam's description, are used ruthlessly through all kinds of weather and terrain. They are expected to perform daily, and maintenance and repairs are usually taken on by a tree runner (the person who delivers caches of trees to planting sites) or (if lucky) a single camp mechanic. But even vehicles in perfect working order will get stuck in mud ruts that reach planters' thighs or will blow tires or break axles on poorly maintained roads, to say nothing of hard use that wears down vehicle-bodies over time. Maintenance of vehicle bodies is an affective investment, an engagement in and witness to ruin, a cultivation of ambivalence, an awareness of the incompetence of human mastery of machines, an attunement to the ways mud is stronger than metal, an awareness of inefficiency equating cost. In other words, there is no knowing when the paperclip will break.

Almost every planter has a story, big or small, about getting stuck or broken down in a vehicle; to that end, Replant.ca, a website and message board for silvicultural workers, maintains a list of "mandatory" items planters should have in their trucks at all times, including items like two extra spare tires (for "simultaneous flats"), a VHF ("very high frequency") radio, jerry cans of gas and diesel, a GPS unit, a cell phone, a satellite phone, a winch controller, extra warm clothes and a sleeping bag, and three days' worth of food and water (Clark 2013). Others mention chains, tow ropes, and boards for digging out trucks that get stuck in mud or sand. Everything here is tied to locality; often, planters' locations are only known as GPS coordinates because there are no roads to orient would-be rescuers and radio signals are unreliable. Such is the life of the truck-body; it commands its own circulations of things and makes clear Pflugfelder's (2017, 4) argument that any form of "transportation is the result of a range of persuasive forces that require the compatibility, coordination, and compliance of many interactions." In Sam's anecdote alone, there are at least as many vehicles as there are humans involved; and materials like chains, winches, and cell phones operate visibly in the lengthy resolution of the problem. Thus while the truck-body is taken as a symbol of speed and efficiency, it is also clear from this description (and others like it) that equally inefficient hours are spent standing and waiting, beholden to geography and metal memory. The truck-body's glitches, in other words, reveal it to be something other than it is, to use Boyle's (2015) turn to the function of glitch in knowledge making. The truck-body promises speed but works against planter notions of efficiency, where even a few extra seconds devoted to a few more stomps around a tree is considered wasting time. The thing-body's promise of efficiency and speed is broken, its thing-power made more visible in its resistance to haste in a planting economy built from a rhetoric of efficiency and humanism. Here both inefficiency and the nonhuman win by virtue of deceleration.

In fact, despite planters' emphases on personal and economic efficiency, the common refrain in planting communities is "hurry up and wait," as tree-planting blogger Luc Forsyth (2013) notes: "So when there are no trees to plant and no one is telling them what is happening, planters have no choice but to wait. Sometimes they wait angrily, sometimes happily, or sometimes introspectively, but in the end they are simply sitting idle until someone tells them otherwise. A good management team can minimize this unprofitable down time, but ultimately patience must be among the virtues of a good tree planter. When confronted with delays, the best planters will simply wait harder."

Planting experts estimate that four to five days out of any season will be waiting time attributed to vehicle maintenance or breakage, frozen trees, fog (in which helicopters cannot fly), or time between contracts (Clark 2017). Thus the degree of self-determination represented by planters' insistence on personal freedom and individual work ethic, as noted in their descriptions of themselves as autonomous actors, is equally constrained by situational modifications by thing-bodies. Even as planters calculate down to the tree centage what they are making per day and focus almost exclusively on economy of movement, they also—often separately—acknowledge that the vehicles they interact with carry a persuasive force that destabilizes the human as the sole determiner of efficiency.

To that end, affects circulate among planter-bodies and thing-bodies, whether in Sam's suggestion that he try to foster "ambivalence" in waiting or Forsyth's (2013) acknowledgment that planters wait angrily, happily, introspectively, or "harder." We might see the ways these affects stick and move to constitute, as in Thayer's following description of getting stuck, a kind of truck persuasion. He relays the story of getting three vehicles stuck in a steep-sided gulley:

> It was quite muddy and slippery, and then there was some type of corduroy road[11] where you just lay logs down at the base of this little bit of a runoff. Anyway, so we drove in. It was sloppy, but we made it, and then our foreman also came in, he had a truck, and then our checker who was with us, he also came in.
>
> And we all made it in fine, planted our last part of the day, and it even went late, so I think maybe that day we planted like a twelve-hour day or something like that, and then after that small area was finished, we were all driving home to go back for dinner and go to sleep. And we all got stuck trying to get out of this area. First our SUV sort of hit these logs that were kind of building the corduroy bridge road, and he [the driver] slid sideways and got thoroughly stuck right against the tree line and spinning his wheels with his nose just facing this big cliff that we had driven down to get in. And then our foreman who's got his big super-duty 350 truck, he got stuck going up the slope. He made it through the bridge, started spinning going up the slope, and then last, the checker, who had a smaller, I think a 250 Ford, he got stuck going up the slope as well, and he had a winch so he thought he was getting out of there no matter what,

but he broke his winch trying to climb that slope. So all three of our vehicles are down in this gulley, the Suburban is totally out of commission, and the other two trucks are stuck trying to go up a muddy hill or cliff, and we all have high-frequency radios but they only base, operate base on line of site, so when you're down in a depression you really don't have any signal. And we didn't; we didn't have any signal. Even if we had been at the top, we were quite far away.

So we had to kind of sit there and sit there and sit there until our supervisor of the camp, this woman S, I don't remember her last name, but she had to realize that "hey, this whole crew's missing, and I've got to go figure out where they were planting today and then see where they're at. You know, did a bomb go off or what?" Anyway, I think it was about 10:00 at night or something. It was pitch black at this point. She showed up, and she's got a little six-cylinder Toyota truck. And we're all kind of just, you know, hanging out there, hoping we don't come across any grizzlies that are interested in anything we smell like or whatever. And yeah, yeah, she comes with her little Toyota truck; we hear her coming. Once she gets within a mile or so, she radios and she's constantly checking us on radio, and yeah, she sees the situation, how we've got these two trucks stuck coming up the hill and the one Suburban truck stuck way down at the bottom, and she uses her tiny little Toyota truck to yank us up this slope and pulls both of us out, both of us, the foreman and the checker who have both big Ford trucks that weigh probably twice as much as this little Toyota. And she uses a tow rope and just yanks these vehicles up, and I've never seen anyone work a truck that way, just driving it until the point that it jumps off the ground pulling these things forward, and [she] pulled both these trucks out. And then we all drove back to the camp, probably got back at midnight, and left the Suburban behind, and I think later on they had to get it out with the helicopter or something like that 'cause it was just thoroughly, thoroughly stuck . . . And yeah, seeing that little truck pull those big trucks up, that inspired me to, I went out and bought that same truck for myself, and now I've had it for years and I love it, but yeah, that just was amazing that night. (T. MacInnis, unpublished data)

It's safe to assume that the human bodies involved in this anecdote likely had some awareness of kinesis being the primary persuasive force, or rhetorical energy, in the situation. Although their vehicles promised speed and time saving, they delivered slowness and delay and in so doing revealed a particular thing-power: the power to strand and isolate human bodies, to cultivate human fear and worry. We have a great deal of detail about various thing-bodies: the corduroy road, the four vehicles (the Suburban, the 350 truck, the 250 Ford truck, and the Toyota truck), the cliff, the broken winch, the useless VHF radio, the mud. In the case of the four named vehicles, we also see the persuasiveness of thing-bodies and their physical force on the landscape: each truck-body has its own physical capacity implicit in its design, separated out by manufacture in terms of carriage, engine, chassis, suspension, and gross axle weight rating.

Each of the three stuck trucks has a larger (eight-cylinder) engine; the Toyota has a smaller, six-cylinder engine. In terms of each truck's towing capacity, the 350 can tow a maximum of 32,000 pounds; the 250, 18,000 pounds; the Suburban, 8,300 pounds; and the Toyota, 6,500 pounds—that is, there is an impression among truck users that towing capacity equals some kind of strength (if not, as in this example, dexterity in handling). The expectation here, in the telling, is that the strongest truck (like the strongest man) will prevail: after the Suburban gets stuck, the anticipation is that the 350 will make it, and then when it, too, gets stuck, the 250 is tried. The surprise, then, is when the smallest truck with the least towing capacity manages to rescue two of the three larger trucks, each weighing between 5,600 and 6,000 pounds. While this is within the V-6 towing capacity of a Toyota truck and thus shouldn't be surprising (given that the vehicle is classed to tow up to 6,500 pounds), it is still, in the narrative of the "Little Engine That Could," the most persuasive thing-body on the landscape. Not only does it provide human rescue and un-stick two of the other trucks, but the rhetorical energy among human-thing-landscape is enough, in Thayer's words, to "inspire" him to go out and buy one for himself in hopes that such replication of a thing-body will similarly ensure his safety and security while maintaining its own longevity. In relaying the description of the truck-human-landscape, Thayer has been persuaded and, more, brought to some emotional being-state with his own vehicle—he loves it for what it has, in his memory and in his relations with it since, come to provide. The story as told is also a story of the love affair humans have with automobility and the patterns it replicates in human habits, dependent upon the attendant infrastructure to support them.

## THE PROMISES OF INFRASTRUCTURE: ROADS AND SPEED

Thus far I've been discussing vehicle thing-bodies (and their human drivers) as though they could stand apart from the infrastructure that carries them—primarily, the logging roads that are constructed for deforestation purposes and provide tree planters with subsequent access to remote areas. Anthropologists and mobility scholars have similarly investigated the invisibility of the thing-power of infrastructure, particularly roads, noting that their mythical imbuement of narratives of progress and development often obfuscates their affective entanglements with human lives. Roads themselves—particularly those in the

West—signify what Penny Harvey and Hannah Knox (2012, 523–24) call "an archetypal technology of post-enlightenment . . . [and] emancipatory modernity" that promise "speed and connectivity," economic prosperity, and political freedom. Most of us familiar with city or country roads recognize them when we see them, as they are materially stable (made of asphalt/bitumen, concrete, or gravel) and of a standard size per lane (12 feet) and per shoulder (4–10 feet, depending). Implicit in any road we come across are the design standards of engineers and the use of specific materials employed to enforce standards of durability, safety, and speed—to say nothing of the accompanying discursive materials we may use to navigate them, such as road signs, traffic signals, and maps. Because we are used to these common infrastructural entities, for the most part, roads as material-discursive thing-bodies remain relatively invisible to us, unless at some point they make themselves more visible (and powerful) by their failure: potholes, spalling, traffic jams, car crashes.

Yet road infrastructure is more than the backdrop to everyday life. As science historian Paul Edwards (2003, 188) notes, such a position is a privileged one; the "notion of infrastructure as an invisible, smooth-functioning background 'works' only in the developed world"—or, in political anthropologist Kregg Hetherington's (2014, 197) words, "infrastructure only works this way at certain times and in certain places." It should come as little surprise that much of the critical scholarship on roads comes out of studies in developing countries: Harvey and Knox (2012) look at roads in Peru; Hetherington (2014) examines roads in Paraguay; Mark Lamont (2017) investigates a rural road in Kenya. For most people who live in North America, roads do function as an unproblematically invisible infrastructure, and they facilitate both speed and connectivity of everyday life, built on the culture of automobility. We can go faster, save time, and have access to greater and farther spaces with the right roads; they indeed are a promise of a particular kind of progress, a particular increase of spatial access, a darling of efficiency. Yet as Hetherington (2014, 196–97) contends, roads are also structures that enable secondary processes to emerge from them, and they work to bifurcate the landscape: "An equally salient feature of infrastructure is the way that it divides the built landscape into temporal priorities to be slotted into a promising narrative of progress. In such a narrative, infrastructure often serves as that which holds nature and culture apart, marking a temporal break between chaos and order."

For Hetherington (2014, 198), roads provide a charged stability, as they "allo[w] people to pass from a state of natural disorder to a civilized order, and then maintain that order against the natural forces of disaster and decay." Thus transportation infrastructure not only represents the promise of stability, speed, connectivity, and access to spaces but also holds steady culture and order (in the form of material development) in the face of a resurgent, chaotic nature (in the form of the environment). Roads are thing-bodies that house within them the environmentalist-developmentalist divide.

Scholarship that looks at transportation infrastructure notes the limitations to assumptions about its promises of modernity that reinforce the nature-culture binary. Harvey and Knox (2012, 523) note the affective impact of poor road maintenance, high numbers of accidents, steep terrain, and little signage on Peruvian roads that instead of increased speed, results in arduous, slow road travel. Such an inversion of affective expectations of roads reveals instead their "fragility and material uncertainty" (Harvey and Knox 2012, 525) and humans' accompanying uneasy reactions to such uncertainty. It is roads' failure to deliver on such promises that I wish to examine as moments that most reveal their thing-power on the planting landscape. Examining planting roads' peculiarities in size, function, and temporality reveals the complexities of their rhetorical operations and offers some promise in recognizing their bodies as agentive negotiations of natureculture rather than bifurcations of nature-culture.

*Logging Roads, Quad Trails, and "They Were Just Swamp":*
*Deactivation/Reclamation and Accessibility*

Most North Americans have acquired their knowledge of road infrastructure by being unnoticeably trained through the history of the modern highway system. Our acknowledgment of what roads should look like, should be made of, and should enable is based on the post–World War II development of over 45,000 miles of roads in the United States and over 20,000 miles in Canada. The development of national and interstate roads has provided particular transportation regulation and safety guidelines, and such roads have been designed to enable the mythos of infrastructure: speed (by softening curves and horizontal and vertical alignment, straightening and flattening, and widening), safety (by providing adequate sight lines for oncoming traffic, providing wide shoulders for a range of movement, and indicating speed minimums and maximums), connectivity (public access to cities and rural areas), economic prosperity,[12] and political freedom.[13] Such roads are built to be durable, dependable, and long-lasting.

Roads take on a completely different meaning for tree planters, one that depends on their uniqueness and separation from the modern commonplace of North American roadways. The roads tree planters use (when they exist) are private, "forest access roads" (also known as "logging roads" or "haul roads") constructed by either the Ministry of Forests (which has allowances from the Crown to develop transport corridors to reach particular forest sites) or logging companies (which have applied to the Ministry of Forests for permits to construct a forest access road). Because these roads are private, they are not held to the same design standards that apply to publicly funded roadways and are not legally usable by the general public—that is, they do not increase public access to space. Logging roads are designed for heavy trucks at low speeds; however, they are unpaved and narrow (one lane, 10–12 feet wide), and they lack sight lines because brush is not required to be cleared to maintain them. Similarly, logging companies create smaller access roads and trails (or "quad trails," primarily for ATV access), each requiring minimal design and often created by "merely pushing down vegetation to clear . . . a narrow right-of-way" (Minister of Public Works and Government Services Canada 2010). In the case of ice haul roads, they are made from snow and are for winter (one-season) use only.

Tree planters are unmistakably aware of the limitations of these different road bodies and make clear reference to them as ambient, sensorial thing-bodies that enable or constrain their work:

> So there's this like smell of like mulch as you walk through these logging roads, which are these, maybe, I don't know, 10-foot-wide dirt roads. They're in varying levels of repair, usually covered in water, but by June or July, you know, you can drive on them or walk on them just fine. (T. Bourlas, unpublished data)

> This block they had given us, the roads weren't accessible during, weren't really accessible during the spring because they were just swamp, so they had brought the trees, so that means we can't really haul trees in, and they didn't want to pay for a helicopter, so they hauled them in during the winter. (S. Dyck, unpublished data)

> 'Cause most of the time where we were, we're on discontinued roads, so there had been logging through there, and then they had come with machinery and dug sort of horizontal trenches to let water run through, and so you don't get the same sort of erosion that you would if you left just flat roads. (T. MacInnis, unpublished data)

> The other thing that's different about B.C. is that there are logging roads that are pretty decent quality that take you right to the block, whereas in northern Alberta it's just muddy nothingness, it's as if you're planting in a muddy bog and there are, you cannot get a truck in to these areas, so it's

*Figure 4.1. Quad trail on cut block (Image credit: Jonathan Clark)*

either heli-work in some cases or ATVs or these Hägglund machines they used to use at one time, which is essentially a Swiss military vehicle on a track; it's a tank for moving people. (R. McCannell, unpublished data)

In northern Alberta, because it's logged in the winter, all the stuff goes up on ice roads. All the forest products come up on ice roads. You're up there in the summer, all the ice roads have melted. It's a swamp. (J. Simpson, unpublished data).

Whether a logging road, an access road, or a quad trail, none of these road types is designed for speed or safety; indeed, some are barely designed at all (figure 4.1). Curves in terrain or hilly slopes are not softened or flattened; access roads do not include high-priced infrastructure like culverts or shoulders (or often even ditches). These roads and trails are private and are not intended for public use or access to forested spaces (and there are often signs that indicate this). They also have a lifespan far different from what most North Americans are used to in transportation infrastructure: they are designed to last only as long as the required access to Crown land that will be logged is needed (sometimes as little as a few weeks), after which they are either "deactivated" or "reclaimed."

While Clark (2016a) notes that the terms *deactivation* and *reclamation* are used interchangeably to describe the process of purposefully making a road unusable or inaccessible, they are procedurally different. A deactivated road is much like the one Thayer MacInnis describes above, where mills deactivate a logging road so that trucks, hunters, and recreational ATV users cannot pass "by putting obstacles such as piles of dirt, piles of logs, or water bars at the entrance to the road" (Clark 2016a, 13). Reclamation, in contrast, "is the process of completely destroying an existing road so future use is impossible" (Clark 2016a, 35). However, because of the long time periods between access, many "deactivated" roads become "reclaimed" over time (figure 4.2). Such a process indicates the impossibility of imagining the road-body as a simple and singular bifurcation of nature and culture; indeed, as figure 4.2 illustrates, there is often no difference at all. There is no clear narrative of progress here, and the temporal break Hetherington claims between chaos and order is ill-defined. These roads are designed in a way that is the opposite of our affectual expectations: they are fleeting; they are made of dirt to be returned to dirt in a short time; they provide private access for transitory populations. Significantly, these populations aren't tree planters but loggers; roads are deactivated or reclaimed as soon as trees are cut and hauled off of blocks and *before* tree planters go in. They have a unique temporality, tied to their intentional liminality and contingent being.

These road-bodies are also uniquely *alive*; while gravel is occasionally brought in for longer-term use, logging roads, many access roads, and all trails are made from the existing terrain—compacted dirt, bush, sticks, rocks—and attendant worms, weeds, insects, larva, fungi, nematodes, algae, bacteria, and microorganisms. Here the road-body defies traditional expectations and mythos of transportation infrastructure and blends instead with plantation flora and fauna, all of which determine tree-planting labor. As Jon notes of his time as logistics coordinator for a planting company, "Depending on the cut site, I would drive in with the truck as far as I could, and, if necessary, I had an ATV to drive them [the trees] in further, and then if the ATV couldn't get further, I would carry them in box by box" (J. Sprohge, unpublished data).

Planting roads continually defy infrastructural expectations and shape the anthropocenic landscape—by influencing access of planter-bodies and tree bodies to particular spaces—often by creating a middle state between order and disorder through inattention and abandonment. As Oliver Rackham (2015, 368) points out, "Neglect is a part of the essential anthropology of plantations," and the road-bodies planters navigate with their own bodies are testaments to how neglect blurs the chaos/order distinction so central to transportation infrastructure elsewhere.

*Figure 4.2. Deactivated road (Image credit: Jonathan Clark)*

Both the unique temporality and the vibrant matter of logging roads, access roads, and trails contribute to their resistance to the efficiency model that dominates tree-planting descriptions. While it's true that planters consistently claim these rhetorics for themselves, the road-bodies they work and travel with consistently push against those discourses with rhetorics of their own. Instead, thing-bodies steadily claim for themselves the thing-power of slowness, of visibility, of obstruction, of resurgence; and they offer a distinct interruption in the efficient use of resources, whether they be time, money, or materials.

*Sonic Roads: Economic Prosperity and Co-Constructing Wilderness*

While I've described the uniqueness of road-bodies planters come across in terms of their defiance of articulated expectations of function (speed, connectivity) and relationship with durability and time, I also am aware that road-bodies do not function independent of their entanglements with others, whether as nematode carrier, caribou corridor, or vehicular surface. Together, roads and vehicles create a particular assemblage that carries suasive meaning for human bodies and contributes to a particular conception of Canadian wilderness as a resource.

One of the ways road-vehicle bodies on the landscape do this is through the use of sound. While most drivers associate driving (that is, the movement of vehicle bodies on roadways) with sight, the system of movement on forest roads is somewhat different. Because these roads are much narrower than traditional roads and are often in various states of reclamation or weather affectation, they are only wide enough for a single lane that has to function as a two-way roadway. There is simply not enough room for two vehicles to pass one another, and often there is not enough sight distance for drivers to know ahead of time that an oncoming vehicle is approaching. Thus drivers on forest roads depend on VHF radios, commercial radios that must be licensed and pre-programmed to very high radio frequencies; they communicate their whereabouts on roads depending on their locality by "calling out" their kilometer marker (when available on an active road), directional reference ("up" or "down" in relation to the mill or log dump), or load ("loaded" or "empty," which indicates a loaded truck headed toward the mill and away from the bush). Without these sonic cues, forest roads would be un-navigable; they enable tree planters to safely traverse landscapes through vehicles' communicative technologies. However, this circulation of bodies also reveals an increased depth of vitality, thing-power, and distributed agency: at the level of electrons and vibrations, radio waves travel in rhythm to make truck travel possible and to save human lives.[14] In doing so, they enable all stages of industrial forestry, fulfilling the promise of economic prosperity through a perpetual and profitable enterprise of plantation.

Yet the sonic road, approached differently, has another impact on the Canadian landscape that is tied deeply to the national economy by way of its connection to tourism, which represents 2 percent of Canada's GDP. A large portion of Canadian tourism is tied specifically to its perception as an unspoiled, or "wild," place; this takes the form of ecotourism (for instance, travel to see the polar bears in Churchill, Manitoba) as well as sports hunting and fishing. The latter activities are dependent on leisure access to "wilderness" as an elite recreational activity (the cost of a week's stay at a fly-in sport fishing outpost is about $3,000, to say nothing of air travel). Sport fishing and hunting outposts are fly-in, which is to say only accessible by air, usually by float plane.

However, logging roads (which are not legally accessible by the public) that surround lodge areas present something of a challenge to the singular idea of wilderness, as Sam explains:

> The sort of literal definition of wilderness is, particularly in northwestern Ontario, somewhat problematic because wilderness implies that no one lives there, so again, with these wealthy Americans who come to hunt and fish in the north and fly in to these outpost camps, those outpost camps

are often very close to logging roads, like maybe, I think they're allowed to cut up to maybe it's 100 meters, I don't know, but there are travel bans. You're not allowed to travel on the logging roads . . . but you're not allowed to travel to the lakes by law using those logging roads, so if you want to fly in, if you're a local you can do that, but they don't have the cash for that, so it's just these [sic] artificial wilderness that's created there. Because essentially what the lodge owners would do, who are mostly American, are [sic] marketing this place devoid of people, and so if you actually hear from, sometimes from the consultations that they conduct in, with forestry management plans, is the lodge owners will complain that some of their customers heard a truck moving a kilometer away and got very upset because it wasn't wild enough. (S. Dyck, unpublished data)

Here Sam illustrates how persuasive the movement of trucks on the logging roads is; through the vibrations and truck rhythms sent through the air, in this case the sound imprint is enough to rattle the economic value of perceived wilderness and generate a complaint that a landscape was not "wild" enough. Here, the mythos of infrastructural connectivity works to co-construct wilderness. These logging roads do not function at all the way roads are expected to; that is, they only connect forest blocks to the closest mill rather than connect people to towns, towns to cities, and cities to cities. Yet the stickiness of their bodies remains: despite the logging road's unique relationship to both vehicles and terrain, the sound of a vehicle on a logging road was enough to uncomfortably remind a consumer through affective upset that an "authentic" wilderness is very much a human-made construct. Thus, despite the road-body as a seeming boundary marker between nature and culture, in Hetherington's terms, it instead garners more thing-power by not doing what it is supposed to do—in this case, remain invisible by its infrastructural silence or appropriately represent itself as a boundary. Instead of holding nature and culture apart, it brings them together, a naturecultural dent in the seamless model of ecotourist prosperity. The assemblage itself co-constructs a particular wilderness that problematizes the nature-as-resource narrative.

*Political Ecologies: Roads, Access, Planting, and First Nations*

A finale suasive tension on the planting landscape in which road-bodies are engaged is what Bennett (2010, 106) terms "political acts" or what Harvey and Knox (2012, 529) might call the "enchantments of political integration" promised by roads. As they note, human expectation is such that roads should function to bring people together, connect people physically to one another, integrate disparate national territories, and bring other infrastructures with them, such as utility poles along road corridor lines. Harvey and Knox use the case of road building in Peru to denote the ways it has historically been tied to integrating the nation-state, imagining cultural and economic singularity, and mitigating sectarian division. Yet by virtue of road-construction programs that promise jobs and connectivity, roads also "operate as technologies for materializing state presence in people's lives" (Harvey and Knox 2012, 529–30). While Harvey and Knox's assertions may be seen to be applicable only in North America in the post–World War II infrastructural boom of interstates and national highway systems, in the particular case of the Canadian north and Indigenous peoples, roads—particularly logging roads—do indeed continue to function as physical mechanisms of integrative state control.

While Canada seems to most people to be a united nation 150 years from confederation, as a nation born from colonialism and genocide by European settlement, it is far from it. Settlements involving Canadian land and who that land belongs to—Crown land, for example, refers to "public" or "state" land that is ultimately held by the British sovereign, Queen Elizabeth at present—are contested, since Indigenous First Nations groups were clearly on Canadian land before European settlers arrived and continue to inhabit their traditional lands. In the late 1800s and early 1900s, Indigenous groups across Canada signed eleven numbered treaties with the Crown that established a system of reserve lands (similarly known in the United States as "reservations") and negotiated hunting and fishing rights, each regulated under the 1876 Indian Act. Because this system often displaced First Nations people from their traditional lands, treaty land entitlement claims (renegotiation of existing treaties and enlarging land claims) are ongoing in many parts of Canada. These claims take the shape of either negotiating un-ceded land—that is, land that was excluded from treaty bargaining and thus has not been relinquished to the Crown by Indigenous groups—or claims made to rectify past grievances under historical treaties (Indigenous and Northern Affairs Canada 2010).

Many of these lands are in remote areas and northern communities, unreachable by roads or connected only seasonally by ice roads. Yet these remote areas, which neighbor Crown land and are often not designated by any visible boundary, are often targeted by resource industries—mining, logging, and drilling—as prime candidates for resource extraction. Struggles among Indigenous groups, provincial governments, and the Crown regarding treaty rights and Indigenous land claims are well represented in contemporary court rulings, such as the 2014 *Grassy Narrows First Nation v. Ontario* case, which ruled that the provincial government could indeed log areas to which the Grassy Narrows First Nation was entitled under Treaty 3 (Supreme Court Judgments 2014). That is, these decisions about land use and integration of national territory—and attendant pop-up resource-industry infrastructure—are not historic in the sense of a temporal past but instead are ongoing. As workers in the last stage of industrial forestry, tree planters are at the forefront of these outcomes and often witness, as Sam put it, "issues with the resource industry and the havoc that it's wreaked on the communities that it leaves . . . You see the cracks in confederation a bit more" (S. Dyck, unpublished data).

First Nations depend on infrastructure as much as any other community; however, they are entitled to their own system of governance that has complicated financial ties to both provincial governments and the federal government. As a result, many First Nations communities are noted as having infrastructure deficits, including underdevelopment of water and wastewater treatment facilities, roads, bridges, electrification, and broadband connectivity (Patterson and Dyck 2015). Thus every road signifies in a different way on reserve land than it does off that land—as something that positively connects people to the resources they need to live but connects them negatively to potentially exploitive acts, such as the extraction of natural resources, with little recourse. Far from engendering the myth of political freedom and polity, roads function instead as political acts do: by generating a particular effect by "catalyz[ing] a public" through their "power to startle and provoke a gestalt shift in perception" (Bennett 2010, 107). To imagine roads as agents on the political spectrum of actions, what Bennett (2010, 108) calls "participants in a political ecology," is to notice them on the planting landscape—which is also Indigenous land—as functioning in persuasive ways, made available by planters' attunement to their role in this ecology.

One of the clearest examples of this is represented by Erin's description of tree planting on illegally logged land in British Columbia:

> There's a contested area of land up near the Houston area in B.C. . . . that belongs to a First Nations group up in northern B.C., and then it's been entitled to them under treaty land, which has been illegally logged in the past, and Enbridge has been trying to, behind their backs, come in and start to pipeline it, basically building a pipeline through their land, and so the people of this valley, there's only [one] road coming into this particular valley, and they've blocked it off with a barricade and have had protesters there for the last many years trying to keep out illegal loggers, trying

to keep out, yeah, mostly Enbridge employees and fairly successfully; it's been one of the most successful barricades, and I wish I could remember the name off the top of my head. But when it was illegally logged about seven years ago, because it's been logged, the logging companies are entitled, because it's been logged, the logging companies by law are required to come in and plant it, and so the logging companies approached the people at the barricade whether we might, or planters might be permitted to come in and plant, and after some debate they decided that we would be, and so our planting company was allowed behind the barricade into the valley that nobody other than this particular family had been allowed in in the last seven years, which was quite the privilege. We actually, I was planting in one area that was along the proposed Enbridge pipeline route and saw a helicopter coming up ahead, and it landed near my plot, and me and my foreman went and approached the guy and said "what are you doing here?" and he was like "oh hi, I'm from Enbridge. I'm here to just chart out a route." And we're like, "You probably better get out of here before anyone comes," and they did. But planting is intricately connected into the land issues that Canada is facing, into who has the right to resources. (E. Sawatzky, unpublished data)

Erin is referring to the Unist'ot'en (C'ihlts'ehkhyu/Big Frog Clan) camp of the Witsuwit'en people, whose traditional lands in the central interior of British Columbia are around the Bulkley River, Morice River, Broman Lake, and François Lake. The Unist'ot'en people have made headlines for erecting a barricade on the only logging road that provides access to the community. The barricade has been erected to control access to this un-ceded land, which has been slated for construction of the Pacific Trails Pipeline (PTP) corridor and is under consideration for eleven more pipelines (McSheffrey 2015). Because there are few people to "guard" the 13,670 $m^2$ swath of Witsuwit'en land (which, as Erin notes, is accessible only by helicopter), the barricade checkpoint on its sole road is the only way the Unist'ot'en can manage access (figure 4.3). Media coverage of the Unist'ot'en checkpoint is filled with descriptions of people "getting lost on logging roads for hours" (Field 2015) "forty miles into the wilderness" (Manno 2016). The 36-member country intergovernmental Organization for Economic Cooperation and Development (OECD) does not consider Unist'ot'en land rural but predominantly rural remote, which is classified as having at least 50 percent of the regional population able to reach a locality of 50,000 people in over an hour (Directorate for Public Governance and Territorial Development 2011). The Unist'ot'en are difficult to reach and are often sought out only for resource extraction.

In this small case, we see how planter-bodies, tree-bodies, truck-bodies, and road-bodies converge on the landscape as an agentic

*Figure 4.3. Unist'ot'en checkpoint (Image credit: Jonathan Clark)*

political assemblage, not only in the singular case of tree planters being allowed to plant on traditional Unist'ot'en land but also in the ongoing struggle for rights to Canadian land, the unequal distribution of power granted to Indigenous people, illegal logging on un-ceded territory, and the fossil-fuel economy. Inasmuch as Bennett (2010, 107) wonders how thing-bodies like sandstorms might enable sectarian violence or how the HIV virus might activate homophobia, we might question here how the only road to the Unist'ot'en camp generates particular political and economic effects: the mobilization of the Unist'ot'en people, carbon offsets (the reason logging companies are required by law to replant trees), Indigenous treaty rights and territory disputes, and global oil dependence. What happens deep in the forest is intimately connected to what happens in NASDAQ; and the circulation of things, people, and affect is what connects these naturecultural ecologies. As Erin shows, tree planters are in a unique position to be among the bodies that are attuned to these circulations and are caught up in producing their effects. As Bennett suggests, nonhuman actors similarly have a distinct role as participants in these political systems, attributable to their materiality and thing-power. In the case of the Unist'ot'en, the road is what enables and constrains a resistance movement—and in Erin's description, the helicopter is what obstructs it.

## ALT-ACCESS: HELICOPTERS AND EFFICIENCY

If thing-bodies like trucks and roads might be said to attune planters to locality, slowness, and thing-power, helicopter modes of access into planting blocks as transportation alternatives in some ways seem to do the opposite. As vehicle bodies, helicopters are as entangled with humans, air, and radio sound as are vehicular bodies on the road landscape. However, as alternative means of accessing areas difficult for humans to reach, even by motor vehicle—whether because of reclaimed roads or no roads at all—as nonhuman actors they consistently tap into planters' discourses of efficiency. Their ability to traverse large areas of difficult terrain vertically and to deliver trees and humans to where they need to be in short amounts of time creates a kind of kinesthetic rhetoric that complements' planters own efficiency values; similarly, their seemingly known expense duplicates the equation of money equaling time in planter's descriptions of working with tree-bodies.

As mentioned, some bush camps depend solely on helicopters; as Thomas noted regarding a few of his planting experiences, "the entire camp had to be transported in by helicopter, everything, all of our tents and buildings and generators and vehicles even. They didn't have many vehicles, just quads, but it would carry them all by helicopter, it was pretty crazy. And in those cases, our commute was always by helicopter everywhere" (T. Kroeker, unpublished data). Cases like Thomas's are echoed by stories like Layla's that began this chapter, in which planting gear carried by a helicopter sling was accidentally detached (again making the glitch of thing-power glimpseable). Ryan suggests that traveling by helicopter was a powerful bodily experience that engaged feelings of isolation. Describing a fly-in bush camp experience, he says: "It was helicopter access only. So I guess we would have driven to a staging area and then flown in a helicopter to the middle of the bush. So since it was my first time doing it, it was a little bit intense to suddenly be in the middle of the forest, helicopter access only, and I think we were there for almost a month, so it was definitely just being thrown into the experience. There was no going back" (R. Boldt, unpublished data).

For isolated camps like the ones Thomas and Ryan describe, helicopters are the only means of connection to food, water, resources, and a return to everyday life. It is possible that flight—specifically, the vertical mobility offered by helicopter travel—fulfills stymied promises of vehicle speed on the planting landscape by delivering on the promises of "freedom and release" offered by air travel, as suggested by Saulo Cwerner (2006, 193). Unencumbered by the limitations of air travel in cities, helicopter travel in remote areas offers what Cwerner (2006, 194) calls "frictionless mobility"—that is, mobility that is unhindered by the structures and regulations that apply to other vehicular mobilities—and "detached mobility": the capacity to "bypass and circumvent the processes, norms, dangers, and conflicts of social and city life." Helicopters allow Virilio's *dromosphere* with far more capacity than do automobiles because they "shrink space" (Cwerner 2006, 194), thus embodying the economic value of the increased importance of travel speed.

Combined with a near lack of restriction on mobility, helicopter bodies help commodify time (Cwerner 2006, 192). This is hinted at in James's description of his coastal planting experiences, which details how much transport is required to access remote areas:

> Access to the blocks is very difficult. There aren't any roads along the coast of B.C. or there aren't obviously many roads on many islands on the north tip of Vancouver Island, so your access is by boat or by float plane or by helicopter and often by a combination of those. Like you'll take a truck to a boat or a boat by a couple of trucks to the side that had been boated in, or you quad to a landing spot, or you get your heli on the top of the mountain. A lot of your time is spent on transport. Probably, you should be compensated, but you aren't. (J. Simpson, unpublished data)

Central to these descriptions are the ways time, distance, and mobility relate: they show how planters are attuned to movement across landscapes and how types of transport (thing-bodies) determine the rate of planter- and tree-bodies' geographic mobility. And certainly, James's description hints at the implicit "price" of the daily commute: these travel times are often long and time is clearly money, yet only planting makes money because time is compensated not by hour but by tree.

Helicopter bodies on the landscape are seen as representatives of the time-money efficiency conundrum: they save time but are extremely expensive bodies whose "cost-effectiveness can only be gauged against large returns, that is, in situations where the significance of time savings is of a similar magnitude in relation to the costs of transportation" (Cwerner 2006, 208). As Ryan notes about his time as a foreman, "You need to be ordering helicopters around, telling them where to drop trees, knowing that a helicopter costs over a thousand dollars an hour to rent or something like that, and you can't waste their time" (R. Boldt, unpublished data). But as James contends, the freedom and detachment of travel by helicopter is a conflicted naturecultural, bodily, human-nonhuman entanglement:

> It's a Stone Age job in a lot of ways. You're using a shovel. That's like the first thing we invented after fire; okay you got fire, here's a shovel. Also, get in this helicopter, which is one of the most advanced pieces

of technology humans have. It's a really odd contrast. Like, you know, you've probably just waded through a swamp, you're covered in crap, all your clothes are ripped. You know, covered, to be blunt, you're probably covered in bodily fluids: sweat, blood, you name it. Flying around in this extremely expensive piece of machinery . . . Tree planters aren't saving the world. They're putting in a lot of trees, but also, you know, flying around burns a lot of gas, and the amount of machinery and equipment that we use to do it is ultimately very destructive. (J. Simpson, unpublished data)

Here James notes that the movement of the helicopter body on the landscape, the planter-helicopter encounter, is contradictory. Planter-bodies are created by their constant contact with low-technology, low-cost shovel equipment at the same time they are created by their mobility on the landscape that enables them to use the shovel to put tree-bodies (which travel in huge helicopter-borne slings, when they work) in the ground. As he points out, the cost of this production—the flying, the machinery operation—does not add up to saving the planet but instead to saving time at a particularly high price that is clearly caught up in the aviation and fossil-fuel industries. Yet the planter-bodies who are bound up in being-with helicopter bodies are nonetheless caught up in their "movement-oriented persuasions," as Pflugfelder (2017, 14) describes them: speed, "frictionless mobility," unlimited access to plantable land, and an infinite number of seconds saved, seconds that can be devoted to planting trees. In this way, helicopters and their vertical movement through air embody the rhetorics of efficiency embedded in planting discourse in a way other vehicular bodies, constrained by terrain, do not.

### THE ROLE OF THE AMBIENT: THING-POWER'S CHALLENGE TO HUMANISM

In turning to the entanglements of planter-bodies with various thing-bodies on plantation landscapes (and airscapes), I've indicated a range of ways tree planters are attuned to movement-oriented persuasions (whether in getting a truck to move on a flooded road, noting the way sound functions between truck and road in constructing ideas of wilderness, or choosing unpaid helicopter commutes) and the ways agency is distributed across a range of human and nonhuman actors. Despite their perceived differences, what these examinations of relevant thing-bodies have in common is their affectual cultivation made possible by their movement on the landscape: through constant motion, modification, and change, trucks, roads, and helicopters each shape particular discourses about nature, about humanism, about efficiency, about mobility. In turn, these persuasive movements, as acts of new materialist environmental rhetoric, have particular effects that often emerge in tension with the expected humanistic outcome or desire.

We might see these effects reflected in a variety of ways: in the case of vehicle bodies, in the way trucks shape notions of time and distance and disrupt expectations of speed, convenience, and personal freedom, making their power more obvious through decay and breakage (and thus slowing planter-bodies down). Questions of mobility, expansion, connectivity, longevity, and political integration are similarly disrupted as promises of infrastructure when the particularities of logging roads, access roads, and trails are seen in connection with planter-bodies, Indigenous people, and intentional time-bound and person-bound road deactivation and decomposition processes. What will become of the Unist'ot'en checkpoint as the only road into the camp disintegrates? What might it mean to listen to that disintegration as an objection? How might that change the conception of a road as a boundary between order and chaos, between nature and culture? Rhetoric, as attuned the material as what animates it, cannot ignore questions such as these.

To imagine thing-bodies as vibrant and agentive in their own right suggests that they may not fulfill the promises and obligations humans make for them. In the case of tree planting, promises of economic prosperity, either individual or national, are enabled or constrained by horizontal forces of terrestriality or vertical forces of aero-nauticality. Represented in the former case by vehicles and roads and in the latter case by helicopters and air, these entanglements of planter, tree, and thing-bodies destabilize the role of the human in each as the determiner of efficiency, thus distributing the agency of achieving "efficiency" across a range of nonhuman actors. If human entanglements with things—as in the case of tree planter, frozen tree, refrigerated truck, forest road, ATV—each sticky with affect, are ultimately what make the decision about how efficiency gets produced, then it is indeed a movement-oriented persuasion born out of distributed agency among human and nonhuman actors, a new materialist environmental rhetoric, that pushes against these common rhetorics of humanism that dominate the tree-planting—the anthropocenic—landscape.

## NOTES

1. An Inukshuk is an Inuit landmark cairn usually made of stone; a recent well-known instance of this icon was used in the 2010 Winter Olympics (and its use was subsequently critiqued by First Nations leaders). For the Inuit, such cairns were meant

to signify directional markers and often, as in this case, were a means for discovery and survival.
2. For a discussion of the turn away from this distinction and toward what Bennett (2010) calls "vibrant materials," see Bennett 2010, 20; Braidotti 2013, 89.
3. Bennett articulates the problem of the "performative contradiction" (2010, 120, 155n29) of humanistic hierarchy inherent in having humans narrate the stories of things, which I recognize in examining the rhetorical agency of things through the discourse of humans as indicated by interview data.
4. The fossil-fuel and forestry industries literally intersect. While they both accept automobility as a given, larger intersections happen specifically between logging ("right-of-way" cuts) and pipeline development and mandates to fulfill reclamation contracts on oil/tar sands; see Batten 2014; Braun and Hanus 2005.
5. One planter relayed the story of a thirty-member tree-planting crew moving into a thirty-person town, effectively doubling its population for the planting season.
6. Depending on the accessibility of the required planting area, trees are often flown in by helicopter or driven in on ice roads (which melt in spring) and dropped in central caches, where they are covered in plastic, then flax straw, sawdust, or woodchips and finally snow to overwinter for spring planting.
7. Relating to the promise of automobilty, speed, and comfort, James noted of Hägglunds, "they float through the muskeg at 5 kilometers an hour, and you get slammed at the back of this thing, you know, this enclosed waterproof space that stinks because you're sitting in it with a bunch of your stinky friends" (J. Simpson, unpublished data).
8. All seedlings have a finite amount of stored carbohydrates they can use to maintain a living state without being planted in soil, and this store is constantly dwindling through respiration. Respiration rate can be controlled by temperature; thus the colder the seedling is kept, the longer it remains dormant and the longer its carbohydrate reserves last. As the temperature of seedling stock rises, they are likely to experience mold or overheating and death (Ebata 1999).
9. Both Braidotti (2013) and Bennett (2012) take issue with the narrow view of assuming a thing's use-value only for humans. Braidotti (2013, 91–94) uses the idea of "becoming-machine" and Guattari's machinic autopoiesis to note the ways machines themselves are "intelligent and generative," while Bennett (2012, 263) argues for a move away from utility and toward things' "noninstrumentalizable aspects or thing-powers.".
10. As Brown (2012, 82) defines it, "The word dromosphere is derived from the Greek *dromos* meaning a race, a racetrack, or the rapid delivery of speech."
11. *Corduroy* is a term for a makeshift road made out of logs that enables passage over a water (or other impassable) source that, in more developed infrastructure, would require a culvert. The name comes from the way the logs look stacked next to one another, as in the wales of corduroy fabric.
12. "Each federal dollar invested in construction generated close to one half-hour of employment" (Lewis 2008) was the report on the American interstate system. Such roads also reduce freight costs, increase retail competition by increasing the geographic range of products, and contribute to creating domestic markets.
13. In the United States, an increased logistical ability to mobilize troops is represented by the US military's STAHNET, or Strategic Highway Corridor Network (Cox and Love 1996).
14. Logging is one of North America's deadliest jobs. British Columbia alone experiences an average of twenty-seven truck rollovers per year (BC Forest Safety Council 2016).

# Conclusion
## FROM ANTHROPOCENE TO CHORACENE
*The Power of a New Materialist Environmental Rhetoric for Staying with the Trouble*

How anthropocenic is the Anthropocene? This is the question we are left with at the end of considering the case of industrial tree planting. As Eileen Crist argues, the Anthropocene is itself a discourse that puts forward a singular story: of a wilderness gone for good, of humans characterized only, as Donna Haraway (2016a, 49–50) summarizes, by "managerial, technocratic, market-and-profit besotted, modernizing, and human-exceptionalist business-as-usual." In the discursive Anthropocene, we accept this story as a given. Our anthropos is always "man," always "not-animal," and the human is always at the cleansed forefront and linguistic neutrality of changing the natural world. As environmental humanities scholars have it, such a view elides darker moments of "destruction, depredation, rape, loss, devastation, deterioration" (Crist 2013, 133). The Anthropocene and its discourse prevails through its silencing of nonhumans in the service of the human enterprise (Crist 2013, 135). Yet this is a bleak, narcissistic story that describes a world we seek to own for as long as we are in it, which has led scholars to point out its use as a reflection of the "poverty of our nomenclature" (Crist 2013, 142) that tells a particular tale of the past and present and severely limits how we might imagine our future.

Scholars have argued for a re-envisioning of this discourse because it reifies a story that has only one possible ending, and such revisionist possibilities are rich—whether through embracing a new discourse of integration (Crist 2013), thinking through problems with anti-fragility as a model (Taleb 2014), imagining tentacular thinking (Haraway 2016a, 2016b), embracing ecological postmodernism (Griffin 1990; Spretnak 2011), fostering cross-species interdependence (Tsing 2012), or listening to narrative agencies (Iovino 2012). A look into the Anthropocene through tree-planting descriptions is also a look into the discourse of

DOI: 10.7330/9781607328551.c005

the Anthropocene itself. For although we are all sincerely caught up in this discourse—tree planters included—a closer look reveals that we, the anthropos, are never acting alone. Even as we claim for ourselves the rational economic man or the hubris of a geological force, our agency is distributed among nonhumans, organic and inorganic, and the non-rational affects that stick to and circulate among them. Yet our investment in the Anthropocene stops us from recognizing the many competing stories we tell and are told. When we pay attention to these stories—the ones we tell and the ones that are told through us—we sense a new environmental rhetoric at work, one that is both human and nonhuman, one attuned to the movement-oriented persuasion of bodies and things, one that listens to dreams and bodythinking, one that sits between savior-environmentalism and endless development, one that is ever embroiled with seeing life in death. Such a new environmental rhetoric turns to the chōra, turns to invention and to placeholding the Anthropocene to better mark it as transitory. It aims to preserve what is entangled rather than imagine such entanglement as problematic. Such a new materialist environmental rhetoric, then, provides a frame to listen *better* to our descriptions in the service of imagining alternate futures, of disrupting the ending to the anthropocenic story we tell.

A fundamental tension is revealed by a look at contemporary tree planting: that we exist in the long tail of an ongoing decision about the trouble we are in. To refer to this trouble is to invoke Haraway's (2016a, 1) appeal to stay with the trouble of the Anthropocene, to not "address trouble in terms of making an imagined future safe, of stopping something from happening that looms in the future, of clearing away the present and the past in order to make futures for coming generations. Staying with the trouble does not require such a relationship to times called the future. In fact, staying with the trouble requires learning to be truly present, not as a vanishing pivot between awful or edenic pasts and apocalyptic or salvific futures, but as mortal critters entwined in myriad unfinished configurations of places, times, matters, meanings."

Rhetoric is one way we might stay with this trouble, and recognizing a rhetorical ontology of nonhuman others, thick with affect—their prominent conflict and tension with human intentions—is one possible way to do so. To that end, it has been my aim to story the staying with this trouble through descriptions of human and nonhuman entanglements in order to examine the potential for an emergent new materialist environmental rhetoric: one that sees humans in a state of being-with devastated landscapes and the nonhuman bodies within them. There are real and lived contestations in the assumption that human experience and environmental awareness are simply "constructed by modern economics" (Killingsworth and Palmer 2012, 5). In turning to the chōra, to placemaking that depends on digression, getting stuck, and acknowledging surrounds, it is possible to acknowledge that as our bodies (and the bodies ever within us or around us) hum through time and space, we are both being unfolded by others and taking part in our own becoming, our own unfolding. As I've hoped to show throughout this book, humans are constantly working through particular tensions—troubles—that come from contradictions in distinguishing between self and other, between nature and culture, between human and nonhuman, between rational and non-rational. Whether we call it the nature-culture divide or the environmentalist-developmentalist tension, it is necessary to see ourselves as inconsistent creatures who make meaning within ambient, persuasive surrounds filled with the underivable rhetoricity of other beings rather than as solely agentive and self-made actors. We stay with the trouble because we live both in and against nature; inasmuch as we claim the boundary between, we are constantly caught up in blurring it.

So it is perhaps the work of the chōra to shrink the Anthropocene and the contribution of new materialism and critical affect studies to rhetoric that together allow us to focus differently on what is often known as situational or contextual "constraints" (Bitzer 1968, 6). A chōra that invents place by allowing the generative potential of specific geographies to bubble up, to arise, is already striving toward the network or constellation rather than the grid, pushing us to listen to the human as only ever one player in a complex linkage of biotic and a-biotic assemblages. This telling is sorely needed as one route out of the Anthropocene; as Haraway (2016a, 48) urges, "one must surely tell of the networks of sugar, precious metals, plantations, indigenous genocides, and slavery, with their labor innovations and relocations and recompositions of critters and things sweeping up both human and nonhuman workers of all kinds."

My attention to the Canadian tree-planting landscape and the choral connections that create it as an ambient plantation-space is one way to attend to Haraway's call. Such a telling has been in the service of hyperopia, an action that allows for far-sighted vision, bringing our attention to rhetoric's "effects that exceed," in Scot Barnett and Casey Boyles's (2017, 1) words, "human agency and intentionality." The work of the silvicultural plantation is more than designing a simple monocultured space; it is a reaching into the past and the future in a constant state of repetition, a constant memory-state of bodily entanglements and forces, a state that is attuned to the persuasive work of rhetorical energy.

I set up a framework for how to listen to planters' descriptions as they gave rise to a particular Canadian landscape: that we consider rhetorical forces as they work through an underivable rhetoricity of bodies; that we allow for circulations of affect to constitute relations among bodies; that we allow for a rhetorical ontology that does not depend on a linguistic, rational detour through logos. All three of these ideas suggest a particular kind of rhetorical attunement: they direct our attention to rhetorical force, to movement, processes, and transitions that offer the possibility of affect and agency distributed among vital bodies. Despite the desolate image of the plantation, among death and ruin there is no standing still. There is constant eating and being eaten. And there is only the possibility to try to make meaning from dwelling in these conditions. *Planting the Anthropocene* has been my attempt to write such a landscape "through its connections and meanings" (Rice 2007, 40), which recognize contemporary plantation spaces as temporal sites of disturbance-based inconsistency among humans and nonhumans. In such an environment, insects make persuasive decisions, roads are political agents, crows determine hypoglycemia, discourses of wilderness are shaped by trucks, tree roots determine labor efficiency, human dreams are made out of repetitive motion, shovels re-engineer the human body.

In recognizing the centrality of humanism and efficiency to tree planters' discourse in chapter 1, it was my intention to point to the explicit and unequivocal ways planters are caught up in discourses of the Anthropocene at the same time they maintain contradictory relations to the environmental dilemma in which they dwell: thick with vernaculars of slash and cream, dirtbags and dead walking, tree planters acknowledge that time is money and strive for a "personal best" at the same time they clearly recognize a landscape in which there is no direct correlation between input and output, in which they deal daily with tree-ghosts. This discrepancy is itself a rhetorical problem, a confusing foray beyond simple reason or rationality to explain human decision-making. It's one that I argue is better approached by scholars who position "rhetoric beyond human symbol use" and allow passage into the realm of what feminist philosopher Avital Ronell calls "contamination," a nature-culture blend so deep that it must disrupt the idea that we can only ever understand human decision-making through a myopic view of the anthropos (quoted in Davis and Ballif 2014, 349).

Allowing for a richer choric view of the Canadian tree-planting landscape required a different approach to thinking about the range of bodies that dwell there; thus chapter 2 located the planter-body (already an assemblage of human-shovel-tree-landscape) among animal bodies and plant bodies, firmly situating the material body as a site of rhetorical power and the space that holds material bodies in relation to one another as a site of distributed agency. What material feminists might call "trans-corporeality" (Alaimo 2014, 187) or "agential realism" (Barad 2007), we might recognize here through rhetoric's sensorium, spoken through the body. Whether expressed through human pain and pleasure, insect seasons or blood nuptials, crow memory or the persuasion of seedling roots, bodythinking provides possibilities for disruption of the discursive Anthropocene. Efficacy at the mercy of plant timescale and descriptions of persuasive interspecies entanglements provide some relief from anthropocenic notions of a nature separate from culture, of animality separate from humanity, of humanscapes separate from plantscapes. Instead, we understand this landscape as created out of these multiple forces and effects that circulate within and among bodies, blurring easy distinction and allowing us to stay with the trouble.

Part of what may allow humans to be present to the potentialities of species-thinking[1] that imagines humans as "mortal critters" sharing space, I argue, is the recognition of the way affect moves among these bodies in motion. On the one hand, the case of the Canadian plantation-scape may be read as a case for the stickiness of forest bodies, for how various bodies are "touched by what they are near," for the mutuality of feeling on bodies. While admittedly the focus on these affective exchanges in chapter 3 is primarily on human bodies (and thus this book would hardly qualify as a serious foray into posthumanism, thing-theory, or object-oriented ontology), the materiality of human affect, the rhetoric through which it is spoken and enacted, and the way it circulates between and among nonhumans is important to the anthropocenic moment for two reasons. The first, perhaps too simple, is that this is a book about humanism, written from the perspective of a scholar in the humanities. As Jane Bennett (2010, 120) notes, it is impossible not to acknowledge the contradiction inherent in the question "is it not, after all, a self-conscious, language-wielding human who is articulating this philosophy"? This book is about language-wielding humans. But it is also about the way humans need to acknowledge their engagement with (or composition of) *things* thought for too long to be somehow too far away from the humanist project. Humanists, in other words, need more of a way *in* to thinking about the role of nonhuman others. Thinking with a new materialist environmental frame allows us to think through the ways affect is generated rhetorically, how it circulates in our words and actions, how it sticks to things and then sticks to us, how it manifests in being touched by what we are near. It is one way in.

The second important contribution affect makes both to rhetoric and to thinning the Anthropocene is one I borrow from Megan Watkins (2010, 269), who, rather than point to the ephemeral structure of affect, instead points to the "capacity of affect to be retained, to accumulate, to form dispositions and thus shape subjectivities." Our affective entanglements with nonhuman others, in other words, have a capacity to stay with us, stay within us, shape us. We not only stay with the trouble, but the trouble stays with us. The cultivation of queer melancholia or deep ambivalence fosters a different *sense* in tree planters. It is possible, of course, that such an affective capacity is fleeting. But the possibility also exists that workers who live and plant among ghosts are not just "clearing away the present and the past in order to make futures for coming generations" (Haraway 2016a, 1). It is possible to view these affective investments as allowing particular transformations that might disrupt the Anthropocene by re-storying it beyond either hope or despair.

Finally, chapter 4 offers an attunement to environs that attends to horizontalizing relations between humans and nonhumans by acknowledging agency distributed among them, embracing a rhetorical ontology that gives rise to the contemporary tree-planting landscape. Rather than view things as separate from biotic beings, I instead view their role through agreement with scholars who note that such attention contains generative potential for acknowledging how rhetorical energy circulates among our entangled nonhuman worlds. Conceptualizing the road-body, truck-body, and helicopter-body as kin, acknowledging their knottedness in material and political relations with humans and their agentive role in both enabling and constraining discourses of the Anthropocene, shows them to be human-nonhuman networks that push against its tenets of "unbounded individualism" or the equation "man plus tool makes history" (Haraway 2016b). Instead, thing-bodies reveal complex relationships with human time, notions of efficiency, and human self-determination. They make promises, make worlds, and make politics, enlarging rhetoric's sensorium by the cultivation of affect, by interspecies mingling, by reminders of timescale, by shrinking or enlarging space, by persuasive kinesis. They also reveal that what we believe to be human situations—ongoing settler-indigenous land claims, ecotourist destinations—are in fact made up of movement-oriented persuasions that stem from a variety of bodies, only some of them human. Rather than make assumptions about how things are supposed to function *for* humans, such a new materialist view of the rhetoric of thing-bodies instead represents humanity as something inseparable from its surrounds. Recognizing the vibrancy of matter, its penchant for resilience, the way we are bound up in its networks, allows us to stay with the trouble because it requires that we learn to be newly present to a naturecultural rhetoric that comes from the world and isn't imposed on it.

## THE CANADIAN CHŌRA

Beyond an argument for changing the anthropocenic narrative, this book has also offered a methodological case for how to invent alternate endings; that is, it suggests that chorography, invention of the "history of 'place' in relation to memory" (Ulmer 1994, 39), is one way to do so. To imagine place as choric, then, is to see it, as Thomas Rickert (2013, 44) suggests, as "less a stable notion than an affective, circulating, and evolving series of encounters." Canadian cultural scholars have come to see the nation as marked by a desire for exploration, one that aspires to universality and shared culture by viewing wilderness as a domestication of nature and relying strongly on the nature-culture divide to do so. Such a divide, as Catriona Sandilands suggests, offers only two relations with nature: developing it or leaving it completely alone to be "wild." The outcome of any derivation arising from this split creates a kind of nature fantasy. Such an "abstract universal land," Sandilands (2000, 181–83) argues, "is not only unnatural but un-Canadian."

The descriptions of encounter offered here represent an attempt to interrupt this view of the developmentalist-preservationist divide that characterizes Canadians' relationships with their nationality and with the land—at least in terms of its universalizing desire to develop relations with "wild" spaces. However, this universalizing desire for a united Canada is the *settler* narrative; it only includes a monocultural desire for Canada as a European-colonial desire to inhabit the Canadian frontier-space and eradicate Indigenous people in doing so. This book, in laying a chorographical foundation for Canadian placemaking, bumps up against this same boundary: let there be no mistake that the tree planters here—and indeed, most industrial forestry workers—are telling settler narratives. It is a valid critique to say we cannot invent a different Canada by listening to the same voices. Yet in invoking the chōra here, I am not only interested in the capacity for such invention to be characterized by instability—the settler nation is an unstable nation—but also in noting that the settler nation represents a *limit* to notions of the "public" and that the chōra is made from bumping up against such limits "while retaining a dependency it wants to overcome" (Rickert 2013, 49). The possibilities of bumping up against the limiting colonial narrative do not come from tree planters themselves; instead, they come from the worlds of encounter they inhabit. The Canadian chōra is invented from mosquitoes, black flies, bears, owls, crows; out of undergrowth, understories, canopies, and emergent layers; out of disturbance and roots and fungus and nematodes and shovels and impermeable rock; out of water and gas and air and machine and compression and movement; out of human entanglement with all of these elements and with each other, all sticky with affects of both "belonging and abjection" (Sandilands 2000, 185). To invent out of these situated encounters is to discover the planter- (human-shovel-tree) body, the deer-fly-biting-at-eleven-o'clock; to bear the brunt of a crow's memory; to experience the isolation brought about by the waiting on vehicular time. It is to invent the Canadian landscape in the Anthropocene, a place that knows that there is no universal but only a constant recognition of human boundaries always in negotiation with the nonhuman. This premise is an obvious one for any scholar working with Indigenous ways of knowing, being, or researching—a web of all our relations that allows for hauntings, ghosts, and "(non)arguments" (Powell 2002); that gathers teachings from the bear, the beaver, the eagle, the turtle, the buffalo, the wolf;[2] that accepts non-linearity, intuition, holism, and matter and mind as inseparable.[3]

Yet this Canada is also a place where indigeneity itself is a modern political site of resistance and resurgence. Because Indigenous ontologies have been suppressed through violence and genocide, the potential for remembering our relations through entanglement, through circulation of affect, through recognition of a rhetoricity of all bodies represents a pushing at the settler narrative that may leave us with, as Sandilands (2000, 185) says, an "anarchic terrain in which one may well find abjection in the company of a human other and a friend in the company of a tree, thus opening the struggle for Canada to a wider variety of interactive/intersubjective possibilities than is currently possible." There is possibility in allowing Canada to be invented anew, to dwell in a site of resistance or anarchy, and to let resistance and resurgence emerge as challenges to, as Haraway (2016b) has it, our current "'unthinkable' theory of relations" that position us only in environmental or developmental camps—in other words, to stand as a dynamic chōra instead of static frontier or wilderness. I hope I have given shape to some of the ways choric thinking helps us move beyond dualisms by asking us to engage in boundary thinking as a wayfaring moment of beginning, a way of locating ourselves as we dwell in the movement of now, whenever that may be.

## EXCEEDING OUR LIMITS: STAYING WITH THE TROUBLE

While the case of Canadian tree planting is unique, the intervention of a new materialist environmental rhetoric as a way to understand how we might reconfigure our understanding of the anthropos in the Anthropocene carries suggestive potential. We might aim to understand a particular place and the material bodies and affects within it as a way to engage in the project of thinning the Anthropocene by tackling an understanding of a variety of naturecultural problems through rhetorical forces and effects. Cases that might be usefully framed this way are those that engage both endangered and invasive species, such as grass carp in the Great Lakes,[4] zebra mussels in hydroelectric dams, cheatgrass and wildfire cycles, knapweed and ranching, and the spread of gypsy moths. We might examine globalized travel and its impact on culture and commodities, such as Rapid Ōhiʻa Death (Ōhiʻa tree fungus) in Hawaii or the coconut rhinoceros beetle. We might use such a frame to think through climate change and its unforeseen impacts, such as the increase of the coffee berry borer, the cultivation of drought-tolerant seed, the breeding of high-yield cattle, or the change in infrastructure design to accommodate 500-year floods that now happen with regularity. Or we might examine contemporary examples of rapidly emergent human-nonhuman entanglements with ecosystems: phytocapping and methane capture in landfills, mercury levels in biomedical waste facilities, synthetic microfibers in oceans, or uranium from tailings ponds and water and soil poisoning. Each of these examples represents a case for which we might invent a specific place through its connections and meanings in time and space; locate ambient rhetorical bodies—humans and nonhumans, biotic and a-biotic—affects, intuitions, technologies, kinesis, and memories within that place; and allow the Anthropocene to be a boundary against which the chōra struggles.

A final possibility for a new materialist environmental rhetoric is to view it as a heuristic through which we might gather and organize scholarship that is assembled under many names and many disciplines. Burgeoning work in a range of fields seeks to examine material expressions of matter, nonhuman and embodied meaning making, unfolding worlds generated in motion, and affective interchanges as they construct contemporary ecological life. Each makes a persuasive case toward a rhetoric of natureculture, even when it does not see itself as belonging to rhetorical frameworks per se. Returning to rhetoric as seeing all available means of persuasion, we might examine how scholars in a range of scientific and humanistic fields that are engaging with natureculture make specific arguments about relational ways of being among humans, biota, and a-biota. It may be possible to speak this rhetoric as a thread through the mantle of interdisciplinary work in environmental humanities, politics, biology, climatology, sociology, feminist studies, anthropology, geography, and hydrology, to name a few of the ways specialists think with and through bodies. In these and other ways, we might work with one another to dynamically re-envision the Anthropocene—whether in terms of the Chthulucene and Plantationocene, as Haraway does, or, as McKenzie Wark (2017) does in imagining new architectural models, the Xenoscene (from *xenos*, the stranger) or the Symbebekoscene (from *symbebekos*, the accident). Invoking a rhetorical ontology through a new materialist environmental rhetoric allows us a way into the Choracene, a "new-where-things-take-place." Perhaps such a revision would allow a way of being that invites us to exceed the boundaries of the Anthropocene, allow us to mark our place by inventing it in a way not measured by the end but by an ongoing commitment to stay with the trouble, to discover the accident, to spend time with the stranger. And to dwell, to *be-with*, all our relations that do so with us.

## NOTES

1. See Chakrabarty 2009, 213.
2. Inclusive of the "Sabe," or human-like figure, these animals represent part of the seven sacred teachings of the Anishanaabe people.
3. See Berkes (1993, 4) and McGregor (2004) for a larger discussion of Traditional Ecological Knowledge (TEK), of which these are the premises.
4. See Sackey 2013.

# Appendix 1
## INTERVIEW QUESTIONS

1. How long have you been a tree planter? What year did you begin/how old were you when you started?

2. Could you tell me how you first got involved with tree planting?
    a. How did you hear about tree planting?
    b. What made you want to try tree planting?
    c. Where were you?
    d. How old were you/what year was it when you first started tree planting?

3. Describe for me a typical day spent planting trees.
    a. Did you return to tree planting after your initial experience?
    b. Did you have to travel to plant trees? Did that impact your experience in any way?

4. Tell me about your experiences planting trees. What was it like?
    a. What was the most rewarding part of your experience?
    b. What was the most difficult part of the experience?

5. What is your most vivid memory from the time you spent tree planting?

6. When you think back on your experiences tree planting and your life, how did your experience tree planting affect you?

7. As I've begun this project, planters have described a complex relationship with what they think of as wilderness or the wild. What would you say has been your relationship to it after your tree-planting experience?

8. What would you want people to know about planting?

# REFERENCES

"About the Regions." Tree-Planter.com. Accessed October 15, 2013. http://www.tree-planter.com/?navigation_id=90&page_id=207.
Agriculture and Agri-Business Canada. 2014. "An Overview of the Canadian Agriculture and Agri-Food System Highlights: 2014." Government of Canada. Accessed December 20, 2016. https://www.flickr.com/photos/aafc_canada/26250839314.
Ahmed, Sara. 2004. *The Cultural Politics of Emotion.* New York: Routledge.
Ahmed, Sara. 2010. "Happy Objects." In *The Affect Theory Reader*, edited by Melissa Gregg and Gregory J. Seigworth, 29–51. Durham, NC: Duke University Press.
Alaimo, Stacy. 2014. "Oceanic Origins, Plastic Activism, New Materialism at Sea." In *Material Ecocriticism*, edited by Serenella Iovino and Serpil Opperman, 186–202. Bloomington: Indiana University Press.
Alaimo, Stacy, and Susan Hekman. 2008. "Introduction: Emerging Models of Materiality in Feminist Theory." In *Material Feminisms*, edited by Stacy Alaimo and Susan Hekman, 1–19. Bloomington: Indiana University Press.
Althusser, Louis. 2003. *The Humanist Controversy and Other Writings.* Translated by G. M. Goshgarian. Edited by François Matheron. New York: Verso.
Anderson, Ben. 2009. "Affective Atmospheres." *Emotion, Space, and Society* 2: 77–81.
Baluška, František, Simcha Lev-Yadun, and Stefano Mancuso. 2010. "Swarm Intelligence in Plant Roots." *Trends in Ecology and Evolution* 25 (12): 682–83.
Barad, Karen. 2007. *Meeting the Universe Halfway: Quantum Physics and the Entanglement of Matter and Meaning.* Durham, NC: Duke University Press.
Barad, Karen. 2008. "Posthumanist Performativity: Toward an Understanding of How Matter Comes to Matter." In *Material Feminisms*, edited by Stacy Alaimo and Susan Hekman, 120–56. Bloomington: Indiana University Press.
Barnett, Scot, and Casey Boyle, eds. 2017. *Rhetoric, through Everyday Things.* Tuscaloosa: University of Alabama Press.
Batten, Tyler. 2014. "I Worked on a Tree-Planting Contract in the Tar Sands." *Vice*, December 4. Accessed April 10, 2017. https://www.vice.com/en_ca/article/qbe5ex/i-worked-on-a-tree-planting-contract-in-the-tar-sands-332.
BC Forest Safety Council. 2016. "2016-09-08: Updated Fatality and Rollover Stats for Forestry in BC." Accessed November 13, 2017. http://www.bcforestsafe.org/node/2848.
Bell, F. Wayne, Shelley Hunt, Jennifer Dacosta, Mahadev Sharma, Guy R. LaRocque, John A. Winters, and Steven G. Newmaster. 2014. "Effects of Silviculture Intensity on Plant Diversity Response Patterns in Young Managed Northern Temperate and Boreal Forests." *Ecoscience* 21 (304): 327–39.
Bennett, Jane. 2010. *Vibrant Matter: A Political Ecology of Things.* Durham, NC: Duke University Press.
Bennett, Jane. 2012. "Powers of the Hoard." In *Animal, Vegetable, Mineral: Ethics and Objects*, edited by Jeffrey Jerome Cohen, 237–69. Washington, DC: Oliphaunt.
Berkes, Fikret. 1993. "Traditional Ecological Knowledge in Perspective." In *Traditional Ecological Knowledge: Concepts and Cases*, edited by Julian T. Inglis, 1–9. Ottawa: International Development Research Centre.
Berlant, Lauren. 2009. "Affect Is the New Trauma." *Minnesota Review* (71–72): 131–36.
Bitzer, Lloyd. 1968. "The Rhetorical Situation." *Philosophy and Rhetoric* 1: 1–14.

Black, Rosemary, and Alice Crabtree, eds. 2007. *Quality Assurance and Certification in Ecotourism*. Oxfordshire, GB: CABI.

Blackman, Lisa. 2012. *Immaterial Bodies: Affect, Embodiment, Mediation*. London: Sage.

Blackman, Lisa. 2015. "Researching Affect and Embodied Hauntologies: Exploring an Analytics of Experimentation." In *Affective Methodologies*, edited by Britta Timm Knudson and Carsten Stage, 25–44. New York: Palgrave Macmillan.

Bodner, John. 1998. "*Slash Romance: An Ethnography and Occupational Folklife Study of an Ontario Tree Planting Camp*." MA thesis, Memorial University of Newfoundland, St. John's, Newfoundland, Canada.

Boyle, Casey. 2015. "The Rhetorical Question Concerning Glitch." *Computers and Composition* 35 (2015): 12–29.

Braidotti, Rosi. 2013. *The Posthuman*. Cambridge: Polity.

Bratta, Phillip. 2017. "Affective Research and Rhetorical Practices with Archives." Paper presented at the *Conference on College Composition and Communication*, Portland, Oregon, March 17.

Braun, Thomas, and Stephen Hanus. 2005. "Forest Fragmentation: Effects of Oil and Gas Activities on Alberta Forests." Accessed April 10, 2017. www.beg.utexas.edu/energy econ/thinkcorner/Forest_Fragmentation_Alberta.pdf.

Brennan, Teresa. 2004. *The Transmission of Affect*. Ithaca, NY: Cornell University Press.

Brockhouse, Charles, and John Kenneth Colbourne. 2007. "The Black Fly (Diptera: Simuliidae) Genome and EST Project." White paper. Accessed February 17, 2016. http://biology.creighton.edu/faculty/brockhouse/SimuliumWhitePaper.pdf.

Brown, Beverly A., Diana Leal-Mariño, Kirsten McIlveen, Ananda Lee Tan, and Sarah K. Loose. 2004. *Land Tenure, Trade, and Community Forestry: The Context for Restoration Forest Work in the NAFTA Region*. Wolf Creek, OR: Jefferson Center for Education and Research.

Brown, James J. 2012. "Composition in the Dromosphere." *Computers and Composition* 29: 79–91.

Buchanan, Brett. 2008. *Onto-Ethologies: The Animal Environments of Uexküll, Heidegger, Merleau-Ponty, and Deleuze*. Albany: State University of New York Press.

Bureau of Economic Analysis. 2016. "Gross Domestic Product by Industry: Second Quarter 2016." US Department of Commerce. Accessed December 20, 2016. http://www.bea.gov/newsreleases/industry/gdpindustry/2016/pdf/gdpind216.pdf.

Callaway, Ragan M., and Bruce E. Mahall. 2007. "Family Roots: Plant Ecology." *Nature* 448: 145–47.

Chakrabarty, Dipesh. 2009. "The Climate of History: Four Theses." *Critical Inquiry* 35: 197–222.

Chamovitz, Daniel. 2013. *What a Plant Knows*. New York: Scientific American.

Chen, Cecilia, Janine MacLeod, and Astrida Neimanis, eds. 2013. *Thinking with Water*. Montreal: McGill–Queens University Press.

Chilisa, Bagele. 2012. *Indigenous Research Methodologies*. Los Angeles: Sage.

Chisolm, Scott. 2009. "About Planting in B.C.'s Interior." Tree-Planter.com. Accessed February 15, 2017. http://www.tree-planter.com/2009/10/about-planting-in-b-c-s-interior/.

Clark, Jonathan. 2000. "Summer 2000." Replant.ca Planting Diaries. Accessed November 11, 2017. http://www.replant.ca/diaries2000.html.

Clark, Jonathan. 2013. "SOPs for Viewing Season." Replant.ca. Accessed April 17, 2017. http://www.replant.ca/phpBB3/viewtopic.php?f=26&t=66072&p=86719&hilit=stuck+truck#p86.

Clark, Jonathan. 2016a. "Dictionary of Planting Terms, and Acronyms." Replant.ca. Accessed April 19, 2017. http://www.replant.ca/dictionary.pdf.

Clark, Jonathan. 2016b. "Section 02: Why Do We Plant Trees?" Replant.ca. Accessed March 24, 2017. http://www.replant.ca/phpBB3/viewtopic.php?t=66639.

Clark, Jonathan. 2017. *Tree Planter Training 06: Camp Life.* YouTube video. Uploaded February 9, 2017. https://www.youtube.com/watch?v=9-ClmMrhNWU.
Clark, Mary E. 1989. *Ariadne's Thread: The Search for New Modes of Thinking.* Basingstoke, UK: Macmillan.
Clement, Stephanie. 2015. "To Plant a Million Trees." Treeplanter.com. Accessed September 24, 2017. http://www.tree-planter.com/2015/10/to-plant-a-million-trees/.
Clough, Patricia Ticineto. 2007. *The Affective Turn: Theorizing the Social.* Durham, NC: Duke University Press.
Cohen, Shaul. 1999. "Promoting Eden: Tree Planting as the Environmental Panacea." *Cultural Geographies* 6 (4): 424–46.
Cohen, Shaul. 2004. *Planting Nature: Trees and the Manipulation of Environmental Stewardship in America.* Berkeley: University of California Press.
Cowell, Douglas. 1982. "Treeplanters." *ForesTalk Resource Magazine* 6 (1): 16–25.
Cox, Wendell, and Jean Love. 1996. "40 Years of the US Interstate Highway System: An Analysis of the Best Investment a Nation Ever Made." *Highway and Motorway Factbook.* Accessed April 19, 2017. http://www.publicpurpose.com/freeway1.htm#def.
Craig, David R., Laurie Yung, and William T. Borrie. 2012. "Blackfeet Belong to the Mountains: Hope, Loss, and Blackfeet Claims to Glacier National Park, Montana." *Conservation and Society* 10 (3): 232–42.
Crist, Eileen. 2013. "On the Poverty of Our Nomenclature." *Environmental Humanities* 3: 129–47.
Cronon, William. 1995. "The Trouble with Wilderness; or, Getting Back to the Wrong Nature." In *Uncommon Ground: Toward Reinventing Nature,* edited by William Cronon, 69–90. New York: W. W. Norton.
Currie, Douglas C. 2014. "Black Flies (Diptera: Simuliidae) of the Prairie Grasslands of Canada." In *Arthropods of Canadian Grasslands, vol. 3: Biodiversity and Systematics, Part 1,* edited by Héctor A. Cárcamo and Donna J. Giberson, 371–87. Biological Survey of Canada.
Cvetkovich, Ann. 2003. *An Archive of Feeling: Trauma, Sexuality, and Lesbian Public Cultures.* Durham, NC: Duke University Press.
Cvetkovich, Ann. 2007. "Public Feelings." *South Atlantic Quarterly* 106 (3): 459–68.
Cwerner, Saulo B. 2006. "Vertical Flight and Urban Mobilities: The Promise and Reality of Helicopter Travel." *Mobilities* 1 (2): 191–215.
Damasio, Antonio. 1994. *Descartes Error: Emotion, Reason, and the Human Brain.* New York: Avon.
Damasio, Antonio. 2000. *The Feeling of What Happens: Body and Emotion in the Making of Consciousness.* New York: Harcourt.
Damasio, Antonio. 2003. *Looking for Spinoza: Joy, Sorrow, and the Feeling Brain.* New York: Harcourt.
Davies, John B. 2016. "Blackfly Biology." Accessed February 16, 2017. http://www.blackfly.org.uk/simbiol2.htm.
Davies, Laura. 2014. "Teaching with Love." *Composition Studies* 42 (2): 30–32.
Davis, Diane. 2011. "Creaturely Rhetorics." *Philosophy and Rhetoric* 44 (1): 88–94.
Davis, Diane. 2014. "Autozoography: Notes toward a Rhetoricity of the Living." *Philosophy and Rhetoric* 47 (4): 533–53.
Davis, Diane. 2017. "Afterwords: Some Reflections on the Limit." *Rhetoric Society Quarterly* 47 (3): 275–84.
Davis, Diane, and Michelle Ballif. 2014. "Guest Editor's Introductions: Pushing the Limits of the *Anthropos.*" *Philosophy and Rhetoric* 47 (4): 346–53.
Davis, Kim, Suzanne Biedenbach, Cara Minardi, Amanda Myers, and Tonya Ritola. 2014. "Affective Matters: Effective Measures for Transforming Basic Writing Programs and Instruction." *Open Words: Access and English Studies* 8 (1).

Deleuze, Gilles. 1988 [1970]. *Spinoza: Practical Philosophy*. Translated by Robert Hurley. San Francisco: City Lights Books.

Deleuze, Gilles. 1991 [1966]. *Bergsonism*. Translated by Hugh Tominson and Barbara Habberjam. New York: Zone Books.

Deleuze, Gilles. 1992. "Ethology: Spinoza and Us." In *Incorporations*, edited by Jonathan Crary and Sanford Kwinter, 625–33. New York: Zone Books.

Deleuze, Gilles, and Félix Guattari. 2003 [1987]. *A Thousand Plateaus*. Tenth printing. Translated by Brian Massumi. Minneapolis: University of Minnesota Press.

Derkowski, Kristel. 2016. *Six Million Trees*. Oakville, ON: Rock's Mills.

Derrida, Jacques. 2008. *The Animal That Therefore I Am*. Edited by Marie-Louise Mallet. Translated by David Wills. New York: Fordham University Press.

Dery, Mark. 2006. "Always Crashing in the Same Car: A Head-on Collision with the Technosphere." In *Against Automobility*, edited by Steffen Böhm, Campbell Jones, Chris Land, and Matthew Patterson, 223–39. Malden, GB: Blackwell.

Descola, Philippe. 2013. *Beyond Nature and Culture*. Translated by Janet Lloyd. Chicago: University of Chicago Press.

Directorate for Public Governance and Territorial Development. 2011. OECD Regional Typology. Organisation for Economic Co-operation and Development. Accessed April 21, 2017. https://www.oecd.org/gov/regional-policy/OECD_regional_typology_Nov2012.pdf.

Donath, Judith. 2011. "1964 Ford Falcon." In *Evocative Objects: Things We Think With*, edited by Sherry Turkle, 153–60. Cambridge: MIT Press.

Doyle, Richard M. 2011. *In Vivo—Darwin's Pharmacy: Sex, Plants, and the Evolution of the Noosphere*. Seattle: University of Washington Press.

Ducey, Ariel. 2007. "More Than a Job: Meaning, Affect, and Training Health Care Workers." In *The Affective Turn: Theorizing the Social*, edited by Patricia Ticineto Clough, 187–208. Durham, NC: Duke University Press.

Duncan, James R. 1997. "Great Gray Owls (*Strix Nebulosa Nebulosa*) and Management in North America: A Review and Recommendations." *Journal of Raptor Research* 31 (2): 160–66.

Dunk, Thomas. 1994. "Talking about Trees: Environment and Society in Forest Workers' Culture." *Canadian Review of Sociology and Anthropology* 31 (1): 14–34.

Du Plessis, Hester, and Gauhar Raza. 2004. "*Linking Indigenous Knowledge with Attitudes toward Science among Artisans in India and South Africa: A Collaboration.*" Paper presented at the conference Bridging Scales and Epistemologies, Alexandria, Egypt, March 17.

Eaton, Allen. 2001. "Black Flies." University of New Hampshire Cooperative Extension. Accessed February 16, 2017. http://www.ultimate.com/washington/wla/blackfly/.

Ebata, Tim. 1999. "6 Stock Handling, Storage, and Transportation." *Silviculture Manual*. Ministry of Forests Forest Practices Branch, Province of British Columbia. Accessed April 17, 2017. https://www.for.gov.bc.ca/hfp/publications/00099/planting/3-PrjMng-05.htm.

Edbauer, Jenny. 2005. "Unframing Models of Public Distribution: From Rhetorical Situation to Rhetorical Ecologies." *Rhetoric Society Quarterly* 35 (4): 5–24.

Edbauer Rice, Jenny. 2008. "The New 'New': Making a Case for Critical Affect Studies." *Quarterly Journal of Speech* 94 (2): 200–212.

Edwards, Paul N. 2003. "Infrastructure and Modernity: Force, Time, and Social Organization in the History of Sociotechnical Systems." In *Modernity and Technology*, edited by Thomas J. Misa, Philip Brey, and Andrew Feenberg, 185–225. Cambridge: MIT Press.

Ekers, Michael. 2012. "'Pounding Dirt All Day': Labour, Sexuality, and Gender in the British Columbia Reforestation Sector." *Gender, Place, and Culture: A Journal of Feminist Geography* 20 (7): 1–20.

Ekers, Michael, and Michael Farnan. 2010. "Planting the Nation: Tree Planting Art and the Endurance of Canadian Nationalism." *Space and Culture* 13: 95–120.

Ekers, Michael, and Brendan Sweeney. 2010. "(Dis)Organizing Tree Planters: Labour and Environmental Politics in the British Columbia Silviculture Industry." *BC Studies* 166: 73–101.

Ekman, Paul. 1995. "Silvan Tomkins and Facial Expression." In *Exploring Affect: The Selected Writings of Silvan S. Tomkins*, edited by E. Virginia Demos, 209–16. Cambridge: Cambridge University Press.

Escobar, Arturo. 2008. *Territories of Difference: Place, Movements, Life*. Durham, NC: Duke University Press.

Evernden, Neil. 1985. *The Natural Alien: Humankind and Environment*. Toronto: University of Toronto Press.

Fatnowna, Scott, and Harry Pickett. 2002. "The Place of Indigenous Knowledge Systems in the Post–Post Modern Integrative Paradigms Shift." In *Indigenous Knowledge and the Interaction of Knowledge Systems*, edited by Catherine O. Hoppers, 257–85. Cape Town, South Africa: New Africa Books.

Field, Dorothy. 2015. "An Inside Look at the Unist'ot'en Camp." *Vancouver Observer*, September 1. Accessed April 21, 2017. https://www.vancouverobserver.com/culture/inside-look-unistoten-camp.

Fitznor, Laara. 1998. "The Circle of Life: Affirming Aboriginal Philosophies in Everyday Living." In *Life Ethics in World Religions*, edited by Dawne C. McCance. Atlanta: Scholars Press.

Fitzsimons, Patrick. 2002. "Neoliberalism and Education: The Autonomous Chooser." *Radical Pedagogy* 4 (2): n.p. Accessed January 5, 2016. http://www.radicalpedagogy.org/radicalpedagogy/Neoliberalism_and_education__the_autonomous_chooser.html.

Forsyth, Luc. 2013. "Always Be Planting: Hurry up and Wait." Accessed April 17, 2017. http://blog.lucforsyth.com/2013/07/always-be-planting-hurry-up-and-wait/.

Foucault, Michel. 1969. *The Archeology of Knowledge*. Translated by Alan M. Sheridan Smith. New York: Routledge.

Fullarton, Catherine. 2014. "Review of *Plant Thinking: A Philosophy of Vegetal Life*." *Dialogue: Canadian Philosophical Review* 53 (2): 377–78.

Gagliano, Monica. 2017. "The Mind of Plants: Thinking the Unthinkable." *Communicative and Integrative Biology* 10 (2): n.p. Accessed March 2, 2017. http://dx.doi.org/10.1080/19420889.2017.1288333.

Galilei, Galileo. 1957. *Discoveries and Opinions of Galileo*. Translated by Stillman Drake. New York: Anchor.

Gaonkar, Dilip Parameshwar. 1997. "The Idea of Rhetoric in the Rhetoric of Science." In *Rhetorical Hermeneutics: Invention and Interpretation in the Age of Science*, edited by Alan G. Gross and William M. Keith, 25–85. Albany: State University of New York Press.

Garzón, Paco Calvo, and Fred Keijzer. 2011. "Plants: Adaptive Behavior, Root-Brains, and Minimal Cognition." *Adaptive Behavior* 19 (3): 155–71.

Gibbs, Anna. 2001. "Contagious Feelings: Pauline Hanson and the Epidemiology of Affect." *Australian Humanities Review* 24. Accessed March 29, 2017. http://www.australianhumanitiesreview.org/archive/Issue-December-2001/gibbs.html.

Gill, Charlotte. 2011. *Eating Dirt: Deep Forests, Big Timber, and Life with the Tree Planting Tribe*. Vancouver, BC: Greystone Books.

Goldman, Michael, and Rachel A. Schurman. 2000. "Closing the 'Great Divide': New Social Theory on Society and Nature." *Annual Review of Sociology* 25: 563–84.

Grassi, Ernesto. 1988. "The Rehabilitation of Rhetorical Humanism: Regarding Heidegger's Anti-Humanism." Translated by R. Scott Walker. *Diogenes* 36 (142): 136–56.

Grassi, Ernesto. 2001. *Rhetoric as Philosophy: The Humanist Tradition*. Translated by John Michael Krois and Azizeh Azodi. Carbondale: Southern Illinois University Press.

Gray, Jonathan M. 2017. "Vultures: Consumptions and Conjurings." *Rhetoric Society Quarterly* 47 (3): 238–46.

Greenwalt, Dustin. 2016. "Affective Capture in Michelle Obama's 'Let's Move' Campaign." Paper presented at the *Rhetoric Society of America Conference*, Atlanta, Georgia, May 27.

Gregg, Melissa, and Gregory J. Seigworth. 2010. *The Affect Theory Reader*. Durham, NC: Duke University Press.

Gries, Laurie. 2015. *Still Life with Rhetoric*. Logan: Utah State University Press.

Griffin, David Ray. 1990. "Introduction to SUNY Series in Constructive Postmodern Thought." In *Sacred Interconnections: Postmodern Spirituality, Political Economy, and Art*, edited by David Ray Griffin, ix–xii. New York: State University of New York Press.

Gross, Daniel M. 2006. *The Secret History of Emotion: From Aristotle's "Rhetoric" to Modern Brain Science*. Chicago: University of Chicago Press.

Grossberg, Lawrence. 1992. *We Gotta Get Out of This Place: Popular Conservatism and Postmodern Culture*. New York: Routledge.

Haber, Samuel. 1964. *Efficiency and Uplift: Scientific Management in the Progressive Era 1890–1920*. Chicago: University of Chicago Press.

Haeussler, Sybille. 1989. "Mounding for Site Preparation." *Synopsis: Topic Summary for the Operational Forester*. Forest Resource Development Agreement Memo 100. Victoria, BC: Government of Canada.

Haff, Peter K. 2013. "Technology as a Geological Phenomenon: Implications for Human Well-Being." In *A Stratigraphical Basis for the Anthropocene*, edited by Colin N. Waters, Jan A. Zalasiewicz, Mark Williams, Michael A. Ellis, and Andrea M. Snelling, 395–403. London: Geological Society of London.

Hall, Matthew. 2011. *Plants as Persons*. Albany: State University of New York Press.

Hammer, Steven. 2017. "More Than a Feeling: Cultivating Affect Studies in Composition and Rhetoric." Paper presented at the *Conference on College Composition and Communication*, Portland, Oregon, March 17.

Haraway, Donna. 2003. *The Companion Species Manifesto: Dogs, People, and Significant Others*. Chicago: Prickly Paradigm.

Haraway, Donna. 2008. "Otherworldly Conversations, Terran Topics, Local Terms." In *Material Feminisms*, edited by Stacy Alaimo and Susan Hekman, 157–87. Bloomington: Indiana University Press.

Haraway, Donna. 2015. "Anthropocene, Capitalocene, Plantationocene, Chthulucene: Making Kin." *Environmental Humanities* 6: 159–65.

Haraway, Donna. 2016a. *Staying with the Trouble: Making Kin in the Chthulucene*. Durham, NC: Duke University Press.

Haraway, Donna. 2016b. "Tentacular Thinking: Anthropocene, Capitalocene, Chthulucene." *E-Flux Architecture* 75. Accessed May 8, 2017. https://www.e-flux.com/journal/75/67125/tentacular-thinking-anthropocene-capitalocene-chthulucene/.

Haraway, Donna, Noburu Ishikawa, Scott F. Gilbert, Kenneth Olwig, Anna L. Tsing, and Nils Bubant. 2016. "Anthropologists Are Talking—About the Anthropocene." *Ethnos: Journal of Anthropology* 81 (3): 535–64.

Haraway, Donna, and Anna Tsing. 2015. "Tunneling in the Chthulucene: Stories for Resurgence on a Damaged Planet." Paper presented at the Association for the Study of Literature and the Environment Conference, Moscow, Idaho, June 25.

Hardt, Michael. 2007. "Foreword: What Affects Are Good For." In *The Affective Turn: Theorizing the Social*, edited by Patricia Ticineto Clough, ix–xiii. Durham, NC: Duke University Press.

Harvey, David. 1996. *Justice, Nature, and the Geography of Difference*. Cambridge: Blackwell.

Harvey, Penny, and Hannah Knox. 2012. "The Enchantments of Infrastructure." *Mobilities* 7 (4): 521–36.

Hawhee, Debra. 2011. "Toward a Bestial Rhetoric." *Philosophy and Rhetoric* 44 (1): 81–87.

Hawhee, Debra. 2015. "Rhetoric's Sensorium." *Quarterly Journal of Speech* 101 (1): 2-17.

Hawhee, Debra. 2017. *Rhetoric in Tooth and Claw: Animals, Language, Sensation*. Chicago: University of Chicago Press.

Hawk, Byron. 2003. "Hyperrhetoric and the Inventive Spectator: Remotivating the Fifth Element." In *The Terministic Screen: Rhetorical Perspectives on Film*, edited by David Blakesley, 70–91. Carbondale: Southern Illinois University Press.

Hawk, Byron. 2007. *A Counter-History of Composition: Toward Methodologies of Complexity*. Pittsburgh: University of Pittsburgh Press.

Hays, Samuel P. 1959. *Conservation and the Gospel of Efficiency: The Progressive Conservation Movement, 1890–1920*. Cambridge: Harvard University Press.

Hays, Samuel P. 1987. *Beauty, Health, and Permanence: Environmental Politics in the United States, 1955–1985*. New York: Cambridge University Press.

Heckman, Davin. 2002. "Glossary." *Rhizomes* 5. Accessed February 9, 2017. http://www.rhizomes.net/issue5/poke/glossary.html.

Heilbroner, Robert L. 1953. *The Worldly Philosophers: The Lives, Times, and Ideas of the Great Economic Thinkers*. New York: Simon and Schuster.

Hemsworth, Wade. 1949. "The Black Fly Song." Accessed February 16, 2017. https://www.youtube.com/watch?v=qjLBXb1kgMo.

Hetherington, Kregg. 2014. "Waiting for the Surveyor: Development Promises and the Temporality of Infrastructure." *Journal of Latin American and Caribbean Anthropology* 19 (2): 195–211.

Holmevik, Jan Rune. 2012. *Inter/vention: Free Play in the Age of Electracy*. Cambridge: MIT Press.

Hood, Eran, Mark W. Williams, and Diane M. McKnight. 2005. "Sources of Dissolved Organic Matter (DOM) in a Rocky Mountain Stream Using Chemical Fractionation and Stable Isotopes." *Biogeochemistry* 74: 231–55.

Indigenous and Northern Affairs Canada. 2010. "Land Claims." Government of Canada. Accessed April 20, 2017. https://www.aadnc-aandc.gc.ca/eng/1100100030285/1100100030289.

Ingersoll, Robert G. 2009 [1990]. *The Works of Robert G. Ingersoll, vol. 8: Interviews*. 12 vols. New York: Cosimo.

Ingold, Timothy. 2000. *The Perception of the Environment: Essays in Livelihood, Dwelling, and Skill*. New York: Routledge.

Iovino, Serenella. 2012. "Stories from the Thick of Things: Introducing Material Ecocriticism." Part 1 of Serenella Iovino and Serpil Oppermann, "Theorizing Material Ecocriticism: A Dipthych." *Material Ecocriticism*. Edited by Heather Sullivan and Dana Phillips. Special issue of *Interdisciplinary Studies in Literature and Environment* 19 (3): 448–60.

Iovino, Serenella, and Serpil Opperman, eds. 2014. *Material Ecocriticism*. Bloomington: Indiana University Press.

Jain, Juliet, and Glenn Lyons. 2008. "The Gift of Travel Time." *Journal of Transport Geography* 16 (2): 1–36.

Jefferson Center for Educational Research. 2003. "Voices in the Woods: Lives and Experiences of Non-Timber Forest Workers." *Pacific West Community Forestry Center*. Accessed October 11, 2013. http://sierrainstitute.us/PWCFC/publications/voices.htm.

Jevons, William Stanley. 1888. *The Theory of Political Economy*. Library of Economics and Liberty. Accessed October 22, 2017. http://www.econlib.org/library/YPDBooks/Jevons/jvnPE.html.

Johnson, Cayden. 2016. "Dirt Bag Geniuses: How Planting Trees Gives Artists Room to Grow." *Martlet*. Accessed January 20, 2017. http://www.martlet.ca/dirt-bag-geniuses-how-planting-trees-gives-artists-room-to-grow/.

Johnson, Maureen, Daisy Levy, Katie Manthey, and Maria Novotny. 2015. "Embodiment: Embodying Feminist Rhetorics." *Peitho* 18 (1): 39–44.

Keller, Robert H., and Michael F. Turek. 1999. *American Indians and National Parks*. Tucson: University of Arizona Press.

Kennedy, George A. 1992. "A Hoot in the Dark: The Evolution of General Rhetoric." *Philosophy and Rhetoric* 25 (1): 1–21.

Killingsworth, M. Jimmie, and Jacqueline S. Palmer. 2012. *Ecospeak: Rhetoric and Environmental Politics in America*. Carbondale: Southern Illinois University Press.
King, Barbara. 2013. "When Animals Mourn." *Scientific American* 309 (1): 62–67.
Kohn, Eduardo. 2013. *How Forests Think: Toward an Anthropology Beyond the Human*. Berkeley: University of California Press.
Lamont, Mark. 2017. "Ruin or Repair? Infrastructural Sociality and an Economy of Disappearances along a Rural Road in Kenya." In *The Making of an African Road*, edited by Kurt Beck, Gabriel Klaeger, and Michael Stasik, 171–96. Leiden: Brill.
Latour, Bruno. 2004. *Politics of Nature: How to Bring the Sciences into Democracy*. Cambridge: Harvard University Press.
Laurie, Timothy. 2015. "Becoming-Animal Is a Trap for Humans: Deleuze and Guattari in *Madagascar*." In *Deleuze and the Non/Human*, edited by Jon Roffe and Hannah Stark, 142–62. New York: Palgrave-Macmillan.
Law, John. 2004. *After Method: Mess in Social Science Research*. New York: Routledge.
Lee, Michael C., and Irene Tracey. 2010. "Unravelling the Mystery of Pain, Suffering, and Relief with Brain Imaging." *Current Pain and Headache Reports* 14 (2): 124–31.
"Let's Talk about Tree Planting!" *Silviculture Canada*. Accessed August 15, 2016. http://www.silviculturecanada.ca/treeplanting.html.
Lewis, Tom. 2008. "Eisenhower's Roads." *Los Angeles Times*, December 26. Accessed April 19, 2017. http://www.latimes.com/la-oe-lewis26-2008dec26-story.html.
Leys, Ruth. 2011. "The Turn to Affect: A Critique." *Critical Inquiry* 37: 434–72.
Liestol, Gunnar, Andrew Morrison, and Terje Rasmussen. 2004. *Digital Media Revisited: Theoretical and Conceptual Innovations in Digital Domains*. Cambridge: MIT Press.
Lindquist, Julie. 2004. "Class Affects, Classroom Affectations: Working through the Paradoxes of Strategic Empathy." *College English* 67: 187–209.
Loe, Kelin. 2016. "The Dog-Star's Skin: Haptic Rhetorics, Ability, and Nonhuman (and Human) Animals." Paper presented at the *Rhetoric Society of America Conference, Atlanta, Georgia, May 28*.
Londo, Andrew J., and Stephen G. Dicke. 2006. "Measuring Survival and Planting Quality in New Pine Plantations." *Southern Regional Extension Forestry*.
Lorimer, Jamie. 2012. "Multinatural Geographies for the Anthropocene." *Progress in Human Geography* 36 (5): 593–612.
Luke, Paul. 2014. "The Pains and Gains of Tree Planters: Five Months of Repetitive Work in Harsh Terrain Can Pay up to $500-a-Day." Vancouver, BC: *The Province*, May 29. Accessed August 15, 2016. http://www.theprovince.com/Pains+gains+tree+planters+Five+months+repetitive+work+harsh+terrain/9894094/story.html.
Luther, Jason. 2017. "Handcrafted Rhetorics: DIY and the Public Power of Made Things." Paper presented at the *Conference on College Composition and Communication, Portland, Oregon, March 17*.
Lynn, William. 1998. "Animals, Ethics, and Geography." In *Animal Geographies: Place, Politics, and Identity in the Nature-Culture Borderlands*, edited by Jennifer Wolch and Jody Emil, 280–98. London: Verso.
Maffi, Luisa, ed. 2001. *On Biocultural Diversity: Linking Language, Knowledge and the Environment*. Washington, DC: Smithsonian Institution Press.
Mailloux, Steven. 2012. "Humanist Controversies: The Rhetorical Humanism of Ernesto Grassi and Michael Leff." *Philosophy and Rhetoric* 45 (2): 134–47.
Manning, Erin. 2010. "Always More Than One." *Body and Society* 16 (1): 117–27.
Manno, Tony. 2016. "Big Oil and Gas Want Them Out, But One Small Clan Is Standing Up to Pipeline Expansion." *Yes! Magazine*, January 19. Accessed April 21, 2017. https://www.yesmagazine.org/planet/big-oil-and-gas-want-them-out-but-one-small-clan-is-standing-up-to-pipeline-expansion-20160119.
Marcus, George E., and Erkan Saka. 2006. "Assemblage." *Theory, Culture, and Society* 23 (2–3): 101–9.

Marcus, Sharon, Heather Love, and Stephen Best. 2016. "Building a Better Description." *Representations* 135: 1–21.
Marder, Michael. 2013a. *Plant-Thinking: A Philosophy of Vegetal Life*. New York: Columbia University Press.
Marder, Michael. 2013b. "What Is Plant Thinking?" *Klesis—revue philosophique* 25: 124–43.
Martin, Gary. 2017. "The Meaning and Origin of the Expression: Dirt Bag." *Phrase Finder*. Accessed January 20, 2017. http://www.phrases.org.uk/meanings/dirt-bag.html.
Martin, Sean. 2017. "25 Wild Stories from Canadian Tree Planting." *Mindful Steward*, May 1. Accessed November 12, 2017. http://themindfulsteward.com/treeplanting-stories/.
Marzluff, John M., Jeff Walls, Heather N. Cornell, John C. Withey, and David P. Craig. 2010. "Lasting Recognition of Threatening People by Wild American Crows." *Animal Behaviour* 79 (2010): 699–707.
Massa, Gioia, and Simon Gilroy. 2003. "Touch Modulates Gravity Sensing to Regulate the Growth of Primary Roots of *Arabidopsis Thaliana*." *Plant Journal* 33: 435–45.
Massumi, Brian. 1995. "The Autonomy of Affect." *Cultural Critique* 31: 83–109.
Massumi, Brian. 2002. *Parables for the Virtual: Movement, Affect, Sensation*. Durham, NC: Duke University Press.
Mazzolini, Elizabeth. 2015. *The Everest Effect: Nature, Culture, Ideology*. Tuscaloosa: University of Alabama Press.
McGregor, Deborah. 2004. "Coming Full Circle: Indigenous Knowledge, Environment, and Our Future." *American Indian Quarterly* 28 (3–4): 385–410.
McNely, Brian. 2017. "Circulatory Intensities: Take a Book, Return a Book." In *Rhetoric, through Everyday Things*, edited by Scot Barnett and Casey Boyle, 139–54. Tuscaloosa: University of Alabama Press.
McNely, Brian. 2017. "Archives, Affects, Ambience." Paper presented at the *Conference on College Composition and Communication, Portland, Oregon, March 16*.
McSheffrey, Elizabeth. 2015. "What You Need to Know about the Unist'ot'en-Pipeline Standoff." *Vancouver Observer*, August 31. Accessed April 21, 2017. https://www.vancouverobserver.com/news/what-you-need-know-about-unistoten-pipeline-standoff?page=0%2C0.
MFA (Manitoba Forestry Association). 2011. "Planting Instructions." ThinkTrees. Accessed March 3, 2017. http://www.thinktrees.org/planting_instructions.aspx.
Micciche, Laura. 2002. "More Than a Feeling: Disappointment and WPA Work." *College English* 67: 432–58.
Micciche, Laura. 2007. *Doing Emotion: Rhetoric, Writing, Teaching*. Portsmouth, NH: Boynton/Cook.
Mills, Gayla. 2011. "Preparing for Emotional Sessions." *Writing Lab Newsletter* 35 (5–6): 1–5.
Mills, William. 1982. "Metaphorical Vision: Changes in Western Attitudes to the Environment." *Annals of the Association of American Geographers* 72 (2): 237–53.
Minister of Public Works and Government Services Canada. 2010. "Northern Land Use Guidelines—Access: Roads and Trails." Northwest Territories Publication. Accessed April 19, 2017. https://www.aadnc-aandc.gc.ca/eng/1100100023568/1100100023583#sub2_1.
Morrison, James. 1994. "Protected Areas in Canada." In *Place of the Wild*, edited by David Clark Burks, 291–307. Washington, DC: Island.
Morrison, Margaret. 2001. "Hypertextuality's Queer Chorography." *Kairos* 6 (2): n.p.
Mortimer-Sandilands, Catriona. 2010. "Melancholy Natures, Queer Ecologies." In *Queer Ecologies: Sex, Nature, Politics, Desire*, edited by Catriona Mortimer-Sandilands, Bruce Erickson, and Stacy Alaimo, 332–58. Bloomington: Indiana University Press.
Morton, Tim. 2011. "Here Comes Everything: The Promise of Object-Oriented Ontology." *Qui Parle* 19 (2): 163–90.

Mucklebauer, John. 2011. "Domesticating Animal Theory." *Philosophy and Rhetoric* 44 (2): 95–100.
Mucklebauer, John. 2017. "Implicit Paradigms of Rhetoric: Aristotelian, Cultural, and Heliotropic." In *Rhetoric, through Everyday Things*, edited by Scot Barnett and Casey Boyle, 30–41. Tuscaloosa: University of Alabama Press.
Natural Resources Canada. 2002. "Fundamentals of Remote Sensing 5.3.1 Clear Cut Mapping and Deforestation." Government of Canada. Accessed September 24, 2017. http://pages.csam.montclair.edu/~chopping/rs/CCRS/chapter5/chapter5_6_e.html.
Natural Resources Canada. 2016. "10 Key Facts on Canada's Natural Resources." Government of Canada. Accessed December 20, 2016. https://www.nrcan.gc.ca/sites/www.nrcan.gc.ca/files/files/pdf/10_key_facts_nrcan_2016-access_e.pdf.
Nealon, Jeffrey T. 2016. *Plant Theory: Biopower and Vegetable Life*. Stanford, CA: Stanford University Press.
Neimanis, Astrida, Cecilia Åsberg, and Johan Hedrén. 2015. "Four Problems, Four Directions for Environmental Humanities: Toward Critical Posthumanities for the Anthropocene." *Ethics and the Environment* 20 (1): 67–97.
Nelson, Julie D. 2016. "An Unnecessary Divorce: Integrating the Study of Affect and Emotion in New Media." *Composition Forum* 34. Accessed April 28, 2017. http://compositionforum.com/issue/34/unnecessary-divorce.php.
Nicotra, Jodie. 2017. "Assemblage Rhetorics: Creating New Frameworks for Rhetorical Action." In *Rhetoric, through Everyday Things*, edited by Scot Barnett and Casey Boyle, 185–96. Tuscaloosa: University of Alabama Press.
Oelschlaeger, Max. 1991. *The Idea of Wilderness: From Prehistory to the Age of Ecology*. New Haven, CT: Yale University Press.
Öhman, Arne. 2006. "Making Sense of Emotion: Evolution, Reason, and the Brain." *Daedalus* 135 (3): 33–45.
Olwig, Kenneth R. 2011. "Choros, Chora, and the Question of Landscape." In *Envisioning Landscapes, Making Worlds: Geography and the Humanities*, edited by Stephen Daniels, Douglas Richardson, Dydia DeLyser, and James Ketchum, 44–54. London: Routledge.
Opperman, Serpil. 2014. "From Ecological Postmodernism to Material Ecocriticism: Creative Materiality and Narrative Agency." In *Material Ecocriticism*, edited by Serenella Iovino and Serpil Opperman, 21–36. Bloomington: Indiana University Press.
Ortega, Milene. 2016. "The Rhetoric of Emotional Suppression as an Index of Civilization in Fin de Siècle American Literature." Paper presented at the *Rhetoric Society of America Conference, Atlanta, Georgia, May 29*.
Outland Reforestation. 2017. "FAQs." Accessed February 15, 2017. http://www.outlandplanting.ca/faqs.aspx#h.
Paharia, Neeru, Anat Keinan, Jill Avery, and Juliet B. Schor. 2011. "The Underdog Effect: The Marketing of Disadvantage and Determination through Brand Biography." *Journal of Consumer Research* 37 (5): 775–90.
Parks Canada. 2016. "Working Together: Our Stories." Accessed October 21, 2016. http://www.pc.gc.ca/eng/agen/aa/te-wt/introduction.aspx.
Parrish, Alex C. 2014. *Adaptive Rhetoric: Evolution, Culture, and the Art of Persuasion*. New York: Routledge.
Patterson, Dennis Glen, and Lillian Eva Dyck. 2015. On-Reserve Housing and Infrastructure: Recommendations for Change. Report, Standing Senate Committee on Aboriginal Peoples. Accessed April 20, 2017. https://sencanada.ca/content/sen/Committee/412/appa/rep/rep12jun15-e.pdf.
Pepper, David. 1996. *Modern Environmentalism*. London: Routledge.
Peters, John Durham. 2015. *The Marvelous Clouds: Toward a Philosophy of Elemental Media*. Chicago: University of Chicago Press.

Pflugfelder, Ehren Helmut. 2017. *Communicating Mobility and Technology: A Material Rhetoric for Persuasive Transportation*. New York: Routledge.

Pilgrim, Sarah, and Jules Pretty. 2010. "Nature and Culture: An Introduction." In *Nature and Culture: Rebuilding Lost Connections*, edited by Sarah Pilgrim and Jules Pretty, 1–20. London: Earthscan.

Plec, Emily, Henry Hughes, and Jackson Stalley. 2017. "The Salmon Imperative." *Rhetoric Society Quarterly* 47 (3): 247–56.

Plummer, Eric. 2012. "A Nostalgic Look at Tree Planting." *Hinton* (Alberta) *Parklander*, July 9. Accessed August 15, 2016.

Powell, Malea. 2002. "Listening to Ghosts: An Alternative (Non)Argument." In *Alt/Dis: Alternative Discourses and the Academy*, edited by Christopher Schroeder, Helen Fox, and Patricia Bizzell, 11–22. Portsmouth, NH: Boynton/Cook Heinemann.

Powell, Malea. 2011. "All Our Relations: Contested Space, Contested Knowledge." Call for Papers, Conference on College Composition and Communication. Urbana, IL: National Council for Teachers of English. Accessed May 3, 2017. http://www.ncte.org/library/nctefiles/groups/cccc/convention/2011/4c_callfor_2011b.pdf.

Pretty, Jules. 2007. *The Earth Only Endures: On Reconnecting with Nature and Our Place in It*. London: Earthscan.

Princen, Thomas. 2005. *The Logic of Sufficiency*. Cambridge: MIT Press.

Probyn, Elspeth. 2010. "Writing Shame." In *The Affect Theory Reader*, edited by Melissa Gregg and Gregory J. Seigworth, 71–92. Durham, NC: Duke University Press.

Rackham, Oliver. 2015. *Woodlands*. New York: HarperCollins.

Rankin, Jim. 2005. "Digging, Screaming, Crying; Every Summer, Thousands of Young Ontarians Travel North to Plant Trees." *Toronto Star*, July 31, AO6.

Rice, Jeff. 2007. *The Rhetoric of Cool: Composition Studies and New Media*. Carbondale: Southern Illinois University Press.

Rickards, Lauren. 2015. "Metaphor and the Anthropocene: Presenting Humans as a Geological Force." *Geographical Research (June)*: 1–8.

Rickert, Thomas. 2013. *Ambient Rhetoric: The Attunements of Rhetorical Being*. Pittsburgh: University of Pittsburgh Press.

Riley, Denise. 2005. *Impersonal Passion: Language as Affect*. Durham, NH: Duke University Press.

Rivers, Nathaniel. 2015. "Deep Ambivalence and Wild Objects: Toward a Strange Environmental Rhetoric." *Rhetoric Society Quarterly* 45 (5): 420–40.

Rivers, Nathaniel. 2018. "Better Footprints." In *Tracing Rhetoric and Material Life: Ecological Approaches*, edited by Bridie McGreavy, Justine Wells, George F. McHendry Jr., and Samantha Senda-Cook, 169–96. New York: Palgrave Macmillan.

Roberts, Delia. 2002. "In-Season Physiological and Biochemical Status of Reforestation Workers." *Journal of Occupational and Environmental Medicine* 44 (6): 559–67.

Robillard, Amy. 2007. "We Won't Get Fooled Again: On the Absence of Angry Responses to Plagiarism in Composition Studies." *College English* 70: 10–31.

Ross, Sean. 2015. "What Percentage of the Global Economy Is Comprised of the Forest Products Sector?" *Investopedia*, January 20. Accessed August 17, 2016. https://www.investopedia.com/ask/answers/030515/what-percentage-global-economy-comprised-financial-services-sector.asp.

Ruyter, Nancy Lee Chalfa. 1999. *The Cultivation of Body and Mind in Nineteenth-Century Delsartism*. Westport, CT: Greenwood.

Sackey, Donnie Jonson. 2013. "*The Curious Case of the Asian Carp: Spatial Performances and the Making of an Invasive Species*." PhD dissertation, Michigan State University, Lansing.

Sandilands, Catriona. 2000. "Domestic Politics: Multiculturalism, Wilderness, and the Desire for Canada." *Space and Culture* 2: 169–86.

Sandilands, Catriona. 2002. "Between the Local and the Global: Clayoquot Sound and Simulacral Politics." In *A Political Space: Reading the Global through Clayoquot Sound*, edited by Warren Magnusson and Karena Shaw, 139–67. Montreal: McGill University Press.

Sarathy, Brinda. 2012. *Pineros: Latino Labour and the Changing Face of Forestry in the Pacific Northwest*. Vancouver: University of British Columbia Press.

Schutten, Julie "Madrone" Kalil, and Caitlyn Burford. 2017. "'Killer' Metaphors and the Wisdom of Captive Orcas." *Rhetoric Society Quarterly* 47 (3): 257–63.

Sedgwick, Eve Kosofsky, and Adam Frank. 1995. "Shame in the Cybernetic Fold: Reading Silvan Tomkins." *Critical Inquiry* 21 (2): 496–522.

Seegert, Natasha. 2014. "Play of Sniffication: Coyotes Sing in the Margins." *Philosophy and Rhetoric* 47 (2): 158–78.

Seigworth, Gregory J., and Melissa Gregg. 2010. "An Inventory of Shimmers." In *The Affect Theory Reader*, edited by Melissa Gregg and Gregory J. Seigworth, 1–25. Durham, NC: Duke University Press.

Selzer, Jack, and Sharon Crowley, eds. 1999. *Rhetorical Bodies*. Madison: University of Wisconsin Press.

Serres, Michel, and Bruno Latour. 1995. *Conversations on Science, Culture, and Time*. Translated by Roxanne Lapidus. Ann Arbor: University of Michigan Press.

*78 Days: A Reforestation Season*. Directed by Jason Nardella. October 16, 2011. https://vimeo.com/62827819.

Sheldon, Rebekah. 2015. "Form/Matter/Chora: Object-Oriented Ontology and Feminist New Media." In *The Nonhuman Turn*, edited by Richard Grusin, 193–222. Minneapolis: University of Minnesota Press.

Sherman, David. 2016. "Toward an Ambient Pedagogy: Mobilizing Affect across Composing Networks." Paper presented at the *Rhetoric Society of America Conference, Atlanta, Georgia, May 27*.

Smith, Linda Tuhiwai. 2012. *Decolonizing Methodologies: Research and Indigenous Peoples*. London: Zed Books.

Spretnak, Charlene. 2011. *Relational Reality: New Discoveries of Interrelatedness That Are Transforming the Modern World*. Topsham, ME: Green Horizon Books.

Stenberg, Shari. 2011. "Teaching and (Re)Learning the Rhetoric of Emotion." *Pedagogy* 11 (2): 349–69.

Stewart, Kathleen. 2007. *Ordinary Affects*. Durham, NC: Duke University Press.

Strathern, Marilyn. 1980. "No Nature, No Culture: The Hagen Case." In *Nature, Culture, and Gender*, edited by Carol P. MacCormack and Marilyn Strathern, 174–222. New York: Cambridge University Press.

Supreme Court Judgments. 2014. "*Grassy Narrows First Nation v. Ontario* (Natural Resources)." Judgments of the Supreme Court of Canada. Accessed April 20, 2017. https://scc-csc.lexum.com/scc-csc/scc-csc/en/item/14274/index.do.

Sweeney, Brendan. 2009. "Sixty Years on the Margin: The Evolution of Ontario's Tree Planting Industry and Labour Force: 1945–2007." *Labour/LeTravail* 63: 47–78.

Sweeney, Brendan, and John Holmes. 2008. "Work and Life in the Clear-Cut: Communities of Practice in the Northern Ontario Tree Planting Industry." *Canadian Geographer* 52 (2): 204–21.

Szasz, Thomas. 1957. *Pain and Pleasure: A Study of Bodily Feelings*. New York: Syracuse University Press.

Taleb, Nassim Nicholas. 2012. *Antifragile: Things That Gain from Disorder*. New York: Random House.

Tavares, Paulo. 2016. "In the Forest Ruins." *e-flux Architecture Superhumanity*. Accessed December 31, 2016. https://www.e-flux.com/architecture/superhumanity/68688/in-the-forest-ruins/.

Thrift, Nigel. 2007. *Non-Representational Theory: Space, Politics, Affect*. London: Routledge.

Tomkins, Silvan S. 1962–63. *Affect, Imagery, Consciousness*. 2 vols. New York: Springer.

Toomey, Melissa. 2016. "'For End to Every Wrong, We Stand as One': How Embracing a Theory of Emotion Helped Perpetuate Social Activism in the Women's Trade Union League (WTUL)." Paper presented at the *Rhetoric Society of America Conference*, Atlanta, Georgia, May 29.
Trainor, Jennifer Seibel. 2006. "From Identity to Emotion: Frameworks for Understanding, and Teaching Against, Anticritical Sentiments in the Classroom." *JAC* 26 (3/4): 643–55.
Trewavas, Anthony. 2003. "Aspects of Plant Intelligence." *Annals of Botany* 92: 1–20.
Trewavas, Anthony. 2009. "What Is Plant Behaviour?" *Plant, Cell, and Environment* 32: 606–16.
Tsing, Anna L. 2012. "Unruly Edges: Mushrooms as Companion Species." *Environmental Humanities* 1: 141–54.
Tsing, Anna L. 2013. "More-Than-Human Sociality: A Call for Critical Description." In *Anthropology and Nature*, edited by Kristen Hastrup, 27–42. New York: Routledge.
Tsing, Anna L. 2015a. "A Feminist Approach to the Anthropocene: Earth Stalked by Man." Barnard Center for Research on Women. Accessed December 21, 2016. http://bcrw.barnard.edu/videos/anna-lowenhaupt-tsing-a-feminist-approach-to-the-anthropocene-earth-stalked-by-man/.
Tsing, Anna L. 2015b. *The Mushroom at the End of the World: On the Possibility of Life in Capitalist Ruins*. Princeton, NJ: Princeton University Press.
Turner, Frederick Jackson. 1920. *The Frontier in American History*. New York: Henry Holt.
Ulmer, Gregory L. 1994. *Heuretics: The Logic of Invention*. Baltimore: Johns Hopkins University Press.
"Vintage B.C. Tree Planting Photos Are the Ultimate Look at Hippie Life." 2014. *Huffington Post B.C.*, October 8. Accessed August 15, 2016. https://www.huffingtonpost.ca/2014/10/08/bc-treeplanting-photos_n_5910600.html.
Virilio, Paul. 2007. *The Original Accident*. Cambridge: Polity.
Walker, Nick. 2015. "Throwback Thursday: Screefer Madness." *Canadian Geographic*, April 16. Accessed March 21, 2017. https://www.canadiangeographic.ca/article/throwback-thursday-screefer-madness.
Wandersee, James H., and Elisabeth E. Schussler. 2001. "Toward a Theory of Plant Blindness." *Plant Science Bulletin* 47 (1): 2–8.
Warhol, Robyn R. 2003. *Having a Good Cry: Effeminate Feelings and Pop-Culture Forms*. Columbus: Ohio State University Press.
Wark, McKenzie. 2017. "From Architecture to Kainotecture." *E-Flux Architecture*. Accessed May 4, 2017. https://www.e-flux.com/architecture/accumulation/122201/from-architecture-to-kainotecture/.
Waters, Colin N., Jan Zalasiewicz, Colin Summerhayes, Anthony D. Barnosky, Clément Poirier, Agnieszka Gałuszka, Alejandro Cearreta, Matt Edgeworth, Erle C. Ellis, Michael Ellis, et al. 2016. "The Anthropocene Is Functionally and Stratigraphically Distinct from the Holocene." *Science* 351 (6269): 137, aad2622-1–aad2622-10.
Watkins, Megan. 2010. "Desiring Recognition, Accumulating Affect." In *The Affect Theory Reader*, edited by Melissa Gregg and Gregory J. Seigworth, 269–285. Durham, NC: Duke University Press.
Whatmore, Sarah. 2002. *Hybrid Geographies: Natures Cultures Spaces*. London: Sage.
Wilson, Shawn. 2001. "Self-as-Relationship in Indigenous Research." *Canadian Journal of Native Education* 25 (2): 91–92.
Wilson, Shawn. 2008. *Research Is Ceremony: Indigenous Research Methods*. Winnipeg: Fernwood.
Winthrop, Henry. 1972. "The Environmental Dilemma: Possible Steps toward Its Dissolution." *American Journal of Economics and Sociology* 31 (4): 387–96.
Wolfe, Cary. 2012. *Before the Law: Humans and Animals in a Biopolitical Frame*. Chicago: University of Chicago Press.

# ABOUT THE AUTHOR

JENNIFER CLARY-LEMON is associate professor of English at the University of Waterloo and past editor of the journal *Composition Studies*. Her research interests include writing and location, disciplinarity, critical discourse studies, and research methodologies. Her work has been published in *Rhetoric Review, Discourse and Society, The American Review of Canadian Studies, Composition Forum, Oral History Forum d'histoire orale, enculturation,* and *College Composition and Communication.*

# INDEX

adaptive rhetoric, 61
affect, 65, 99(n18), 102–3; body-mind, 122, 125, 131(n3); and emotion, 104–5; and entanglement, 129–30; inside-out models, 103; outside-in models, 103; and planter-body, 115–16; transmission of, 101, 119–20. *See also* critical affect studies
affect studies, 21
agency: hubris and, 9–10; in new materialist environmental rhetoric, 135–36; nonhuman, 85–89, 172
agonism, environment as, 13. *See also krisis*
Ahmed, Sara, 15, 20, 104, 105, 106, 109; on emotions, 107–8, 118
Ainsworth, Lindsay, 34, 38, 41, 44, 51, 91, 112
Alaimo, Stacy, 9
Alberta, 12
Algonquin Park, 30
ambient, 56
animal bodies, animals: agency of, 85–89; encounters with, 75, 76, 114–15; and environment, 80–81; persuasive energy of, 77–85
animal studies: rhetorical forces in, 63–64
Anthropocene, 4, 5, 6, 22(n7), 35, 167–68, 176; as boundary event, 10–11
anthropocentrism, 21, 167; environment and, 122–23
*anthropos*, 34, 45, 167
aquatic habitats, 81–82
Arron, 132
artist-dirtbags, 39
atmospheres, 120
automobility, 137–38, 166(n7); thing-power of, 140–42; planter time, 142–44; and tree-planting camps, 139–40

bag-up times, 50
Banff National Park, 30
Barad, Karen, 15
Barnett, Scot, 61, 133, 134
Basic Emotions Paradigm, 103
bears, encounters with, 87–88
becoming, 64–65
being-in-the-world, 80

Bennett, Jane, 10, 15, 20, 39, 129, 133, 166(n3), 171; on metals, 144–45; on roads and politics, 157, 159; on thing-power, 140–41; on vital materialism, 134, 135
Bergson, Henri, 103
Best, Stephen, 15
biodiversity, vs. plantation planting, 93–94
birds, encounters with, 114
Blackfeet, and Glacier National Park, 30
black flies, 77; persuasive energy of, 79–85
"Black Fly Song, The," 80
Blackman, Lisa, 103
Bodner, John, *Slash Romance*, 35
bodies, 61, 98, 121, 135; human and nonhuman, 67, 172; interactions of, 116–17; plant, 89–90; rhetoric of, 60, 62–64, 76; as sets of relations, 64–66. *See also* planter-bodies
body-mind, 125, 131(n3)
body thinking, 19, 76, 78, 100, 171; animal, 88–89
body topologic, 109
Boldt, Ryan, 34, 44, 70, 73, 82, 91, 112, 121, 122, 126, 127, 163; emotional responses of, 107, 114; on good and bad land, 40–41; on motion-memory, 106, 109, 110; on planting process, 49–50
boundary, 174; culture-nature, 12–13
boundary event, Anthropocene as, 10–11
Bourlas, Tamir, 34, 36, 37, 44, 49, 54, 58, 69, 72, 96, 117, 152; on costs of trees, 46–47
Boyle, Casey, 61, 133, 134, 146
Braidotti, Rosi, 15
brain-body-world processes, 108
breaks, 74
Brennan, Teresa, 15, 100–101, 103, 105, 106, 119
British Columbia, 39, 166(n14); illegal logging in, 159–60; tree planting in, 11–12
Brown, Max, 39
Buchanan, Brett, 19, 64, 80
bugging out, 82–85

camp life, 120
camps: isolated, 162–64; tree-planting, 139–40

# INDEX

Canada, 14, 17; forest industry in, 6–7, 11–12; nature narratives, 28–29
capital, trees as, 19
carbon offsets, 5
carbon sequestration, black flies, 82
caribou, 114
CAS. *See* critical affect studies
change, 136
Chappell, Georgia, 34, 44, 56, 68, 77, 83, 93, 116, 125; emotional attachment/response, 112, 114, 115; on land qualities, 40, 42; on personal efficiency, 53, 54; on pleasure/pain, 73, 74; on tree planting, 36, 39, 51, 92
Cheater, Dan, 34, 44, 58, 83, 93, 95, 114
choice, 38–39
chöra, 169, 173–74
chorography, 14–15, 17, 21, 23(n24), 108; of landscape, 170–71
Clark, Jonathan, 107
Clark, Mary, 46, 51–52
Clement, Stephanie, 16, 50; "To Plant a Million Trees," 3
climate change, 5
Clough, Patricia Ticineto, 102, 103
colonialism/colonization, 29, 173–74
communications, with animals, 87–89
*comunidades indigenas*, 6
consciousness, community, 38, 39
Coole, Diana, 15
Corax, 86
cream, creamy, 40, 43
Crist, Eileen, 167
critical affect studies (CAS), 18, 102, 103, 104, 107–8
critical description, 16
Cronon, William, 8, 19, 29, 30
crops, trees as, 13
cross-species encounters, 76; persuasive energy of, 77–85
Crown lands, 158
Crow people, and Yellowstone, 30
crows, 99(n26); encounters with, 86–87
culture, 4, 9. *See also* natureculture
cut blocks, 75, 128; emotional responses to, 111–15, 128–29; forest layers and, 93–94
Cwerner, Saulo, on helicopter travel, 162–63

Damasio, Antonio, 102, 103
Davies, John, 80
Davis, Diane, 15, 19, 76; animal studies, 63–64
deactivation, road, 153–54
deer, 113, 114
Deleuze, Gilles, 15, 99(n18), 103, 105, 109; on becoming, 64–65
dependency, on automobiles, 138, 142–44
Derkowski, Kristel, *Six Million Trees*, 122
Derrida, Jacques, 60
Dery, Mark, 144
developing countries, roads in, 150
developmentalists, 32
dirtbags, 39
discourse, 25
distance, and time, 144
disturbance, human, 93
Donath, Judith, 141
dromosphere, 144, 163, 166(n10)
dualisms, Cartesian, 63
Ducey, Ariel, 129
Dunk, Thomas, loggers, 12
duration, 105
dwelling, 8, 18, 19, 20, 26
Dyck, Sam, 34, 37, 44, 46, 54, 69, 93, 111; on plantations, 95, 128; on roads, 152, 156–57; on vehicles, 143, 145; on weather, 116–17

Earth System science, 10
ecocentrism, 21
ecologists, vs. environmentalists, 5
ecology, 10; rhetoric of, 19–20
economics, 4, 59; efficiencies of, 48–52; injury and, 68–69; of pleasure/pain, 74; trees and, 46–48
economy of movement, 48–49
ecosystems, health of, 81–82
ecotourism, 156, 172
Edbauer Rice, Jenny, 19–20, 76, 102–3, 104
Edwards, Paul, 150
efficiency, efficiencies, 25, 170; injury and, 68–69; in *krisis*, 97–98; Nature as Resource in, 46–48; personal, 52–55; rhetorics of, 33, 44–55
efficiency logics, 75
egalitarianism, 38
*ejidos*, 6
Ekman, Paul, 103
*élucubrations*, 59; bodies as sets of relations, 64–66; rhetorical human and, 60–62; rhetoricity of bodies and, 62–64
embeddedness, in nature, 25
emotion, 101–3, 131(n5); and affect, 104–5; and happiness, 120–21; of planters, 111–12; of planting, 106–7
employment, in tree planting, 11–12
Enbridge company, 159–60
encounters: multi-species, 113–15
endangered species, 175

entanglements, 113, 124, 127, 172; affect and, 129–30; automobility and, 141–42; human-nonhuman, 122, 135; road-vehicle, 155–56; with thing-bodies, 136–37; weather- and planter-bodies, 118–19
environment, 13, 17, 18, 31; animal and, 80–81; black fly, 81–82; destruction of, 124–29; and human hubris, 9–10; humans and, 25–26, 33; mourning over, 122–25; tree planting and, 129–30
environmental humanities, 21
environmentalism, 5, 31, 92; humanistic, 9–10; rhetorics of nature, 28–29
environmentalists: vs. developmentalists, 31–32; vs. ecologists, 25
environmental protections rules, 48
environmental quality, 31
equipment, 146
ethics, 37–38
Evernden, Neil, 26, 27

feeling(s), 101, 104, 120, 131(n5)
feminist science studies, 21
fill blocks, 41
First Nations, 174; land issues, 158–59; logging and, 159–61; and "wilderness," 29–30
forest layers, 93–94
forestry industry, 4, 166(n4); and Indigenous lands, 159–61; labor in, 6–7; planter critique of, 125–27; tree planting in, 5, 39
forestry management, plantation cultivation, 94–95
forests, 4, 129; emotional attachment to, 111–12
Forsyth, Luc, 146–47
fossil fuel industry, 160, 161, 166(n4)
Foucault, Michel, on discourse, 25
foxes, encounters with, 87
Frank, Adam, 103
frictionless mobility, 163
Friesen, Sam, 34, 37, 41, 50, 53, 69, 74, 95, 113, 114, 143; on environmental destruction, 126–27; on motion-memory, 109, 110
Friesen Hughes, Nik, 34, 54, 74, 83, 88, 106, 113, 121, 143; crow encounters, 86, 87; on soil type, 42–43; on weather, 119, 120
Frost, Samantha, 15
fungal argument, 61

Galileo Galilei, nature-culture divide, 26
geography: good and bad land, 40–44; of tree planting, 24, 35, 36–37

Glacier National Park, and Blackfeet, 30
*Grassy Narrows First Nation v. Ontario*, 159
Gray, Jonathan, 62
Gregg, Melissa, 100, 103, 104, 107
grief, over environmental destruction, 123–25
Grossberg, Lawrence, 103
Grover, Jan Zita, 123, 127
Guattari, Félix, 15; on becoming, 64–65

Hall, Matthew, 90
happiness, 40, 57(n20), 120–21
Haraway, Donna, 13, 15, 18, 21, 28, 61, 167, 168, 169, 176
Harvey, David, 19, 25, 31, 46, 47
Harvey, Penny, on roads, 150, 151, 157, 158
Hawhee, Debra, 18, 19, 63, 76
Hawk, Byron, 17
Hays, Samuel, 31
Heidegger, Martin, 15, 80
Heilbroner, Robert, 45
Hekman, Susan, 9
helicopters, 166(n6), 172; bush camps, 162–64
Hetherington, Kregg, on roads, 150–51, 154
"Hoot in the Dark, A" (Kennedy), 63
human-animal dichotomy, 63
humanism, 19, 25–26, 55–56; efficiency and, 97–98, 170; rhetorical, 33, 34–35; of tree planters, 37–38
humanness, 15–16
human-nonhuman interaction, 19, 21, 172, 174
humans, and environment, 25–26. *See also* planter-bodies; tree planters

ice haul roads, 152
identity, tree planters, 37, 39
Indian Act (1876), 158
Indigenous peoples, 174; land issues, 158–59; logging and, 159–61; and "wilderness," 29–30
individualism, of tree planters, 37, 38
inductive reasoning, 28
industry, Western, 28
inefficiencies, of things, 145–46
infrastructure, 140, 151, 159; road, 149–50, 166(nn11, 12, 13)
Ingold, Timothy, 8, 108
inhabitant, 32
injury, 134; animal bodies and, 78–79; and pain, 68–72
insects, persuasive energy of, 77, 78–85, 135
intensity, intensities, 101, 107–8

198   INDEX

intense rhetorics, 129
interspecies relationships, 61
invasive species, 175
Iovino, Serenella, 15

Jain, Juliet, 144
Jarman, Derek, 123
Johnson, Maureen, 67
J-rooting, 91–93

Kailen, 24, 35, 43–44, 48
*kairos*, 117
Keeseekoowenin Ojibway, 30
Kennedy, George, "A Hoot in the Dark," 63
Killingsworth, M. Jimmie, Nature as Spirit, 27–28
kinesthetic rhetoric, 62, 116, 142, 145
Knox, Hannah, on roads, 150, 151, 157, 158
Kohn, Eduardo, 81, 122
*krisis*, 13, 97–98
Kroeker, Thomas, 1, 34, 84, 92, 115, 162; on land quality, 41, 42; on pain and injury, 68, 70, 71–72

labor, 11, 48; in forestry industry, 5, 6; personal efficiency of, 52–55; personal satisfaction of, 129–30; of tree planting, 35–37
Lac la Croix Ojibway, and Algonquin Park, 30
Lamont, Mark, 150
land, 113, 114; good and bad, 40–44; Indigenous peoples, 158–61
land claims, 30, 172
landscape(s), 4, 20, 102, 108; choric view of, 170–71; multi-species, 75–76, 80, 114–15; rhetorics of, 169–70
Latinos, 4
Latour, Bruno, 28
Laurie, Timothy, 35
Law, John, 22
Layla, 132, 133, 162
Leys, Ruth, 103
liminal space, 6
loggers, logging, 12, 166(n14); illegal, 159–60; and Indigenous lands, 160–61
logging roads, and wilderness, 152–53
Love, Heather, 15
Lynn, William, 27
Lyons, Glenn, 144

MacInnis, Thayer, 13, 34, 43, 91, 96, 111; on roads, 152, 154; on tree planting, 112, 124; on vehicles, 143, 147–48, 149

macroinvertebrates, aquatic habitats, 81–82
Mailloux, Steven, 60
management, forest, 4, 5, 33, 54
Manitoba, Riding National Park, 30
Manning, Erin, 103
Marcus, Sharon, 15
Marder, Michael, 15
market, and tree planting, 95–96
Massumi, Brian, 102, 103, 109, 131(n6)
materialism, vital, 10, 134, 135
McCannell, Ross, 34, 44, 51, 70, 84, 107, 109, 120, 128, 143; on roads, 152–53
melancholia, 124, 127
memory, 124, 173; and movement, 105–6, 109–11
metals, 144–45
Mexicans, as forestry labor, 6
microbiomes, 135
migrants, undocumented, 5
migrant workers, 39
Ministry of Forests, 152
mobility, frictionless, 163
Mol, Annemarie, 15
money, nature as, 46–48
monoculture, 5, 92, 93
moose, persuasive energy of, 78, 79
Morrison, James, 29, 30
Mortimer-Sandilands, Catriona, 102, 127; environmental mourning, 122–24. See also Sandilands, Catriona
Morton, Tim, 124
mosquitos, persuasive energy of, 77, 78, 83, 84, 135
motion-memory, 109–11
motivation, 78; of tree planters, 36–37
movement, motion, 108; and landscape, 113–15; and memory, 105–6; of planter-bodies, 106–7, 110–13, 116; of planting, 109–10
Mucklebauer, John, 19, 59, 61, 64; rhetoric as practice, 76–77
Muir, John, 29
multi-species landscapes, 80; encounters in, 75–76, 114–15
mysticism, 28

Nakota/Assiniboine, land claims, 30
nature, 4, 9, 13, 18, 24, 25; as disordered, 150–51; market value of, 32–33; as resource, 45, 58; separation from, 26–27
nature-as-other, 25, 26–27
Nature as Resource, 45, 58; trees as capital, 46–48
Nature as Spirit, 27–28

natureculture, 9, 19, 23(n29), 100, 104, 129, 170
nature-culture divide, 9, 12–13, 20, 26
Nealon, Jeffrey, 19, 64
Nelson, Julie, 104–5
neurobiology, plant, 90
neuroscience, 103, 105, 131(n6)
new material environmental rhetorics, 56, 59, 129, 135–36, 175–76
new materialism, 21
Nicotra, Jodie, 135–36
nonhumans, 98, 172; agency of, 85–86
non-rational, as source of dwelling, 20
nostalgia, 29, 108

object-qualities, 26
object, nature as, 26–27
OECD. See Organization for Economic Cooperation and Development
Oelschlaeger, Max, 32
Öhman, Arne, 103
oil industry, 160, 161, 166(n4)
Ojibway, land claims, 30
Ontario, 12, 30
Opperman, Serpil, 15
Organization for Economic Cooperation and Development (OECD), 160
Owls, Great Gray; planter encounters with, 88–89
ownership, of planted trees, 43–44

Pacific Trails Pipeline (PTP) corridor, 160
pain, 82; planters and, 68–72; pleasure and, 72–75
Palmer, Jacqueline, Nature as Spirit, 27–28
Parks Canada, 30
Parrish, Alex, 61
patchiness, 94
PBs, 53–54
Pepper, David, objects in nature, 26–27
persuasion, 60–61
persuasive energy, 135; of black flies, 79–85; cross-species encounters, 77, 78–79
Peters, John Durham, 117
Pflugfelder, Ehren Helmut, 116, 142, 164; on transportation, 143–44, 146
Pilgrim, Sarah, 28
*pineros*, 6
place, 173; emotional attachment to, 111–12
placeholding, 6
placemaking, 4, 59, 76, 100, 169
"Plant a Million Trees, To" (Clement), 3
plantations, 5, 114; choral connections of, 169–70; critique of, 125–27; environmental destruction in, 127–28; environmental issues, 93–94; and forestry management, 95–96; neglect in, 154–55; simplified environment of, 33–34; success of, 96–97
plant blindness, 89, 99(n27)
plant-bodies, 89; efficiency and, 90–91; and planter-bodies, 92–97
planter-bodies, 67, 130, 174; and animal agency, 85–89; as form, 70–71; and insect bodies, 81–85; injury and pain in, 68–70, 71–72; J-roots and, 91–92; motion of, 106–7, 108–10, 111–16; motion-memory, 110–11; and plantations, 94–96; and plant bodies, 92–97; pleasure/pain in, 72–75; as sets of relations, 64–66; things and, 133–34; weather and, 116–19
plants, 90, 99(n32); J-rooting, 91–92
plant seeing/plant sense, 90, 92
pleasure, and pain, 72–75
political ecologies, 133
politics, of roads, 157–58
postmodernism, 9
prep blocks, 41
preservation, management and, 32–33
Pretty, Jules, 28
pride, 39, 54
Princen, Thomas: on automobility, 138, 139; on efficiency, 44–45, 54
Probyn, Elspeth, 101–2, 130
process, 106
PTP. See Pacific Trails Pipeline corridor

quad trails, 152, 153(fig.)
Quetico Provincial Park, and Lac la Croix Ojibway, 30

Rackham, Oliver, 94, 95–96; on plantation neglect, 154–55
ravens, 99(n26); encounters with, 86, 87
reclamation, of roads, 153–54
reforestation, in Canada, 6, 11–12
Rempel, Luke, 34, 36, 46, 53, 70, 82, 96, 142; on motion-memory, 110, 111; on wasp encounters, 78–79
Replant.ca, 146
replanting, illegally logged land, 160, 161(fig.)
resource: nature as, 27, 45, 46–48, 58
responsibility, of tree planters, 37–38
rest, pleasure in, 73–74
resurgence, 18
rhetorical-magical thinking, 62
rhetorical ontology, 133
rhetoricity of being, 15

rhetoricity of bodies, 18
rhetorics, 4, 5, 7–8, 14, 17, 35, 129, 168; of ecology, 19–20; *élucubration* and, 60–62; kinesthetic, 116, 142, 145; of landscape, 169–70; of practice, 76–77
Rice, Jeff, 17
Rickards, Lauren, 10
Rickert, Thomas, 17; on persuasion, 60–61; on rhetorics, 8, 19, 35; on thing-bodies, 134, 136; on Toronto Island, 138–39
Riding National Park, 30
Rivers, Nathaniel, 9–10, 102
road-bodies, 172; neglect and abandonment of, 154–55
roads, 149–61, 166(nn11, 12); as civilized order, 150–51; deactivated and reclaimed, 153–54, 155(fig.); and First Nations, 158–61; politics of, 157–58; private/logging, 152–53; and wilderness, 156–57
road-vehicle bodies, 155–56
Roberts, Delia, 87
Ronell, Avital, 170
ruin, 4

Sandilands, Catriona, 28–29, 173. *See also* Mortimer-Sandilands, Catriona
Sawatzky, Erin, 34, 37, 77, 96, 109, 115, 121; and animal encounters, 87–88; on black flies, 83–84; on illegal logging, 159–60
*schnarb*, 43
scholarship, 61, 151
Schussler, Elisabeth, on plants, 89–90
seasons, seasonality, 77, 99(n25)
Sedgwick, Eve, 103
Seegert, Natasha, 76
Seigworth, Gregory, 100, 103, 104, 107
self-identity, of tree planters, 37–38
Seniw, Jane, 34, 113; on plantation cultivation, 95, 96; on plant bodies, 92–93
sequestration, 5
settler narratives, 173–74
Sheldon, Rebekah, 65
Shoshone, and Yellowstone, 30
shovels: as extension of affect, 115–16; thing-power of, 134–35
silviculture, 14; human disturbance and, 93–94
Simpson, James, 34, 39, 46, 50, 53, 73, 78, 95, 107, 112; on helicopters, 163–64; on roads, 153, 166(n7)
*Six Million Trees* (Derkowski), 122
slash, 40, 42(fig.)

*Slash Romance* (Bodner), 35
Smith, Adam, *Wealth of Nations*, 45
sociality, 17; process of, 120–21
social relations, 120–21
soil type, 42–43
sonic roads, 156, 157
species-thinking, 171
Spinoza, Baruch, 15, 65, 103
Spirit, Nature as, 27
Sprohge, Jon, 34, 37, 47, 48, 74, 96, 110, 111, 112, 120, 136, 154; on environmental destruction, 126, 127; on mosquitos, 77–78, 135
standard of living, and environmental quality, 31
stenosing tenosynovitis, 71, 134
stickiness: affective, 111–16, 118, 119, 129; of automobility, 141–42
Stoney/Nakoda people, and Banff National Park, 30
stress, 107
students, 6–7, 11
success, of plantation cultivation, 96–97
Szasz, Thomas, 68

Taylor, Frederick Winslow, 45, 48
temporality, cross-species interactions, 84
*tempus*, 117
thing-bodies, 20, 63, 133, 151, 155, 165, 172–73; entanglements with, 136–37; power of, 134–35
thing-power, 135, 155, 164–65; automobility of, 140–42; of vehicles, 148–49
things: inefficiencies of, 145–46; interactions with, 136–37; planter-bodies and, 132, 133–34
ticks, *umwelt* of, 81
time: travel and, 143–44; waiting, 146–48
timescale, 19
Tomkins, Silvan S., 103
topography, and land quality, 41–42
*topos*, 13, 17, 28
Toronto Island, 138–39
tourism, 156
transformation, 121
transportation, 146; infrastructure, 150–51, 166(nn12, 13); of planters, 142–44; to remote areas, 162–64
travel time, 143–44
tree-bodies, J-rooting, 91–92
tree planters, 13, 34, 166(n5); acts of memory and, 105–6; bodies as sets of relations, 64–66; characteristics and values of, 37–38; efficiency of, 48–52; employment in, 11–12; environmental loss, 124–25; good and bad land,

40–44; industrial, 3–4; injury and pain, 68–72; interviews, 16–17; and things, 136–37; workday/work ethic of, 35–37. *See also* planter-bodies
trees, 4, 13; as capital, 46–48; care for, 112–13; efficiency of, 48–52; in plantation system, 95–96; planting of, 90–91; as sticky bodies, 113–14
Trewavas, Anthony, 15
*tropos*, 13
trucks, 156, 157, 166(n14), 172
Tsing, Anna, 18, 21, 23(n27), 55, 60, 75, 93; on humanness, 15–16; on plantations, 33–34
Turner, Frederick Jackson, 29

Uexküll, Jakob von, 81
Ulmer, Gregory, 14
*Umwelt*, 80–81
underivable rhetoricity, 59–60
Unist'ot'en (C'ihlts'ehkhyu/Big Frog Clan), Land issues, 160–61
use value, and automobility, 138, 139
utility, 75

value(s), 4, 166(n9); monetary, 46–48; tree planters, 37–38
vehicle-bodies, 144
vehicles: dependence on, 142–44; performance of, 145–46, 147–48; and roads, 155–56; thing-power of, 140–42, 148–49, 165
vibrant things, 39
Virilio, Paul, 144, 163

waiting, vehicles and, 146–48
Wandersee, James, on plants, 89–90
Wark, McKenzie, 176
wasps, encounters with, 78–79
Watkins, Megan, 172
*Wealth of Nations* (Smith), 45
weather, and planter bodies, 116–19
wilderness, 18; concepts of, 7, 8–9, 29–30; logging roads and, 156–57
wild imaginings, 59. *See also élucubrations*
Witsuwit'en people, 160–61
work ethic, 35–37

Yellowstone National Park, Indigenous peoples and, 30

www.ingramcontent.com/pod-product-compliance
Lightning Source LLC
Chambersburg PA
CBHW030443090526
44586CB00044B/581